Helen Prejean, C.S.J., is a writer, lecturer and community organizer who was born in Baton Rouge and has lived and worked in Louisiana all her life. She has lectured extensively on the subject of capital punishment and has appeared on *ABC World News Tonight, 60 Minutes*, BBC World Service radio and an NBC special series on the death penalty. Her articles have appeared in publications including the *San Francisco Chronicle*, the *St Petersburg Times*, the Baltimore *Sun*, and the *St Anthony Messenger*. She is a member of the Sisters of St Joseph of Medaille.

D1347086

To my mother, Gusta Mae,
and my father, Louis,
who loved me into life

DEAD MAN WALKING

An Eyewitness Account of the Death Penalty
in the United States

Helen Prejean, C.S.J.

Fount

An Imprint of HarperCollins*Publishers*

Fount Paperbacks is an Imprint of
HarperCollins*Religious*
Part of HarperCollins*Publishers*
77-85 Fulham Palace Road, London W6 8JB

First published in 1993 by Random House, Inc, New York
and simultaneously in Canada by
Random House of Canada Limited, Toronto
This edition published in Great Britain
in 1994 by Fount Paperbacks

1 3 5 7 9 10 8 6 4 2

Copyright © 1993 Helen Prejean

Helen Prejean asserts the moral right to
be identified as the author of this work

A catalogue record for this book
is available from the British Library

ISBN 0 00 627814-0

Printed and bound in Great Britain by
Hartnolls Limited, Bodmin, Cornwall

CONDITIONS OF SALE

This book is sold subject to the condition that it shall not,
by way of trade or otherwise, be lent, re-sold, hired out or
otherwise circulated without the publisher's prior consent
in any form of binding or cover other than that in which it
is published and without a similar condition including this
condition being imposed on the subsequent purchaser.

All rights reserved. No part of this publication may be
reproduced, stored in a retrieval system, or transmitted,
in any form or by any means, electronic, mechanical,
photocopying, recording or otherwise, without the prior
permission of the publishers.

Grateful acknowledgement is made to the following for
permission to reprint previously published material:

ALFRED A. KNOPF, INC: Excerpt from *Resistance, Rebellion and Death* by Albert
Camus, translated by J. O'Brien. Copyright © 1960 by Alfred A. Knopf, Inc. Five
lines from 'The Warning' from *The Panther and the Lash* by Langston Hughes.
Copyright © 1967 by Arna Bontemps and George Houston Bass. Reprinted by
permission of Alfred A. Knopf, Inc.

ACKNOWLEDGMENTS

I want to thank those who helped me write this book.

Jason Epstein, my editor at Random House, took a chance on a first-time author and guided me through three revisions. Finding him was a great surprise. I didn't know that a top-notch editor at such a large publishing house cared enough to work so patiently with a neophyte author. Julie Grau, Maryam Mohit, and Mallay Charters, Jason's coworkers, have also been immeasurably helpful. Gloria Loomis, my energetic, dedicated literary agent, with her coworkers, Kendra Taylor and Nicole Aragi, have been a steady source of encouragement and support during the two years it has taken to write this book. Jason DeParle, Lisa and Michael Radelet, Bill McKibben, and Sue Halpern have been with me through all three revisions, offering invaluable advice.

A host of people read the manuscript and offered suggestions: Liz and Art Scott, Tom Dybdahl, Judy Rittenhouse, Mary Riley, Millard Farmer, Ronald J. Tabak, Leigh Dingerson, Richard Dieter, Hugo Adam Bedau, Ronnie Friedman Barone, Bill and Debbie Quigley, Magdaleno Rose-Avila, Charles McGowan, Rosemary Lewis, and members of my religious community — Sisters Jane Louise Arbour, Julie Sheatzley, Barbara Hughes, and Jean Fryoux.

Many helped me get information: Neal Walker, Nicholas Trenti-

ACKNOWLEDGMENTS

costa, Gary Clements, Barbara Warren, Alice Miller, Howard Zehr, Russ Immarigeon, Marc Mauer, Wilbert Rideau, Ron Wikberg, Sam Dalton, Ginger Berrigan, Michael Kroll, Dianne Kidner, Gerald Bosworth, C. Paul Phelps, Howard Marsellus, Peggy Norris, Pam and Keith Rutter, Allen Johnson, Jr., Jonathan Eig, Janet Yassen, Jonathan Gradess, Dennis Kalob, Michael Small, John Craft, Bob Gross, Bill Pelke, Karima Wick, Lloyd LeBlanc, and Elizabeth and Vernon Harvey.

I have received immeasurable support and encouragement from the staff at Hope House in New Orleans: Odessa Carew, Idella Casimier, Don Everard, Sister Lilianne Flavin, O.P., Ethel George, Brother Virgil Harris, S.C., Elaine Henry, Jarldine Johnson, Shirley Lemon, Patricia Robinson, Patrick Stevenson, Thero Stevenson, Melvin Thompson, and Brother Brendan Wilkinson, F.S.C.

Joan Benham, Shelley Garren, and Dennis Ambrose at Random House painstakingly worked on the manuscript and Walter Weintz, Bridget Marmion, Carol Schneider, and Becky Simpson worked hard to publicize the book.

Finally, I am grateful for the love, friendship, and moral support I have received from my religious community, the Sisters of St. Joseph of Medaille, and from my family, and my good friend, Ann Barker.

ABOUT THE TYPE

The text of this book was set in Janson, a misnamed typeface designed in about 1690 by Nicholas Kis, a Hungarian in Amsterdam. In 1919 the matrices became the property of the Stempel Foundry in Frankfurt. It is an old-style book face of excellent clarity and sharpness. Janson serifs are concave and splayed; the contrast between thick and thin strokes is marked.

CONTENTS

Acknowledgments	*v*
Introduction	*ix*
CHAPTER ONE	3
CHAPTER TWO	23
CHAPTER THREE	43
CHAPTER FOUR	68
CHAPTER FIVE	96
CHAPTER SIX	118
CHAPTER SEVEN	141
CHAPTER EIGHT	157
CHAPTER NINE	175
CHAPTER TEN	212
CHAPTER ELEVEN	223
Notes	*246*
Index	*271*

INTRODUCTION

I've heard that there are two situations that make interesting stories: when an extraordinary person is plunged into the commonplace and when an ordinary person gets involved in extraordinary events. I'm definitely an example of the latter. I stepped quite unsuspectingly from a protected middle-class environment into one of the most explosive and complex moral issues of our day, the question of capital punishment.

It began ten years ago when I wrote a letter to an inmate on Louisiana's death row and the man wrote back. Thus began a ten-year journey that led me into Louisiana's execution chamber and then into advocacy groups for homicide victims' families. I began naively. It took time — and mistakes — for me to sound out the moral perspective, which is the subject of this book.

There is much pain in these pages. There are, to begin with, crimes that defy description. Then there is the ensuing rage, horror, grief, and fierce ambivalence. But also courage and incredible human spirit. I have been changed forever by the experiences that I describe here.

I went right along, not fixing up any particular plan, but just trusting to Providence to put the right words in my mouth when the time come: for I'd noticed that Providence always did put the right words in my mouth, if I left it alone.

— *Huckleberry Finn*
Mark Twain

CHAPTER

1

When Chava Colon from the Prison Coalition asks me one January day in 1982 to become a pen pal to a death-row inmate, I say, Sure. The invitation seems to fit with my work in St. Thomas, a New Orleans housing project of poor black residents. Not death row exactly, but close. Death is rampant here — from guns, disease, addiction. Medical care scarcely exists.

I've come to St. Thomas to serve the poor, and I assume that someone occupying a cell on Louisiana's death row fits that category. I had learned that back in 1977 at a lecture by John Vodicka, one of the founders of the Louisiana Coalition on Jails and Prisons where Chava now works. I had also learned that the death penalty in the United States has always been most rigorously applied in Southern states — mostly toward those who kill whites. The Prison Coalition office is near Hope House, where I teach high-school dropouts, and Chava and I run into each other fairly often.

After he has written the name of the death-row inmate he says, "Maybe I ought to give you someone else. This guy is a loner and doesn't write. Maybe you want someone who will answer your letters."

But he's already written the name and I say, "Don't change it. Give me his name." I don't know yet that the name on this tiny slip

3

of white paper will be my passport into an eerie land that so far I've only read about in books.

I look at the name and address that Chava gave me: Elmo Patrick Sonnier, number 95281, Death Row, Louisiana State Penitentiary, Angola.

Almost all the killings here in St. Thomas seem to erupt from the explosive mixture of dead-end futures, drugs, and guns. But when Chava describes what Sonnier has done, my blood chills. On November 4, 1977, he and his younger brother, Eddie, abducted from a lovers' lane a teenage couple, David LeBlanc and Loretta Bourque. They raped the girl, forced the young people to lie face down, and shot them in the head.

I look down at the name in horror. Do I really want to know such a man?

"He's a Cajun from St. Martinville, Louisiana," Chava says.

Which makes the murders all the more vicious, because St. Martinville, at the center of Acadiana, is one of the friendliest, most hospitable places on earth. Here and in the surrounding towns French-speaking people, mostly farmers and fishermen, cook good food, swap stories and recipes, and dance the two-step and the zydeco. They love to talk, even to strangers. If murders are prone to happen anywhere on the face of the earth, this is the place one would least expect.

I wonder what I can say to this man. What will he have to say to me?

"We have files at the office," Chava says, "if you want to read about the case."

I take the piece of paper with the name on it back to the apartment in the project where I live with five other nuns.

A year ago, in June of 1981, I had driven a small brown truck loaded with my personal possessions to the apartment on 519 St. Andrew Street and hoped to high heaven I wouldn't be shot. We were practically the only whites — all women — among one thousand five hundred residents in the six square blocks of beige brick buildings tucked between the central business district and the garden district. After my first night in the project apartment, I wrote in my journal:

"Didn't sleep much. Noisy until about 3:00 A.M. People standing on the corner talking and drinking. Feel nervous, unsettled. Heard a gunshot. Had checked when I got into bed to make sure my bed was *under* the windowsill in case a bullet came through.

"Is this New Orleans? I feel like I'm in another country."

DEAD MAN WALKING

I came to St. Thomas as part of a reform movement in the Catholic Church, seeking to harness religious faith to social justice. In 1971, the worldwide synod of bishops had declared justice a "constitutive" part of the Christian gospel. When you dig way back into Church teachings, you find that this focus on justice has been tucked in there all along in "social encyclicals." Not exactly coffee-table literature. The documents have been called the best-kept secret of the Catholic Church. And with good reason. The mandate to practice social justice is unsettling because taking on the struggles of the poor invariably means challenging the wealthy and those who serve their interests. "Comfort the afflicted and afflict the comfortable" — that's what Dorothy Day, a Catholic social activist said is the heart of the Christian gospel.[1]

In 1980 my religious community, the Sisters of St. Joseph of Medaille, had made a commitment to "stand on the side of the poor," and I had assented, but reluctantly. I resisted this recasting of the faith of my childhood, where what counted was a personal relationship with God, inner peace, kindness to others, and heaven when this life was done. I didn't want to struggle with politics and economics. We were nuns, after all, not social workers, and some realities in life were, for better or worse, rather fixed — like the gap between rich and poor. Even Jesus Christ himself had said, "The poor you will always have with you." Besides, it was all so complex and confusing — the mess the world was in — with one social problem meshed with other problems. If you tried to get a handle, say, on improving housing for poor people, you found yourself in a morass of bureaucracy and waste in government programs, racist real estate and banking policies, unemployment — a mess.

Enlightenment had come in June 1980. I can remember the moment because it changed my life. My community had assembled at Terre Haute, Indiana, to grapple with directions of our ministries for the 1980s, and the chief speaker was Sister Marie Augusta Neal, S.N.D.deN. A sociologist, she described glaring inequities in the world: two thirds of the peoples of the world live at or below subsistence level while one third live in affluence. Did we know, she asked, that the United States, which comprises about 6 percent of the world's population, consumed 48 percent of the world's goods? What were we to do about such glaring injustices? She knew her facts and I found myself mentally pitting my arguments against her challenge — *we were nuns, not social workers, not political.* But it's as if she knew what I was thinking. She pointed out that to claim to be apolitical or neutral in the face of such injustices would be, in actuality, to uphold the status quo — a very political position to take, and on the side of the oppressors.

But it was the way she presented the message of Jesus that caused the most radical shift in my perspective.

"The Gospels record that Jesus preached good news to the poor," she said, "and an essential part of that good news was that they were to be poor no longer." Which meant they were not to meekly accept their poverty and suffering as God's will, but, instead, struggle to obtain the necessities of life which were rightfully theirs. And Jesus' challenge to the nonpoor, she emphasized, was to relinquish their affluence and to share their resources with the dispossessed.

Something in me must have been building toward this moment because there was a flash and I realized that my spiritual life had been too ethereal, too disconnected. I left the meeting and began seeking out the poor. This brought me one year later to the St. Thomas housing development.

I had grown up in Baton Rouge, Louisiana, in the 1940s and 1950s in as solid and loving a family as one could hope for — a mother and father who lavished attention and affection on their children and a brother, Louie, and sister, Mary Ann, whom I could spar with and tease and argue with and love. We grew up in a spacious two-story house, were educated in Catholic schools, and traveled extensively across the United States, Canada, and Europe.

As a child, at Mama's urging, I knelt by my bed at night for prayers and always included "poor people who have no place to sleep tonight." But poor people occupied a land somewhere out there with Cinderella and Hansel and Gretel. I did not have any direct experience with poor people.

I did not then consider the "colored" people who worked for us as poor. They were just, well, "colored" people doing what "colored" people did, which was working for white people, and living where "colored" people lived, which was usually in shacks out in the country or, in "nigger town" in the city. In my early childhood a black couple lived in the "servants' quarters," a small house behind ours. The man took care of the yard, the woman in a white uniform helped in the house. They never used the family bathrooms and they always ate in the kitchen. Only whites went to the elementary and high school I attended, and in our church blacks could sit only in a niche of pews over to the side and had to wait until last to receive communion. They had to sit at the back of the bus, and it was a great dare for a white kid to go to the back of the bus and sit with the blacks *for five seconds*. I had taken on the dare more than

6

once, then rushed back to the front of the bus to amused, giggling friends.

Yet, even when I was a child there was something in black people that drew me to them. Once, when I was five years old, I remember making my way over to the group of black men Daddy had hired to remove a stump from our front yard, and I watched and listened as they swung axes in fluid motion and moaned bluesy songs and swapped stories about women and drinking and going to jail. This was life so raw, so earthy, so uncushioned, yet so vibrant, so tenacious, so enduring. I was fascinated. Mama was not. She spotted me and told me to get inside.

I was twelve years old the first time I witnessed physical violence against a black person. Elise Gauthier, my friend and classmate, and I rode the bus one December day in 1952 to Third Street to do our Christmas shopping. We were in seventh grade; everything was funny that year, and we had a great time on the bus, teasing and laughing uproariously over twelve-year-olds' jokes. The bus stopped at the end of Third Street and everyone on the bus was getting out when Elise and I heard the bus driver shout an obscenity to a young black woman and saw him kick her with his *foot* off the bus and onto the sidewalk. She landed on her hands and knees and her purse flew open and coins rolled all over. She didn't say a word, did not even look at the bus driver, just picked herself up and walked away.

I felt awful. My parents never acted *mean* to black people, even though they never questioned the system of racial discrimination that permeated every aspect of life. Daddy, an attorney, represented a slew of black clients, charging them five dollars for his services, and he helped several families buy property and, eventually, own their own homes. It would take me a long time to understand how systems inflict pain and hardship in people's lives and to learn that being kind in an unjust system is not enough.

Now, here in St. Thomas, I am learning plenty about systems and what happens to the people in them, here in a state whose misery statistics are the highest in the nation — where residents bring home an average yearly income of $10,890, where half the adult population has not completed high school, where one in every six persons is a food-stamp recipient, one of every three babies born has an unwed mother, and the violent crime rate is ninth highest in the nation.[2]

I am meeting seventeen-year-old girls who have had one, sometimes two children. Without a chance for college, a senior trip to Florida, the possibility of a career, and the independence and mobility that a car gives, they are vulnerable to the first young man who looks at them. Sixteen-year-old Lily, swaying with the blanketed bundle in her arms as if she were holding a doll, tells me the familiar story that she wanted a baby so she could have "something of my very own."

With paper and pencil I am helping Shirley, a single mother, compute how to make ends meet for herself and her child on an AFDC (Aid to Families with Dependent Children) check of $138 a month and $123 in food stamps. I witness her agony of deciding if she should give up AFDC and get a job, which means losing medicaid, the only health insurance she has for her child. The cashier's job at a supermarket which she is considering pays minimum wages and is part-time — thirty-five hours a week (the policy of most supermarkets in the city), which means that she won't get medical or retirement benefits. The St. Thomas residents who do find full-time work usually receive minimum wages, which amounts to about thirty-five dollars a month above the AFDC income level. (1990 Census Bureau statistics reveal that *full-time* minimum-wage earners received $8,840 a year.) Plus, mothers like Shirley, who choose work instead of welfare, face additional costs of child care, medical bills, an increase in rent (proportionate to income), and transportation expenses. I had always thought that jobs were the way *out* of poverty. Now I'm learning the meaning of *working poor*. (In 1989 37.3 million working Americans, accounting for 39 percent of total tax returns, received incomes below $15,000.)[3]

At the supper table at night I am listening to the stories Sister Therese St. Pierre tells of the three- and four-year-olds in her preschool group who do not know words like "over" or "lettuce" or "sofa." Most of these children will hit the overpopulated, under-staffed, ill-equipped public schools with "failure by third grade" stamped on their foreheads.

I am watching how easy it is for a teenage boy to "run a bag" of cocaine down the street for an easy twenty bucks. (If he gets an after-school or summer job, his income will be deducted from his mother's AFDC check.)

I am seeing, with my own eyes — shocked, disbelieving — bags of white powder peddled in the open with no police in sight. Sister Lory Schaff, who began Hope House in 1969, tells of meeting in 1972 with a high-ranking city official to express her concern about the freewheeling dope peddling in St. Thomas, and of being met with, "Well, now, Sister, we know drugs are going to pop up *somewhere* in every city. At least we know where they are."

I also notice that when residents of St. Thomas are killed, the newspaper barely takes notice, whereas when white citizens are killed, there is often a front-page story.

But the most frightening revelation is the treatment of neighborhood residents by the police. Story after story, incident after incident is told of people, especially young men, picked up, verbally abused, handcuffed, beaten, and sometimes killed. I've witnessed such scenes myself, watching young men thrown forcefully against police cars, handcuffed, pushed into the car and driven away. One called out to another Sister and me as we watched in disbelief, "Sisters, ya'll are my witnesses. I got no drugs on me. They gonna stick it in my pockets. I got no drugs." According to a 1984 – 1990 U.S. Department of Justice survey, New Orleans logged more complaints against its police than any other city in the country.[4]

I think of lines from a poem by Langston Hughes:

> Negroes
> Sweet and docile,
> Meek, humble, and kind:
> Beware the day
> They change their mind . . .[5]

Meanwhile, I watch Reagan slash funds for prenatal and child care, low-income housing, employment training, and food subsidies. And as social programs are slashed, new prisons are built. Between 1975 and 1991 Louisiana expanded its adult prisons from three to twelve, with prison populations increasing by 249 percent. Throughout the 1980s Louisiana ranked first, second, or third in the nation as the state incarcerating the greatest number of its residents — at an annual cost per inmate of $15,000, and that doesn't include the cost of prison construction, about $50,000 for the average prison bed. Louisiana's exponential prison expansion is part of a national trend. In 1980 about 500,000 Americans were behind bars; in 1990, 1.1 million — the highest confinement rate in the world. And if parole and probation systems are included, in 1990 the United States had in its criminal justice system 1 of every 43 adults, 1 of every 24 men, and 1 of every 162 women, at the cost of $20 billion a year. Between 1981 and 1991 the federal government cut its contribution to education by 25 percent (in real dollars) and increased its allocation for criminal justice by 29 percent.[6]

Almost every family I meet in St. Thomas has a relative in prison. (In 1989 one in four black men in the twenty-to-twenty-nine age group was under the control of the criminal justice system.)[7] As one woman put it, "our young men leave here either in a police car or a hearse."

I feel like I've entered a war zone or a foreign country where the language and customs and rules are different from anything I have ever encountered.

"This ain't no place to raise kids," a mother says to me, her eyes glinting with anger. "But where can I go? Where else can I go and be able to pay the rent and light bill? This place is like a reservation."

Yet, it is from some of the residents themselves that I receive hope. They remind me of those plucky little flowers you see growing straight up through asphalt.

Here is a young teenage boy who works in a drugstore after school to help his single working mother buy clothes for his younger sisters. Here is a twenty-two-year-old man who after a short stint in parish (county) jail steadily comes to the Adult Learning Center for fifth-grade reading lessons. Here is a young woman whose mother has worked at two jobs so that she can attend college. Here is an ex-convict organizing a boys' club in the neighborhood. Here is a college-educated, articulate young man helping tenants organize self-help programs.

I keep thinking of the gifts of my own upbringing, which I once took for granted: I can read any book I choose and comprehend it. I can write a complete sentence and punctuate it correctly. If I need help, I can call on judges, attorneys, educators, ministers. I wonder what I would be like if I had grown up without such protections and supports. What cracks would have turned up in my character? What makes me think that I wouldn't have been pregnant at seventeen? How law-abiding would I be?

In some mysterious way my living and working in St. Thomas is paring me down to essentials and liberating my spirit. Even living without air-conditioning is good for me. Intense heat slows you down. You choose essential tasks. You become grateful for small breezes and seek the company of trees. You appreciate a cool bath, ice water. Simple things. Good things. And for the first time in my life I have the opportunity to enjoy the friendship of black people. I realize how deprived my life was in the all-white-just-like-me social circles I used to frequent.

But I am out of joint with the times. This is the eighties, when social activists from the sixties are supposed to be experiencing the "big chill," and here I am just warming up to the action.

DEAD MAN WALKING

I am reading people like Gandhi, Alice Walker, Albert Camus, Dorothy Day, and Martin Luther King, and even the way I pray is changing. Before, I had asked God to right the wrongs and comfort the suffering. Now I know — really know — that God entrusts those tasks to us.

After getting the name of the death-row inmate from Chava, that very night after supper I write my first letter. My new pen pal is a white man, a Cajun from St. Martinville. That's a surprise. I had assumed he would be black. I tell Mr. Sonnier a little about myself and where I work and that if he doesn't want to write back, that's okay, I'll keep writing to him anyway.

I send him three photos. One is of me on a pony out in the woods (it is the only photo that I have and Chava had said to be sure to include a photo of myself). I also send a color photograph of the blue, shimmering water at Bay St. Louis, Mississippi, and a picture of Christ on the cross.

As I address the envelope, I pause. What an address: "Death Row." What's it like to live on Waiting for Death Street? And what's it like to have done something really bad, really evil, something irreparable? I can't bear myself when I hurt someone. I had felt terrible in eighth grade when a group of us during a slumber party called up a fat girl and made fun of her. When I was eight I had had nightmares after I helped torture an opossum some neighborhood boys had cornered. I had wanted to be tough like the guys and I had taken my turn hitting the animal with a stick until the opossum had begun to bleed from the mouth. I dreamed that night of the bloody head. Perhaps there were baby opossums waiting for their mother to return with their food.

But this is my sensitivity, not Sonnier's. Maybe he doesn't care about the pain he inflicts on others. Maybe he doesn't even realize that his victims' families, cursed with memory of their slain loved ones, will forever occupy a "death row" of their own because of him. Maybe violence is natural to him. Maybe he's a brute.

As I seal the envelope I wonder what his two young victims were like, and I think of their parents. I can't imagine the pain of losing children to a wanton murderer. I think of how my mother would suffer if Mary Ann or Louie or I were killed. She would rather die herself. Those poor parents. I wonder what I might do to comfort them. But the murders happened five years ago, and I assume that by now the Bourques and LeBlancs have tried to put the pain behind them and want nothing to do with someone befriending their children's murderer. Later, Lloyd LeBlanc will berate me for not seeking him out at the beginning, and the Bourque family will be outraged and hurt over the "Church's" attention to their daughter's murderer. "Why didn't [she] come and talk to our family, to understand how we felt?" Goldie Bourque will say of me to a newspaper reporter.[8] I will meet the Bourques and the LeBlancs a year and a half from now at Pat Sonnier's Pardon Board hearing a few days before his execution. And several years down the road Elizabeth and Vernon Harvey, whose daughter, Faith, was murdered by Robert Lee Willie (another death-row inmate whom I befriend), will bring me with them to victims' meetings and I will find a way to help the victims' families, too. But not yet.

A week after my letter to Sonnier I receive a letter from the Louisiana State Penitentiary at Angola. It is from prison authorities, who tell me I have not observed the rule which specifies the size of photographs that are permitted in inmate mail. The photographs of Christ and the scene of Bay St. Louis that I had enclosed with my letter have exceeded the required size and are being returned.

A few days later another letter from Angola arrives.

This is from the man who is never supposed to answer letters.

In the letter Sonnier says that, yes, he would enjoy exchanging letters with me. He has tried going it alone, figuring he is going to die anyway, so why try to be close to anyone? But it is "just too hard" and, yes, my letters will be most welcome. He says that at first he had thought the guard had made a mistake when he flipped the letter onto the floor of his cell. Who would be writing to him? Helen? Did he see "Helen" in the corner of the envelope? His ex-"old lady," Helen? He wanted nothing to do with her. Things were bad between them. If this was her letter, he would tear it up unopened. But then he had looked more carefully at the envelope. Sister Helen? A nun? He didn't like the nuns who had taught him catechism in grade school. Plenty hits with a ruler on young hands and knuckles.

The fierce irony makes me smile.

"Who is God?"

Whack, whack, whack.

"God is *love*. Remember that." *Whack, whack.*

He says that he chuckled, seeing my picture on the pony. Was that poor pony's legs buckling from my weight on him? The other nuns he had known wore habits. Did I ever wear one too?

He asks, "Can we just talk to each other in regular words?" He had had a spiritual adviser who had spoken to him in "scriptures" from the Bible. He couldn't hold up his end of the conversation and the relationship soon ended.

Sure, we can just talk regular, I tell him. It's the only way I know how to talk.

We soon become steady correspondents, and I begin to think of him as a fellow human being, though I can't for a moment forget his crime, nor can I reconcile the easygoing Cajun who writes to me with the brutal murderer of two helpless teenagers. Sometimes I include newspaper articles about world events in my letters, sometimes clippings from the comics. He tells me about how he organizes his cell. His life is lived twenty-three out of twenty-four hours a day in a space six feet wide and eight feet long. On one wall is a bunk, on the back wall a stainless steel toilet and washbasin, a stainless steel plate above the washbowl instead of a mirror. He keeps all of his stuff in a footlocker under his bunk. He uses the footlocker for weight lifting. It's hard not to gain weight in this place, he says. Plenty of potatoes, rice, pancakes, and beans. He is allowed out of his cell for one hour a day (the time of day varies; the earliest is 5:00 A.M.) and then he can visit with the other eleven men on the tier if he chooses, but relations are often tense. If another inmate has it in for you, he explains, he can throw hot water on you through the bars of your cell, or he can take batteries out of his radio and sling them at you, or he can sling feces.

He says that he tries to keep pretty much to himself and that the man in the cell next to him is sometimes hard to get along with. "The black dude sees racism in everything. We argue."

I notice his letters are stamped "indigent" in a little red box on the envelope. I learn that he is given two such stamped envelopes a week for correspondence. He is not allowed to work as other prisoners are, and so has no income. If he were allowed to work, his pay would be two and a half cents an hour. (The abolition of slavery in the Thirteenth Amendment of the Constitution does not extend to the incarcerated.)[9] I ask if I can send him stamps. "Sure," he says, "then I could write to you more often." He begins drawing pictures on his envelopes: alligators, ducks, squirrels.

I learn that his mother lives in St. Martinville but seldom comes to see him. "Her health isn't too good, and it's hard for her to come to this place," he says, excusing her. His younger brother Eddie is also at Angola, serving a life sentence.

One day, after we have been writing each other for a couple of months, he includes in his letter a photo of himself taken after he was incarcerated. It is the first time I see his face: he's not scowling exactly but there is something about the bushy eyebrows and the way they slant downward. I feel a sliver of fear. I feel safer knowing he is behind bars.

So far he has not mentioned his crime.

I telephone Chava and ask if I might come to the Coalition office to read the Sonnier files.

When I arrive, Chava has several thick manila folders and a stack of trial transcripts waiting for me on a table. He says he doesn't mind if I take the documents home, and explains that these word-for-word transcripts of the trial are what attorneys examine when they represent death-row inmates in their habeas corpus appeal, the review by federal courts to assure that state courts have upheld the constitutional rights of the defendant. (Federal court review of capital cases results in a high percentage of reversals — between 1976 and 1990, 40 to 60 percent of such cases were reversed.)[10] Chava says that within a week of his arrival on death row, Patrick Sonnier had received two pieces of mail — one from the trial judge announcing the date of his execution in six weeks and one from his court-appointed attorney terminating his services. He explains that here in Louisiana, court-appointed attorneys are required to represent clients only in the state courts, not on federal appeal.[11] "And of course, none of the guys on the Row can afford to hire their own attorney," he says, "so you can imagine the frantic telephone calls we get from death-row inmates, begging us to find them attorneys. In this state only when the petition for postconviction relief is filed can there be a stay of execution. One of our biggest challenges here is recruiting lawyers to represent these death-row inmates — free of charge, of course — and these petitions take hours and hours to prepare. Attorneys aren't exactly lining up outside this door for the job."

I ask who volunteers to take these cases.

"People who believe in fairness," Chava says and explains that sometimes even attorneys who support capital punishment take a postconviction capital case because they believe that no one, no matter how despicable the crime, should be deprived of a habeas review. He says that more than half of the attorneys recruited are from out of state, but Sonnier's attorney is a native Louisianian who telephoned and offered to take the case.

I don't know anything about the legal issues in these cases. Once Pat mentioned that he had got a letter from his attorney, but only in passing, and he has never mentioned legal issues. I gather that he has a lot of confidence in his attorney. Since the man offered on his own to take the case, I assume he must be good at what he does.

I look down at the mound of documents.

As Chava leaves he says, "Pull the door behind you when you leave. It'll lock," and he's gone.

There are seven volumes of transcripts. I slide them to one side of the table and open a folder labeled "Correspondence." I find a letter from Eddie Sonnier, Pat's brother, written from parish jail.

"These lawyers we have, I'm not sure what all they're doing for me and my brother because we hardly ever see them. Can you help us?"

I open the top folder full of newspaper clippings.

"Leads are few in murder here," the November 7, 1977, front-page headline of the *New Iberian* announces, and I look down upon the smiling faces of a teenage couple. The young man has laughing eyes and the young woman, a serene half-smile. The article tells how on the Friday evening before the murders, David LeBlanc, age seventeen, and Loretta Bourque, eighteen, had been "just two happy faces in the crowd at Catholic High School's homecoming football game." The couple had each been shot three times at close range in the back of the head with a .22-caliber rifle.

The day after the bodies of the couple are discovered, the *Iberian* runs an editorial, which says in part, "It's hard to imagine that there may be somebody in this fine community of ours who could contemplate, much less carry out, this vilest of vile deeds."

It takes a month to capture the killers. Their sneering faces appear on the front page of the *Iberian* December 2 issue: Elmo Patrick Sonnier, age twenty-seven, and Eddie James Sonnier, age twenty. The article says that the brothers are being held in neighboring parish jails without bond and have been given attorneys to represent them at the court's expense.

In addition to the murder charges, the Sonnier brothers face ten counts of aggravated kidnapping and one charge of aggravated rape. Law enforcement authorities have revealed that a number of teenage couples in the area, six weeks before the murders, had been attacked at the local lovers' lane. Two men, posing as security officers, would handcuff the men and molest the women. Most of the couples were too afraid or too ashamed to come forward, parish deputies said, but now, in the wake of the killings, the young people are revealing what happened to them and identifying the Sonnier brothers as the assailants.

As the trials take place, the horror of David LeBlanc's and Loretta Bourque's last evening of life unfolds: the Sonniers rabbit hunting with .22 rifles, the couple parked in a lovers' lane, the Sonniers posing as security officers, the young people accused of "trespassing" and handcuffed together in the back seat of a car and driven twenty miles down dark, abandoned roads, the car stopping in an abandoned oil field and the girl taken off by herself in the woods and raped, the couple being ordered to lie face down on the ground.

That would be their last physical sensation before the shots were fired: the cold, dew-laden grass. The coronor testifies that they died instantly.

The brothers' confessions are riddled with contradictions. At first, Patrick Sonnier says he shot the young people because he didn't want to go back to Angola, where he had served time in 1968 for stealing a truck, and he was afraid the couple would identify him to the police. He confesses to the murders not once but two, three, four times over several days. He takes law officers to the scene of the crime and points out the place where he stood as he fired the gun. But then at his trial he says he confessed because he was afraid of the police and that in fact it was his brother who had gone "berserk" and killed the teenagers. But Eddie Sonnier at his brother's trial testifies that it was Patrick who had committed the murders, that he had been afraid of him and had held the flashlight while Patrick shot the youngsters. Both admit to the kidnapping; Patrick denies raping the girl, but Eddie says his brother did have sex with the girl and admits to having sexual intercourse with her himself but claims she was "willing."

At separate trials each brother is found guilty of first-degree murder and sentenced to death, but Eddie Sonnier's death sentence is overturned by the Louisiana Supreme Court, which holds Patrick Sonnier to be the triggerman and Eddie, the younger brother, not as culpable. Patrick Sonnier's death sentence is also overturned by the Louisiana Supreme Court because of the judge's improper jury instruction.[12] At Patrick's second sentencing trial, Eddie, declaring, "I want to tell the truth and get everything off my chest" testifies that it was he who had killed the teenagers, that he had "lost it," because the boy's name was David and shortly before the killings his girlfriend had spurned him for a man named David — not the victim — and something the boy had said had triggered his rage, something had "come over him," and the two Davids had blurred in his mind and the gun was in his hand and he had fired.

16

But the prosecutor discredits this confession of guilt, arguing that Eddie Sonnier, his death sentence now overturned by the court, is transparently trying to save his brother from the electric chair. The jury readily agrees with the prosecutor and resentences Patrick Sonnier to death.[13]

Information about the Bourque and LeBlanc families filters through the news articles.

"The Sonniers exterminated the LeBlanc name," Lloyd LeBlanc tells a reporter. He and his wife, Eula, are older and do not expect other children. David was their only son. The LeBlancs are Catholics who attend Mass regularly and send their children to Catholic schools. They have one other child, Vickie, who is attending college.

Loretta Bourque was the oldest daughter of Godfrey and Goldie Bourque's seven children. The Bourques' youngest child, Hubert, age five, was born with severe brain damage and cannot walk, talk, or feed himself. He lives in a crib in the Bourques' living room and the family calls him God's "special angel." The Bourques are devout Catholics.

The sun is setting and a shaft of orange filters through one of the tall windows. I close the folder and put my head in my hands.

A boy and girl, their young lives budding, unfolding. Snipped.

And their parents, condemned to wonder for the rest of their lives about their children's last tortured hours; sentenced for the rest of their days to fear for their families, their other children; startled out of their sleep at night by dreams of the terror that ripped their children from them.

The details of the depravity stun me. It is like the spinning merry-go-round that I had once tried to climb aboard when I was a child, but it was spinning too fast and it threw me to the ground.

You may take the documents home, Chava had said, but I do not want to take them home. I know enough. More than enough. I leave the documents on the table and walk across the dying sunlight to the door and close it behind me, the words of Jeremiah welling within me:

> A voice was heard in Ramah,
>   sobbing and lamenting:
>   Rachel weeping for her children,
>   refusing to be comforted
>   because they were no more.
>   (31:15)

A few days later a letter from Pat Sonnier arrives. It brims with small details: that the grits for breakfast had been hard that morning, that he hoped for scrambled eggs soon, that he had lent ten cigarettes to a guy on the tier, giving him a second chance, because the last time he had lent this guy cigarettes he had not returned the favor. But he would give the guy "one more chance." It ends as all his letters end, thanking me for my love, my care. He has sketched and colored a green and blue duck on the envelope.

Between the lines of his letters about eggs and cigarettes and daily routine I sense words he does not say, a reality he scrupulously omits. He never talks about the death the state has in store for him.

Louisiana used to hang its criminals until the state legislature in 1940 decided that electrocution would be more humane and efficient. Hanging didn't always work. As the noose was placed around the condemned's neck, the knot had to be positioned exactly right, or the victim died a slow death by strangulation — or worse, decapitation, if the distance of the drop was disproportionate to body weight.

Death by electrocution was introduced in the United States in 1890 at Auburn Prison in upstate New York, when William Kemmler was killed by the state of New York. The *New York Times* described the new method as "euthanasia by electricity," and the U.S. Supreme Court, upholding the state appellate court's decision that death by electricity was not cruel and unusual punishment, had concluded: "It is in easy reach of the electrical science at this day to so generate and apply to the person of the convict a current of electricity of such known and sufficient force as certainly to produce instantaneous and therefore painless death."

A reporter for the *New World* newspaper who witnessed Kemmler's execution reported:

"The current had been passing through his body for 15 seconds when the electrode at the head was removed. Suddenly the breast heaved. There was a straining at the straps which bound him. A purplish foam covered the lips and was spattered over the leather head band. The man was alive.

"Warden, physician, guards . . . everybody lost their wits. There was a startled cry for the current to be turned on again . . . An odor of burning flesh and singed hair filled the room, for a moment, a blue flame played about the base of the victim's spine. This time the electricity flowed four minutes . . ."

That was in 1890.

DEAD MAN WALKING

On October 16, 1985, the electrocution of William Vandiver by the state of Indiana took seventeen minutes, requiring five charges of electricity.

On April 22, 1983, as the state of Alabama electrocuted John Louis Evans, the first electrical charge burned through the electrode on the leg and the electrode fell off. The prison guards repaired it and administered another charge of electricity. Smoke and flame erupted from Evans's temple and leg but the man was still alive. Following the second jolt, Evans's lawyer demanded that Governor George C. Wallace halt the proceedings. The governor refused. Another jolt was administered. It took fourteen minutes for Evans to die.

On May 5, 1990, as the state of Florida killed Jesse Tafero, flames shot six inches from the hood covering his head. The executioner interrupted the standard two-minute 2,000-volt electrical cycle and officials later determined that a sponge on Tafero's head had caught fire.

The only man to walk away from an electric chair alive was seventeen-year-old Willie Francis. On May 2, 1946, he was strapped into Louisiana's portable electric chair in the jail in St. Martin Parish. As the current hit his body, witnesses reported that the youth's "lips puffed out and he groaned and jumped so that the chair came off the floor, and he said, 'Take it off. Let me breathe.' " The officials applied several more jolts, but Francis was still alive. They then helped him back to his cell to recuperate from the ordeal.

The U.S. Supreme Court, considering whether it could be considered "cruel and unusual punishment" or "double jeopardy" to subject Francis to electrocution a second time, rendered a split verdict. On May 8, 1947, Louisiana officials once again strapped Willie Francis into the chair, but this time they succeeded in killing him.[14]

Witnesses over the years have rendered graphic descriptions of state electrocutions, which Justice William F. Brennan, in *Glass v. Louisiana*, included in his dissenting opinion:

"The hands turn red, then white, and the cords of the neck stand out like steel bands . . . The prisoner's limbs, fingers, toes, and face are severely contorted . . . The force of the electric current is so powerful that the prisoner's eyeballs sometimes pop out on his cheeks . . . The prisoner often defecates, urinates, and vomits blood and drool . . . Sometimes the prisoner catches fire . . . There is a sound like bacon frying and the sickly sweet smell of burning flesh

19

... when the post-electrocution autopsy is performed the liver is so hot that doctors said it cannot be touched by the human hand ... The body frequently is badly burned ...[15]

It is a common opinion that persons subjected to 2,000 volts of electricity lose consciousness immediately and feel no pain. But Dr. Harold Hillman, director of the Unity Laboratory in Applied Neurology, University of Surrey, England, thinks otherwise. Hillman, who studied autopsies of thirteen men electrocuted in the Florida and Alabama electric chairs from 1983 to 1990, concluded that such executions are "intensely painful" because the prisoner may for some time retain consciousness. For death to be instantaneous, he maintains, the full force of the electrical current would have to reach the brain. Instead, he says, only a small percentage of the current may be reaching the brain because the greater portion travels through and over the skin to reach the other electrode. The autopsies of electrocuted prisoners which he studied reveal that there was minimal damage to the brain in comparison to massive burns to the skin.

He adds, "The massive electric current stimulates all the muscles to full contraction. Thus, the prisoner cannot react by any further movement, even when the current is turned off for a short period, and the heart is still beating, as has been documented in numerous cases of execution by electrocution. It is usually thought that the failure of the convict to move is a sign that he cannot feel. He cannot move because all his muscles are contracting maximally."[16]

Later, in the months ahead, Patrick Sonnier will confide his terror to me of the death that awaits him, telling me of a recurring nightmare, always the same: the guards coming for him, dragging him screaming toward the chair, strapping him in with the wide leather straps, covering his face with the hood, and he is screaming, "No, no, no ..." For him there can never again be restful, unbroken sleep, because the dream can always come. Better, he says, to take short naps and not to sink into deep sleep.

I cannot accept that the state now plans to kill Patrick Sonnier in cold blood. But the thought of the young victims haunts me. Why do I feel guilty when I think of them? Why do I feel as if I have murdered someone myself?

In prayer I sort it out.

I know that if I had been at the scene when the young people were abducted, I would have done all in my power to save them.

I know I feel compassion for their suffering parents and family and would do anything to ease their pain if I knew how. I also know that nothing can ease some pain.

I know I am trying to help people who are desperately poor, and I hope I can prevent some of them from exploding into violence. Here my conscience is clean and light. No heaviness, no guilt.

Then it comes to me. The victims are dead and the killer is alive and I am befriending the killer.

Have I betrayed his victims? Do I have to take sides? I am acutely aware that my beliefs about the death penalty have never been tested by personal loss. Let Mama or my sister, Mary Ann, or my brother, Louie, be brutally murdered and then see how much compassion I have. My magnanimity is gratuitous. No one has shot my loved ones in the back of the head.

If someone I love should be killed, I know I would feel rage, loss, grief, helplessness, perhaps for the rest of my life. It would be arrogant to think I can predict how I would respond to such a disaster. But Jesus Christ, whose way of life I try to follow, refused to meet hate with hate and violence with violence. I pray for the strength to be like him. I cannot believe in a God who metes out hurt for hurt, pain for pain, torture for torture. Nor do I believe that God invests human representatives with such power to torture and kill. The paths of history are stained with the blood of those who have fallen victim to "God's Avengers." Kings and Popes and military generals and heads of state have killed, claiming God's authority and God's blessing. I do not believe in such a God.

In sorting out my feelings and beliefs, there is, however, one piece of moral ground of which I am absolutely certain: if I were to be murdered I would not want my murderer executed. I would not want my death avenged. *Especially by government* — which can't be trusted to control its own bureaucrats or collect taxes equitably or fill a pothole, much less decide which of its citizens to kill.

Albert Camus' "Reflections on the Guillotine" is for me a moral compass on the issue of capital punishment. He wrote this essay in 1957 when the stench of Auschwitz was still in the air, and one of his cardinal points is that no government is ever innocent enough or wise enough or just enough to lay claim to so absolute a power as death.

> *Society proceeds sovereignly to eliminate the evil ones from her midst as if she were virtue itself. Like an honorable man killing his wayward son and remarking: "Re-*

ally, I didn't know what to do with him" . . . *To assert, in any case, that a man must be absolutely cut off from society because he is absolutely evil amounts to saying that society is absolutely good, and no one in his right mind will believe this today.*[17]

Camus addresses the moral contradiction inherent in a policy which imitates the violence it claims to abhor, a violence, he says, made more grievous by premeditation:

> *Many laws consider a premeditated crime more serious than a crime of pure violence* . . . *For there to be equivalence, the death penalty would have to punish a criminal who had warned his victim of the date at which he would inflict a horrible death on him and who, from that moment onward, had confined him at his mercy for months. Such a monster is not encountered in private life. (p. 199)*

I am beginning to notice something about Pat Sonnier. In each of his letters he expresses gratitude and appreciation for my care. He makes no demands. He doesn't ask for money. He does not request my phone number (inmates at Angola are allowed to make collect phone calls). He only says how glad he is to have someone to communicate with because he has been so lonely. The sheer weight of his loneliness, his abandonment, draws me. I abhor the evil he has done. But I sense something, some sheer and essential humanness, and that, perhaps, is what draws me most of all.

In my next letter I ask him if anyone ever comes to see him, and he says, no, there is no one. So I ask how I might go about visiting him.

CHAPTER
2

*P*at's return letter *brims with excitement and he explains that he must* put me on his visitor list so the prison can do a security check. I am to send my birth date and social security number. He tells me that he went back and forth in his mind about which category of visitor to put me in — friend or spiritual adviser — but he has decided on spiritual adviser. I have no idea what difference the category will make. I later learn that a spiritual adviser may remain with the condemned man in the death house after 6:00 P.M., when relatives and friends must leave. The spiritual adviser is allowed to witness the execution.

Nothing happens for months, and then I receive a letter from a Catholic priest who serves as chaplain at the prison. He says he has to interview me before I can become Pat's spiritual adviser. I drive to Angola for the interview.

It is July 1982. I set out around nine in the morning. My interview is set for the early afternoon. I have a poor sense of direction, so I have carefully written down the route to the prison, which is at the end of a circuitous road, about three hours from New Orleans.

It feels good to get out of the steamy housing project onto the open road, to see sky and towering clouds and the blue, wide waters of Lake Pontchartrain.

Highway 66, which dead-ends at the gates of the prison, snakes through the Tunica hills, a refreshing change of terrain in pancake-flat Louisiana. It is cooler and greener in the hills, and some of the branches of the trees arch across the road and bathe it in shadow.

I think of the thousands of men who have been transported down this road since 1901, when this 18,000-acre prison was established. About 4,600 men are locked up here now, half of them, practically speaking, serving life sentences. "Wide-stripes," they used to call the lifers.

Louisiana deals out harsh sentences. In 1977, when the death penalty was reinstated by the state legislature, the life-imprisonment statute was reformulated, effectively eliminating probation, parole, or suspension of sentence for first- and second-degree murder. An eighteen-year-old first-time offender convicted of distributing heroin faces a life sentence without possibility of probation or parole; and the habitual-offender law, aimed at reducing "career criminals," imposes a life sentence on offenders even for nonviolent crimes.

About five miles from the prison I see a hand-painted sign nailed to a tree: "Do not despair. You will soon be there." I make a sharp S-curve in the road and see a clearing, an open sky, and the Louisiana State Penitentiary — Angola. I drive up to the front gate. Several armed, blue-uniformed guards occupy a small, glassed-in office and one of them comes to the car and I show him the letter from the chaplain. They inspect my car — trunk, glove compartment, seats — put a visitor's sign on my dashboard, and direct me to the administration building about a quarter of a mile inside the prison grounds.

There are red and yellow zinnias all along the road, and the grass is neatly trimmed. Mottled black-and-white cattle browse in a field of green. I see a column of inmates, most of them black, marching out to soybean and vegetable fields, their hoes over their shoulders. Behind and in front of the marching men, guards on horseback with rifles watch their charges. In antebellum days three cotton plantations occupied these 18,000 acres, worked by slaves from Angola in Africa. The name Angola stuck. Since its beginnings in 1901, abuse, corruption, rage, and reform have studded its history.

In 1951 eight inmates, known as the "Heel-string Gang," inaugurated the first reform at Angola by slitting their Achilles tendons with razor blades rather than go to the "long line" in the fields, where they were systematically beaten or shot by guards. The *Shreveport Times* and the New Orleans *Times-Picayune* carried the heel-slashing story, and the ensuing publicity brought a gubernatorial investigative commission to the prison and the first rudimentary reforms. But as recently as 1975 it took a federal court to prod state officials to enact needed reforms of Louisiana penal institutions. Before then, at Angola, men were still being kept in the "Red Hat," a disciplinary cell block made of tiny concrete cells (including a cement bunk) with only a slit of a window near the ceiling. After prisoners were moved out, prison authorities converted the facility into a dog kennel.[1]

I wait in the front foyer of the administration building for the chaplain. Soon he comes in from one of the offices along the side wing of the building. He is an elderly man. His face is kind. His voice seems tired. Why, he asks, do I want to become Sonnier's spiritual adviser? I say I want to visit him because he has no one else and visiting prisoners is a Christian work of mercy.

The chaplain says that "these people," I must remember, are the "scum of the earth," and that I must be very, very careful because they are all con men and will try to take advantage of me every way they can. "You can't trust them," he says emphatically. "Your job is to help this fellow save his soul by receiving the sacraments of the church before he dies," he says.

He is strictly an old-school, pre-Vatican Catholic, and he shows me a pamphlet on sexual purity and modesty of dress that he distributes to the prisoners. Later I will be the source of such stress to this man that the warden will tell me, "That old man is going to have a heart attack because of you." Later, the chaplain will try to bar me and other women from serving as spiritual advisers to death-row inmates.

But for now, on this July afternoon, we chat pleasantly. As I am leaving he urges me to wear my habit when I visit the inmates. It's the modesty thing, I think, but, no, it isn't that. "The inmates know," he says, "that the Pope has requested nuns to wear the habit, and for you to flout authority will only encourage them to do the same." Which amazes me. I have serious doubts that Angola inmates know — or care — what dress code the Pope recommends for nuns.

I have not had one of these "habit" conversations in a long while. There had been much discussion when we had changed to ordinary clothes back in 1968. Seeing us dress like regular people had been upsetting for many Catholics, who said that when they saw us in our long, flowing robes, dressed like "angels," it had made them think of God.

Actually, for me, discarding the habit probably increased my life expectancy. As a student teacher my veil had caught on fire from a candle during a prayer service and I had almost gone up in smoke before my wide-eyed class. I tend to move quickly, and more than once my long black veil, flowing behind me, had caught on a door knob and stopped me dead in my tracks. The garb had covered us completely — except for face and hands — and once, when a member of my community, Sister Alice Macmurdo, was in a fabric shop she felt small tugs at her veil and turned to face an embarrassed woman who had mistaken her for a bolt of material.

But this dear old priest will not like these stories. I thank him for his time and his advice and on the drive home I take some of his wariness of prisoners to heart. I could never call inmates "scum," but I know I'm inexperienced and he's right — I do need to be on guard against being conned. Until today I have never been inside a prison, except for a brief foray into the Orleans Parish Jail in the late sixties during the days of the "singing nuns" ("*Dominique-nique, nique*" — that crowd). I could plunk out a few chords on my guitar and another Sister and I had gone once or twice to entertain the prisoners. When I suggested "If I Had a Hammer" for our opening number, the inmates sang it with great relish, and, as the song progressed, made up spirited verses of their own: "If I had a crowbar; If I had a switchblade . . ." The guards rolled their eyes.

And I think again of the sliver of fear I felt when I first saw the photo of Patrick Sonnier, the cruel slant of the eyebrows. What will he be like in person? My heart tightens. How did I get involved in this bizarre affair? Where is this going to take me?

Early in September I receive approval from prison authorities to become Elmo Patrick Sonnier's spiritual adviser. I set a date for our first visit: September 15, 1982.

Along with the letter of approval, I receive the Louisiana Department of Corrections regulations for visitors. The most alarming rule is that by entering the corrections facility, you are subject to "searches of your property, automobile, and person" including "pat-down searches, inspection by dogs, and strip searches of your body, including your body cavities."

Maybe I'm an exception since I'm a nun. But I can't be sure. I have heard ugly stories of strip searches of visitors in Georgia. But I remind myself that I have been in other scary situations. Shoot-outs in the neighborhood, for instance. I am learning to face things as they come, not stepping out ahead of grace, as one of the spiritual maxims of my community counsels.

On September 15 I drive to Angola for my first visit with Pat. The summer heat has not yet lifted, though some of the trees along the highway are looking dry and yellow. I have a thermos of coffee. I have my approval papers and a picture ID.

I arrive at the prison at about 10:00 A.M. There are mostly women guards inside the visitor center, and they seem friendly, respectful. There are several bouquets of plastic flowers on the wall, probably their warming touch. A sign on a trash can catches my attention. It says, "It will be grateful if you throw your butt's in the butt can."

I show the guards my ID and letter of approval. One of the women searches my billfold (no purses are allowed) and the pockets of my suit. She does a few quick pats of my front and sides. Not bad. I breathe easier. I notice my fingertips are cold.

Death row is located in a building near the prison entrance. I walk past the guard's station and wait outside the gate of the fenced-in yard surrounding the death-row building. A woman guard in a nearby watchtower opens the gate electronically from a control switch. I hear a loud click. I walk through and the gate clangs shut behind me. There are flowers along the sidewalk leading to the building, and a small pond with ducks swimming. It looks like a quiet little park.

Inside the building I am accompanied by a guard through a series of gates down a hallway. "Woman on the tier," he yells, warning prisoners to steer clear of the hallway. Gate one, *clang*, gate two, *clang*, gate three. Metal on metal. It is all green and cement and bars. And it is stiflingly hot. Too many blocked-off spaces. No way for the air to circulate. I see a green metal door with a barred window and above it red block letters: "Death Row."

The guard is unlocking a door to my right. I am to go inside. "Wait here. They'll get your man for you," he says, then closes the door and locks me in the room.

I look around. I feel a tight band of ice around my stomach. In the room are six visiting booths the size of telephone booths constructed of heavy plywood painted stark white. A heavy mesh screen separates visitors from inmates. On the visitor side is a loud, whirring fan. There are plastic chairs stacked in a corner and several large tin cans painted red which serve as trash cans. I am the only one in the room. The place gives me the creeps.

The reality of this waiting place for death is difficult to grasp. It's not a ward in a hospital where sick people wait to die. People here wait to be taken out of their cells and killed. This is the United States of America and these are government officials in charge and there's a law sanctioning and upholding what is going on here, so it all must be legitimate and just, or so one compartment of my brain tells me, the part that studied civics in high school, the part that wants to trust that my country would never violate the human rights of its citizens.

The red block letters say "Death Row."

My stomach can read the letters better than my brain.

I pace slowly back and forth in the room and keep trying to take deep breaths, to settle down. I am allowed two hours for my visit. That seems like a very long time. I'm doubly tense. One, I am locked behind four — I count them — doors in this strange, unreal place. Two, I'm about to meet and talk to someone who killed two people. Letters are one thing, but just the two of us like this talking for two hours?

I hear him before I see him. I can hear the rattle of chains on his legs scraping across the floor and I can hear his voice. He is laughing and teasing the guard. I detect a Cajun accent.

"Hi, Pat, I made it," I say.

"Am I glad to see *you*, Sister," he says.

He is freshly shaven and his black hair is combed into a wave in the front. A handsome face, open, smiling. Not the face I had seen in the photo. He has on a clean blue denim shirt and jeans. His hands are cuffed to a wide brown leather belt at his waist. He has brought me a gift: a picture frame made out of intricately folded cigarette packages. "I made it for you," he says, and he explains that the biggest challenge had been collecting enough of the wrappers from the others on the tier. He is bright and talkative and tells me of some recent letters from college students whom I have referred to him.

"I was always a loner growing up. I've never had so many friends," he says, and he tells in detail what each pen pal has said and how he has responded. He keeps a checklist: "letters received — letters answered" and the date next to each.

He smokes one cigarette after another and he has to lean his head far down to reach the cigarette because his hands are cuffed to the belt. He is obviously very happy to have someone to talk to. Contact with someone in the outside world goes a long way in this place, where, as I soon learn, mail is rare and visits rarer.

As we talk I find myself looking at his hands — clean, shapely hands, moving expressively despite the handcuffs as he talks. These hands that made the nice picture frame for me also held a rifle that killed. The fingernails are bitten down to the quick.

He tells again of receiving the first letter from me and how the name Helen had made him think at first it was from his ex-"old lady," and he wanted to have nothing to do with her because she was the one who had told the sheriff where to find him, warning that he was dangerous and heavily armed, and the scowl is there and he stares past me as he talks. He can't believe his good fortune, he says, that I have come into his life out of the blue like this, and he thanks me profusely for making the long drive to come and see him.

The way he was teasing the guard and the way he thanks me and is talking to me now — I can tell he likes to please people.

He hasn't done well with women, he admits — lived with several but always "busted up." He has a little girl, Star, eleven years old, but she is with foster parents and her mother is in Texas and he says that his child was born when he was serving time in Angola for stealing a truck, and the first time he laid eyes on her was the day he got out of prison because he went right to where his "first old lady" was living and there was the child, playing in the front yard, and he had swooped her into his arms and said, "I'm your daddy," and her mother had appeared at the front door with a shotgun because she thought someone was trying to kidnap the child and and he had called out to her, "It's me. I'm back. I want to see my kid." But the first thing he had done when he stepped out of the gates at Angola was to get a case of beer, and by the time the Greyhound bus had pulled into St. Martinville he was pretty "tanked" and he and the woman had "gotten into it" that night and he smashed up some furniture and she threw him out and he had gone to his mother's.

He never has been one to share his feelings, he says, because when he was a kid growing up his mother and father used to fight a lot and they separated when he was six and his sister was three and Eddie was just a baby. His mother went on welfare because his daddy never did come through with child support and the welfare check would run out and they'd be hungry and he and Eddie would hunt deer and rabbit. He chuckles remembering how his mother would help them with the rabbit hunt and it was always her job to put the dead rabbits in a sack and to "finish them off" with a stick if they weren't dead yet. "And we'd be stalking along and behind us we'd hear *whack*, *whack*, *whack* — Mama beating the hell out of those rabbits."

I cringe, but he tells the incident nonchalantly. I am thinking of the clobbered rabbits. He is thinking of the food.

Once, he says, he and Eddie couldn't find a deer so they shot a neighbor's cow and skinned it and brought it home. "Mama knew this was no more a deer than the man in the moon, but she didn't say nothing 'cause we were all so hungry. She fixed us up a good roast that night and you could smell it cooking all through the house."

They often hunted at night. "Isn't it against the law to hunt at night?" I ask. "Yeah," he says, "but we didn't worry about that."

As kids they moved from mother to father and back again, he says, and by the time he was fourteen he had changed schools seven or eight times. He got only as far as eighth grade, dropped out when he was fifteen, forged his mother's signature on an application form, and went to work as a roustabout on the oil rigs. Later, he got his license and drove eighteen-wheelers and he had liked that best. From the age of nine, he says, he was on probation with juvenile authorities for burglaries, disturbing the peace, trespassing. "Mama couldn't do anything with me and she'd have Daddy come get me out of trouble."

His daddy was a sharecropper and one of the best things he got from him, he says, is his love of work. At the age of seven he picked cotton, potatoes, and peppers alongside his father, and as he got older, when it was harvesting time for the sugar cane, "there I'd be walking to school and see those open fields and I'd drop my books on the side of the road and head out into the fields." He hopes that maybe some day he can "hand back the chair" and work in the fields here, driving one of the tractors.

He stands up and I try to adjust my view of him because it is hard to see through the heavy mesh screen and he tells me to look down sometimes. "This screen can really do a number on your eyes."

He talks and talks and talks, and I am easing up inside because I was wondering how much I'd have to keep the conversation going, and now I can see that all I have to do is listen.

"Daddy took me to a bar when I was twelve and told me to pick my whiskey and there were all these bottles behind the bar and I pointed and said I'd take the one with the pretty turkey on it and the guys in the bar laughed and Daddy laughed too." He laughs. "We got drunk as a couple of coots and there we were at one in the morning trying to make it home on our bicycles, weaving and hitting every garbage can along the road."

He has feelings for his father, I can tell by the way he speaks of him, and he says that when he and his cousin, Robert, had been arrested for stealing a truck (the plan was to run away to Texas and start a new life) Robert's father had come to the jail to talk to the authorities and had gotten his boy off, but by then his own father was dead — cancer of the liver — and so Pat served time in Angola. "But you can bet your bottom dollar that if Daddy had been living, he'd been there to get me out," he says.

The guard announces that visiting time is over.

I rise to leave. I thank him for the picture frame and promise to come back in a month, and again he thanks me for making the long drive. "Be careful on that highway," he says. "People drive crazy."

I have a roaring headache when I emerge from the prison, and I take two Bufferins before I begin the drive back. Pure tension. I have never been in such a strange place in my life. When I get home, I promise myself, I'm going to take a bath to wash the place off me.

Freedom. How blessed it is to be outside the bars, and the windows are down in the car and the road is open before me and I take deep gulps of the fresh, good air. I wonder how I would bear up day after day, month after month in such a tiny cell.

I notice — the omission is glaring — that Pat said nothing about the crime. Maybe he's blocked it out or feels no remorse for what he did. Or maybe he just can't talk about the worst thing he ever did in his life to someone he meets for the first time. I have no right to demand that he confess to me his terrible sin. That kind of revelation demands trust and should be freely offered. I respect that.

His words drift back: what he said about his ex-wife turning him in to the police and his getting drunk and smashing furniture and her warning the sheriff that he was dangerous. If I had lived in St. Martinville I probably would have been terrified to meet him on the streets.

But I am not meeting him on the streets. I am meeting him in a crucible, and I am surprised by how human, even likable, he is. Despite his friendly letters I had half expected Charles Manson — brutish, self-absorbed, paranoid, incapable of normal human encounter.

But even if he were unlikable and repulsive, even if he were Manson, I still maintain that the state should not kill him. For me, the unnegotiable moral bedrock on which a society must be built is that killing by anyone, under any conditions, cannot be tolerated. And that includes the government.

Ten years have passed since I first met Patrick Sonnier. Over the years I have clarified my perspective. Back in 1982 I was an exuberant activist, having just joined the fray against social injustice, and

I see now that I devoted my energies exclusively to Pat Sonnier's plight when I should have shouldered the struggles of victims' families as well. I should have reached out to the Bourques and LeBlancs immediately and offered them love and comfort, even if they chose to reject it. Now, as I befriend each new man on death row, I always offer my help to his victim's family. Some accept my offer. Most angrily reject it. But I offer.

I also realize how naive I was about the criminal justice system. I had always known, of course, that there were imperfections in the system, but I honestly thought that when a person faced death, he or she would at least be given adequate legal defense. I thought the Constitution promised that. It took me longer than it should have to realize the shamefully inadequate legal counsel that Pat Sonnier and others like him get. By the time I sought remedial legal help for him it was too late. If I had acted sooner, I believe he would be alive today — imprisoned at Angola where he should be, but alive.

"The truth arrives disguised; therein the sorrow lies." So wrote Jimmy Glass, executed by the state of Louisiana in 1987.

Pat Sonnier and I continue to write, and every month I visit. He talks to me often about Eddie. The prison doesn't allow the brothers to visit each other, and I figure that since I'm making the long trip to the prison I can visit two people instead of one. Eddie keeps receiving disciplinary write-ups, which land him in the "hole," a stripped-down disciplinary cell with no TV or radio, nothing to read except the Bible, minimal writing materials.

"He's got to learn to control his temper in this place. He blows up too easy," Pat says. "That'll get you killed here, you can't afford to have enemies, but he just won't learn, and I can't be there to calm him down the way I used to on the streets."

Since his arrival on death row three years ago, Pat has never received a disciplinary write-up. No small feat in such a confined space where tensions run high, not only between inmates and guards, but among inmates as well.

"You have to learn each 'free man' [guard]," he says. "You learn which ones you can tease and which ones you can't and which ones blow hot one day and cold the next."

Pat has written to Eddie about me, preparing the way for my first visit. "She's a nun, but she talks natural and doesn't quote the Bible all the time."

In March of 1983 I visit Eddie for the first time. He reminds me of a caged panther. He is thin, tight, his eyes narrow slits. His hands tremble. He makes me feel tense, wary. I feel afraid of him and sorry for him at the same time. Clearly he's a tortured man.

He's on a lock-down tier, not yet in "big yard," where inmates sleep in a sixty-man dormitory, eat in a cafeteria, and have access to a recreation room. He shares a cell with one other person and he stays in this cell at all times except when he works in the fields. Meals are served in the cell. This is the normal track when inmates first come to Angola. Prison authorities keep a man in the fields until he "adjusts."

"Adjusting" does not come easily to Eddie Sonnier. Later, when I know him well, I will ask him why he got all those write-ups and he will answer with a wry smile, "Because I didn't have no understandin'."

A stack of Eddie's disciplinary reports will be among Pat's personal possessions, shipped to me by prison authorities after his execution.

The visiting room in the main prison where I visit Eddie is much more agreeable than the death-row visiting room. The room is spacious and air-conditioned. You can have a private conversation at a small table at the far end of the large room. You can touch. You can get a hot dog or hamburger and a cold drink at one of the concession stands run by inmate clubs. You can get a Polaroid picture taken. You can get an ice-cream cone.

But the visiting room does not give Eddie much consolation. First of all, because he doesn't see much of it. I am his first visitor. Prison is torture for him. He hates waiting while guards do the "count." He tells me how every inmate at every minute of the day has to be accounted for. Before going to work you wait for the count. After work you wait for the count. Before eating, before you go to sleep, when you first wake up at 5 A.M. He hates being thrown side by side with "all kinds of people." On the streets he had kept to himself, avoided crowds. He is afraid in "this place." You never know, he says, when someone might "lose it" and stab you with a radio antenna or a blade someone's buddy made for him in the welding shop. He's already been sent to the "hole" because someone with a grievance had put contraband under his mattress. He had protested his innocence but to no avail. "You got no defense in this place." And he says it's okay with him if they keep him on a lock-down tier forever "because you only have to deal with one cellmate, but in the dorms, if you have enemies, they can follow you when you go to the bathroom at two or three in the morning and beat you up or stab you or rape you and if the free man on duty isn't quick to intervene, you're dead meat, you're history."

Periodically, inmates are strip-searched. Eddie points to the door in the visiting room through which inmates return to the prison. Behind that door is a room and a guard. After a visit the inmate removes all of his clothes. He opens his mouth and sticks out his tongue. He turns his head from side to side so the guard can check his ears. He raises his arms above his head and stands spread-eagled, then he turns his back to the guard, bends over, and opens the cheeks of his buttocks. Finally, his back still toward the guard, he raises his feet one at a time for the guard to inspect the soles of his feet, his toes. If a guard suspects drugs he may do a "finger wave" of the inmate's rectum.

I shudder to think of myself in this type of situation, and I remember reading Dorothy Day's account of her experience in jail for civil disobedience. She told how the woman who conducted her physical exam had been "brutal" and how shocking it was to hear other women inmates shouting vulgar invitations to her and her young companions as they were led down the tier to their cells.

I can't imagine.

Sometime in July 1983, I receive a phone call from Pat. That morning a guard had entered the tier, stopped in front of his cell, and handed him a paper to read and sign. The paper was entitled "Warrant of Execution in Capital Case," and he had found himself reading his own name after the words "the condemned person to be put to death," and the date of his death, "the 19th day of August, 1983."

His voice cracks. "This is my second date," he tells me, and I remember that Chava had mentioned his receiving an execution date shortly after his arrival at Angola.

On my fingers as I talk to him I count the days. How many Fridays left? Thursdays? Sundays?

"I'll be moving to Cell 1 any time now," he tells me. An inmate on "countdown" for execution is put in the cell nearest the guard station. That way the guards, trained to spot desperate behavior — suicide, escape — can look in on him and make notes in a log book on how he is bearing up. Tranquilizing medication is offered to the inmate if he desires it. Pat refuses medication.

I step up the visits and begin seeing Pat once a week. I write to him more often and tell his other pen pals about the execution date so they can write to him also. A week or so after the delivery of the death warrant he tells me that a couple of guards had appeared unannounced at his cell one morning. They had shackled his hands and feet and taken him to a scale. "What's this for?" he asked. "Ya'll starting a Weight Watchers program around here?" But the guards had not answered and did not smile. One guard recorded his weight while another measured his height. Then the guards returned him to his cell.

"What was that all about?" I ask.

"They wouldn't say," he answers. "Some of the guys on the Row say they're measuring us for our coffins."

Later, Warden Frank Blackburn will explain to me that a guard, matching the inmate's height and weight, does a dry run from the cell to the chair to make sure the "Tactical Team" can "contain" the condemned prisoner should he put up a fight. "Some of these guys are pretty big and strong," he explains. "Once the guards get the inmate in the chair, they use the leather straps on the chair to hold him, then remove the leg irons and handcuffs."

Albert Camus:

> Long in advance the condemned man knows that he is going to be killed and that the only thing that can save him is a reprieve . . . In any case, he cannot intervene, make a plea outside himself, or convince. Everything goes on outside him. He is no longer a man but a thing waiting to be handled by the executioners . . . This explains the odd submissiveness that is customary in the condemned at the moment of their execution. (pp. 201–202)

Pat is scheduled for execution on Friday, August 19. That really means the evening of Thursday the eighteenth, because the execution is scheduled for just after midnight. I go to visit him on Wednesday the seventeenth. Warden Ross Maggio has granted me a special four-hour visit. Just before entering the prison I use the public telephone outside the gates to call the Coalition office to see if perhaps the courts have issued a stay of execution. Execution is about forty hours away. They have not yet moved him to the death house, where the electric chair is located about five miles deep inside the prison.

Pat looks thin, sallow. He has dark circles under his eyes. He has not been able to keep his food down and has lost thirty pounds in two weeks. He keeps going on coffee and cigarettes.

"My stuff is packed, ready to go," he tells me when I walk in.

Any minute the prison authorities might summon him to move to the death house. He has packed what they allow him to bring: a toothbrush and toothpaste, a change of underwear, cigarettes, his Bible, his address book, some stationery and a ballpoint pen. No radio. Music stirs emotions, and prison authorities want as little emotion as possible in this process. There will be a television for him to watch. There will be a telephone on the wall near his cell from which he can make collect calls. Some men on the Row have recently made this move to the death house, but they have all come back alive, receiving stays of execution from the courts. There hasn't been an execution in Louisiana since June 1961.

I tell him that I have just spoken with the Prison Coalition by phone and Tom Dybdahl, who has replaced Chava, has told me to assure him that his attorney has filed his petition and he will surely get a stay from the courts any minute now. I tell him I will visit with him for a couple of hours, and if by then word of a stay has not come, I will ask the major to let me use the phone in his office to call the Coalition office again.

I hope Tom knows what he is talking about. I know nothing of legal issues. I'm practicing blind faith that the attorney knows what he's doing.

"How sure are you about the stay?" I had asked Tom. "Ninety-five percent sure," he had said. That reassures me. But he had also said, "You're never absolutely sure about what the courts will do." How does one deal with this kind of waiting? How keep one's poise, one's sanity? Even if he had said 99.9 percent sure, there's that one tenth of 1 percent.

The simplest surgery can go wrong. Delivery of babies can go wrong. Anything that human beings do can go wrong.

To pass the time I do what I do best. I talk to him. I ask him questions, tell him stories. He talks about hunting in the woods, driving the big trucks, working on a hog farm in Texas, how his mama cooks venison and rabbit stew with a lot of onions and thick gravy, what it is like to work on oil rigs and what makes it dangerous work, some close calls he's had, some bad accidents he's seen.

We talk for two hours. We do not talk about death and dying. We will if the time comes, but for now the talking helps pass the time and maintain sanity until the time when the phone will ring and the guard will come in and say, "Sonnier, you got a stay."

Pat is hyped, at times full of bravado. "They want to see me break. Well, they'll never break me." He had talked to one of the guards about getting some barbecue corn chips and a Dr Pepper from a snack machine for me. "We'll celebrate when we get news of the stay," he told me. "Ole Maggio [the warden] thinks he's got me this time, but I'll show him. My attorney will pull off the stay at the last minute. Maybe I'll even get a good 'last' meal off of him," and he laughs. But the laugh is forced. It comes from his diaphragm. He is talking and laughing like this and I can see the terror in his eyes.

"Be a man my son." The line from Hemingway's "Big Two-Hearted River" wells up in my mind, the words of a priest to Sam Cardinella, who loses control of his anal sphincter muscle on the way to the gallows.

As if one can be brave by simply willing it. I wonder what kind of dignity I would muster if I were facing my executioners.

It's surreal, all of it. My mind keeps casting about for something familiar to reassure myself that it is just a question of time before the stay of execution comes, that this is all a bad dream. Unreal.

At about two o'clock I go to the major's office to make the phone call.

"Sorry," Tom says, "no word yet from the court. You just have to help him wait it out."

I go back to the visiting room. He is standing up, peering eagerly through the heavy mesh screen. "No word yet," I tell him. "Would you like to pray?"

He nods his head. I don't remember the exact words of the prayer — a prayer, I'm sure, of essentials: forgiveness, courage, sustenance for the final big step if it should come.

When the prayer is over I say to him, "If you die, I want to be with you."

He says, "No. I don't want you to see it."

I say, "I can't bear the thought that you would die without seeing one loving face. I will be the face of Christ for you. Just look at me."

He says, "It's terrible to see. I don't want to put you through that. It could break you. It could scar you for life."

I know that it will terrify me. How could it not terrify me? But I feel strength and determination. I tell him it won't break me, that I have plenty of love and support in my life.

"God will give me the grace," I tell him.

He consents. He shakes his head. It is decided. I will be there with him if he dies.

He says, "If only I knew I'd die right away when the first jolt hits me. Will I feel it? They say the body burns. (Later, his death certificate will record that death took four to five minutes.)[2] My poor mother . . ."

Yes, his poor mother. She had been raised by her grandmother, lived out in the middle of cane fields, and at a young age had married an older man. The marriage had brought a trail of sorrows, no companionship, just poverty. Once, Eddie, her "baby," had cried for two days and two nights with a toothache because she had no money for a dentist. And then had come the ultimate tragedy – her sons' terrible deed, the trial, the sentencing. She did not come much to Angola, but when her sons were awaiting trial in the parish jail close to home, she had brought them home cooking. She had earned money by sitting at night with an elderly sick man so she could get them cigarettes and warm winter clothes. But she has been able to visit death row only once or twice. It makes her ill to see her son here.

Pat says, "When they put that hood on my head, I don't want that 'Lord is my shepherd' prayer. It will only delay things. I just want to get it over."

I ask him if he believes God has forgiven him or does he feel condemned forever for what he has done? Now, for the first time, he talks to me about the murders.

"At first, no," he says, "I felt that even God hated me, but I know now that God forgives me. I went to confession to the old priest.

"Nobody was supposed to get killed. Eddie was upset. We had just gotten him out of jail. He had come unglued over a girl who was pregnant with his child. She wouldn't marry him, and he had gone to her house with a sawed-off shotgun, cut the telephone wires, and threatened to shoot her and her whole family. They had him put in jail and every day Mama was calling me at work. 'Get your brother out. Get my baby out.' We got him out, got the charge dropped, but his nerves was messed up. Something I think the boy David said to him teed him off and he shot the kids. I should've known he could blow. I shouldn't have let us get mixed up in the bad things we was doing."

He has his head down. The cigarette hangs limp between his fingers. The smoke comes up in a thin, curling line. It is very quiet.

"I read the articles about it at the Prison Coalition office," I say. "Those poor children. Those poor parents. They must be in hell."

"I will go to my grave feeling bad about those kids," he says. "Every night when they dim the lights on the tier I kneel by my bunk and pray for those kids and their parents. Nobody was supposed to get killed."

His voice is barely audible.

Later, one of the trusties [trustees], who served meals on death row, will tell me that he never saw anyone with more remorse than Patrick Sonnier. "The guy wouldn't eat when he first got here. He didn't sleep much. The guy was eaten up by what he did."

Later, I will find out that after his arrest, while in the parish jail, he had attempted suicide by slitting his wrists.

But now I just look at him. I'm not sure how to measure his sincerity. I see the young people getting down on their knees and lying down in the cold wet grass. Even if he didn't do the shooting, he participated in the kidnappings — not just this couple. There had been others.

The silence is heavy. And then he says with anger in his eyes, "I didn't rape Loretta. I never touched her."

He had confessed to the murders, he tells me, because it was their plan, his and Eddie's — each would say he did it and the authorities wouldn't know who had done it, and he was afraid of the police. Two of the police officers had taken him into an office, his hands cuffed behind his back, and one of them had taken off his jacket, revealing a holstered gun. He was afraid that they were going to pistol-whip him with the gun. He figured that he could do the time at Angola, he said. He had served time when he and his cousin had stolen a truck. "In the confession I said I killed the kids because they might identify me and I didn't want to go back to Angola, but I had done good at Angola, and I could do it again."

The murders and the arrest had happened in 1977, he tells me, shortly after the reinstatement of the death penalty by the Supreme Court, but he had not "kept up too good with the news. If I had known then I could get the chair, no matter what they did to me, I would never have confessed."

He tells me these things all in a flow, all at once, no break in the words, his eyes down most of the time or looking past me to a place I cannot see. He seems to accept that he is responsible for what had happened, even though he claims not to have killed the teenagers. He does not press his innocence. Nor does he seem to harbor any bitterness toward his brother. A week before his execution he will face off with the warden over his right to visit with his brother before he dies.

I remember the old chaplain's words: "These people are the scum of the earth, and they'll try to con you."

I simply do not know what to make of what he is telling me. I suspend judgment. With the electric chair waiting, with death close like this, who the triggerman was seems not the point. Two people are dead, and soon three people will be dead. That for now is the only point.

It is 3:00 P.M. — thirty-six hours away from execution. The guard comes in and tells me visiting time is up. No call has come from the Coalition office. I tell Pat I am going to Baton Rouge to my mother's house (about an hour's drive from the prison). If he does not get a stay I will come back to the death house to be with him. I brace myself inside.

About fifteen miles from the prison I hear on the car radio that he has been granted a stay pending a review of his petition by the Fifth Circuit Court of Appeals.

I try to comprehend the meaning behind the words. He will live. He will not die. He will be served his supper on the tier with all the others. The trays will come and one will be for him. He can unpack his toothbrush, his underwear, his paper bag of stuff, and put his things back into their regular place in his cell. Over the next days and weeks he will get his taste for food back, and perhaps he will be able to sleep when he climbs into his bunk for the night.

In a letter I quote to him lines from Psalm 107. "It was written for you," I tell him.

> . . . Some, driven frantic by their sins,
> made miserable by their own guilt
> and finding all food repugnant,
> were nearly at death's door.
> Then they called to Yahweh in their trouble
> and he rescued them from their sufferings . . .
> he snatched them from the Pit . . .

He, too, has a favorite psalm, Psalm 31, he tells me in his next letter. After his death I will see this psalm highlighted in his worn Bible. He will hand me this Bible shortly before he dies.

> . . . I am contemptible,
> loathsome to my neighbors,
> to my friends a thing of fear . . .
> I am forgotten, as good as dead in their hearts,
> something discarded.
> . . . as they combine against me,
> plotting to take my life.
> But I put my trust in you, Yahweh . . .

DEAD MAN WALKING

On my next visit to the prison I follow the routine I have set up over the last several months — visiting Pat first, then Eddie.

When Eddie comes into the visiting room he looks almost as bad as Pat looked a couple of weeks ago when he had come close to execution. He greets me somberly. He is carrying a heavy load. His shoulders slump. His hands are shaking. As we sit down at one of the tables, he lights a cigarette. "I've got something really, really bad to tell you," he says. I assume that Pat must have written him a letter, telling him that he had told me about the murders.

I reach over and put my hand on his arm. He is swallowing and his Adam's apple moves up and down in his throat. He is trying hard to say the words. He is trying to push the words out with sheer willpower.

I say, "I think I know, Eddie. Pat told me you're the one who killed those children."

I say it first, but he needs to say it. Does he absorb it, take it in, own it? One moment like that. Six small pieces of metal from his hand destroying two human beings? And he is trying to find the words to tell me that he has done this.

He speaks in a measured, flat voice like a cancer patient, giving the history of his illness again and again to this doctor and that. How many times, I wonder, has he gone over these events in his mind trying to make sense of them, trying to grasp the catastrophic consequences: two families with two dead children, a brother facing the electric chair, and himself sitting here in this blue denim shirt and the bars, gates, fences, and guards that will be around him for the rest of his life.

He seems remorseful about the killings, but I can tell his most tangible regret is his own fate behind bars. Self-survival seems to dominate his moral horizon.

He lays out the facts of the crime, and I can only guess what they mean to him: his girlfriend pregnant, his offer of marriage spurned, the "coldness like a deep-freeze" by her family when he had gone to her house to ask to marry her, she in the back room, refusing even to come out and talk to him, another man in her life named David who's now her boyfriend; going home enraged and coming back to the girl's house with his shotgun, cutting the telephone wires to the house, threatening to kill them all, the arrival of the police, arrest, jail; then some talking back and forth, an agreement reached, his release on bond, the record expunged; at home again, rabbit hunting, the kids in the car, the abduction, the boy, David saying, 'Put down that gun and I'll show you who's a man,' rage, the two Davids blurring, the gun in his hand. *Snap.*

I see no reason to doubt Eddie. The weight on him is tangible. I can see the pain and bewilderment in his eyes at the enormity of the evil he has done.

I have heard that this is the way most murders happen — an explosion of passion, not a cold, calculated, premeditated act.[3]

"What words could I ever say to the families of those kids?" he asks me. "I'm sorry? What good are those words now? No words can bring those kids back. I've been over it in my mind a million times. If I could turn back the clock . . ."

He looks up at me.

I miss the moment. I should say to him, *Yes, yes, apologize. As weak and ineffective and futile as your words of remorse and sorrow may seem, say them.* Only later will I learn from Lloyd LeBlanc, David LeBlanc's father, what such an apology means. He will later tell a reporter that his main reason for attending Patrick Sonnier's execution was to hear an apology.

"Why did you testify in court against Pat?" I ask. It had shocked me when I read this. What kind of man would testify against his own brother?

He explains that before their arrest they had planned what each would say, but he had understood one thing and his brother another. Pat had understood that they would each confess to the murders, but he had understood that they would each accuse the other. Pat's attorney, he says, had not interviewed him before calling him to testify at Pat's trial. "I was real, real nervous up there trying to keep everything consistent and not contradicting myself, and I was coming unraveled right there on the stand and Pat could see that, he could see I was about to blow, and he told his attorney to stop the questioning. His attorney didn't know what the hell was going on. He didn't know what I was going to say when I got up there."

I am astonished that in a first-degree murder trial an attorney would call a witness to the stand, much less such a crucial one, without talking to him or her first.

In October 1983, I hear that the Fifth Circuit Court in New Orleans has denied Pat's appeal. He is running out of time. In talk around the Coalition office I have heard of an attorney in Atlanta named Millard Farmer who defends death-row inmates. I decide to call him.

CHAPTER
3

Poor Millard Farmer. I am pleading with him: "a man on death row running out of time ... even though you're busy ... help him, please, help him."

I telephone him in early November 1983, about a week after Pat's denial by the Fifth Circuit Court of Appeals. I have heard that he is a native Georgian, but I am surprised by how thick his accent is. After a short pause: "Okay, we'll 'hep' you. Send me the transcripts." And he gives me the address and I thank him profusely. I waste no time in mailing the papers to him.

After a moratorium of twenty-two years, executions have once again become a reality in Louisiana. On December 14, 1983, the state executed Robert Wayne Williams, a young black man who had shot and killed a black security guard during a robbery. The execution was scheduled for midnight, but just as Williams approached the chair, news came of a delay so a legal question could be settled. Williams went back to wait in his cell, then, one hour later, was executed.

In Louisiana it's unusual for a black man to be executed for killing another black man. Although the majority of victims of homicide in the state are black (90 percent of homicide victims in New Orleans in 1991), 75 percent of death-row inmates are there for killing whites. And when blacks do get death for killing other blacks, their victims typically fit a certain demographic profile: police or security guards, children, more than one person, or, more rarely, women.[1]

Tom Dybdahl, now heading the Prison Coalition office, comes over to use the Hope House photocopying machine and tells me about Williams's funeral and that Robert Wayne's mother would not let the embalmers hide the burns on her son's body.[2] "The casket was open and you could see the deep burn marks on his head and the calf of his leg," Tom says.

About a week after the Williams execution I visit Pat. His eyes are dark and he looks pale. He's having trouble sleeping, he says. He had seen an artist's sketch of the Williams execution in the Baton Rouge newspaper (no cameras or recording devises are allowed) and noticed that Williams was barefooted.

"If they take me, I'm going with my shoes on," he says.

Millard Farmer has reviewed Pat's transcripts and is preparing petitions for the Fifth Circuit Court of Appeals and the U.S. Supreme Court. Pat receives a letter from Michael Baham, his volunteer attorney, who has represented him thus far in his appeals. Baham tells him, "I think it is indeed fortunate that Mr. Farmer is now involved in your case . . . While I like to think that I am very dedicated to your case, I also realize that dedication — no matter how deep and sincere — is no proper substitute for experience and the resources needed to satisfactorily handle the important pleadings necessary at this time."

Millard Farmer's associate, Kimellen Tunkle, drives from Atlanta on Christmas day to meet me in Baton Rouge. "Time is short," she tells me. "We expect that the Supreme Court is not going to give Pat a hearing." Kimellen is young, has straight long brown hair, speaks quietly. She takes rapid notes as I tell her what I know about Pat Sonnier. She wants to know about his family and people in the community who might be able to speak for his life should he have to appear before the Pardon Board. I know the Pardon Board is the last appeal before execution.

On January 18 Millard picks me up around 7:30 A.M. and we drive to Angola to see Pat. Millard is a tall, thin man with a long face and grizzled gray hair. All the way to Angola we talk.

Though my daddy was an attorney, I tend to avoid lawyer talk, with all its jargon and razor-thin distinctions and counterdistinctions. But now I want to know and understand everything about the legal issues in Pat's case. I feel that we're in a boat in the rapids and we're trying to throw out an anchor that will catch solidly on a rock.

I am hoping that, even though it's very late, Millard and his team will find an anchor issue.

What I learn first about the legal system is that it's a system of gates that shut like one-way turnstiles, and you can't go back in once you've come out. Millard explains that if the trial attorney does not raise an issue or make an objection, the higher courts say the defendant has waived his/her rights to raise the issue later on.

In looking through the voir dire — the interviews with prospective jurors at Pat's trial — Millard has seen that the prosecutor used too many "strikes" — excusing jurors without having to give a reason. He used eight strikes. He was entitled to six. It was up to the defense attorney to notice and to object. "Too late now," Millard says, and explains that one rule of thumb he uses to determine the quality of defense counsel is how long the jury selection process lasts. If it lasts several weeks or a month, he says, you know you have a strong attorney. The jury selection in Pat's trial took two days.

Millard has also discovered that the prosecutor during the sentencing portion of the trial told the jury that Pat was incapable of rehabilitation and would kill again and the only way to protect other prisoners or society at large would be to execute him.[3] That kind of rigid prediction of future dangerousness, which cannot be supported by evidence, is inappropriate, he explains, but again it was up to defense counsel to object, which would have assured a review of the issue on appeal. But it's too late now. Gate closed.

Introducing these issues in a federal court now, after all this time, will almost surely evoke "abuse of the writ" from the courts, he says, and explains that the court wants to protect itself from defendants filing issues piecemeal, which would keep cases before the courts indefinitely.

"But can't you explain that it's the attorneys' fault, not Pat's, that these issues have not yet been raised?" I ask. "Shouldn't the courts be interested in the substance of the issues, not who raised them and when?"

In the past, Millard says, defense attorneys used to be able to count on the federal courts to monitor and check errors and abuses in state courts. It was the authority of the federal courts, he explains, which put legal teeth into the civil rights movement in the 1960s, and he believes that if it had been left to state legislatures to enact social legislation on their own, Jim Crow might still be the law of the land today. Then in *Gregg v. Georgia* in 1976, he says, the high court, by removing the constitutional protection against capital punishment, essentially said that if states wanted to kill their citizens, they wouldn't stop them. The Court interpreted the Constitution as saying that putting someone to death was not forbidden by the Eighth Amendment, which forbids cruel and unusual punishment. "I believe, though," he says, "the political motive behind this decision was a power struggle between the federal government and states' rights — that old struggle, as old as the Constitution itself. Southern states were mad as hell about the federal enforcement of desegregation in the sixties. And then they were mad as hell again with the *Furman v. Georgia* ruling in 1972, which said the application of the death penalty was 'arbitrary and capricious,' which looked like the Court might permanently overturn the death penalty. The South has always been a proponent of strong law-and-order measures,[4] mainly to keep blacks in line, and they were not about to let the feds in Washington tell them how they could or couldn't punish their criminals. They prevailed."

He laments the courts' turn to the right in recent years. "They're so interested in speeding up executions that it doesn't seem to matter that they're running roughshod over people's constitutional rights," he says. "They keep tightening procedural requirements so that it's harder and harder to get a hearing in these death-penalty cases. Our clients might have the most substantial issue in the world — even new evidence of innocence — but the courts say, 'Sorry, filed too late' and refuse to hear the case."

Later, the issue of procedural requirements for federal appeals in death-penalty cases will be played out with dramatic force in the case of Roger Keith Coleman, convicted in Virginia of murdering his sister-in-law. His attorneys filed his post-conviction appeal to the Virginia Supreme Court *one day late* — violating a procedural requirement, which the state court said precluded an evidentiary review of the case even though new evidence suggested the possibility that Coleman may not have been the murderer.[5] The federal courts refused to overturn that ruling, and Coleman was executed in May 1992.

And more radically, on May 4, 1992, in *Keeney v. Tamayo-Reyes* the U.S. Supreme Court gutted federal habeas appeal when it ruled that federal courts are not required to hold evidentiary hearings where state courts did not hold hearings, even if the prisoner can show that inadequate counsel prevented crucial parts of the case from being heard — despite the fact that federal judges find constitutional errors in at least 40 percent of the death-penalty cases they review.[6]

Millard explains that he'll raise the issue that Pat's attorney was ineffective, but he doesn't have much hope that the courts will agree with him. It's rare nowadays in capital cases, he says, for the courts to concede that defense attorneys are ineffective. "I mean, there are cases where defense attorneys in capital cases have actually shown up for trial drunk, or so ill prepared they told the judge they didn't know what they were doing, and even then the appeal courts wouldn't concur on ineffectiveness of counsel."[7] He points out that public defenders, especially in Southern states, have so many clients to defend they can scarcely manage to interview them before trial, much less do the time-consuming investigation that capital cases require.[8]

It's not a fluke, Millard says, that 99 percent of death-row inmates are poor. "They get the kind of defense they pay for." He explains that the high court's stringent standard of judging ineffectiveness of counsel now puts the burden of proof on a defendant's appellate attorney to demonstrate that defense counsel blunders directly affected the jury's verdict, and that minus those blunders the jury would have returned a different verdict. "But how are you going to demonstrate that, of all the variables in a case, a mistake of the defense counsel caused the jury to render a certain verdict? The court just comes back and says that the attorney's mistakes were 'harmless error' and the jury would have returned a guilty verdict anyway. Every person is supposed to have a constitutional right to effective assistance of counsel, but the courts, by imposing such impossible procedural strictures have reamed out that right to an empty shell."[9]

Pat's trial attorney failed him most of all during the sentencing part of the trial, Millard says. "That's when you want to try to get family, friends, employers, clergy, who know your client, to speak for him. If the jury can see your client as a human being, no matter what terrible crime he or she may have done, your client has a chance to live." In Pat's first trial, he says, other than the attorney, there was no one to speak for his life — only a photocopied report of a psychologist who wasn't even in the courtroom.

"And then, during the second trial for sentencing," he says, "when the attorney had a whole new chance to do it right, instead he reintroduces guilt and innocence all over again by getting Eddie up there, who claimed he did it, not his brother, which was not credible to anybody and probably made the jury angry."

I had always thought that the lengthy appeals process virtually assured fair review of these cases. Now I'm learning just how much depends on the skills of defense attorneys. There's now not a doubt in my mind that if Millard had been Pat's defense attorney, Pat wouldn't now be facing the electric chair.

We are wending our way to Angola. I do not much notice the scenery. I am thinking of Millard Farmer and how much he knows and wondering what it is going to take to keep Pat Sonnier alive. I am looking across the front seat of the car at this impassioned man and wondering what makes a man like this — obviously an excellent lawyer who could be making an awful lot of money — defend people like Pat Sonnier. I ask him.

He tells me that when he studied law there was a block called "poverty law," and he began going into housing projects and jails and "just talking to people, you know what I mean?" (He says "you know what I mean" a lot.) There he witnessed case after case of black men tried by all-white juries, and he asks me if I know that here in Louisiana every juvenile that has been executed has been a black whose victim was white and who had an all-white jury[10] and that every man executed for rape in Louisiana has been black (the death penalty for rape was declared unconstitutional by the U.S. Supreme Court in 1977.)[11] When a black defendant is on trial in these capital cases, he explains, even though the Constitution promises a right to a jury of one's peers, it's common practice for prosecutors to try to eliminate blacks from the jury because blacks are less likely than whites to impose death, and unless there's a strong defense attorney the prosecutor will succeed.[12]

I say that at least Pat, who is white, doesn't have to contend with racism.

But Millard says the crucial race factor in Pat's case is that his victims were white. "The sad, terrible truth," he says, "is that if he and Eddie had killed two black kids, chances are they would never have been sentenced to death."

He asks if I've ever heard of the Gaskin case in Bossier Parish here in Louisiana. I haven't.

The case, he says, has to do with a crime that happened in 1980. Three young men with juvenile records of violent crime, including several armed robberies, kidnapped a fourteen-year-old girl, Virginia Smith, beat her, robbed her, forced oral sex on her, and while giving a Confederate yell, slit her throat, stabbed her numerous times and left her to bleed to death in the woods. Two of them got life sentences and one got thirty years.[13]

Virginia Smith was black. Her assailants were white.

He contends this is not an isolated case and explains that prosecutors, judges, and juries, most of whom are white, are far more outraged when white people are murdered than when black people are. "White people identify more with other white people, you know what I mean?" he says.

Later, when I become involved with victims' families I will find out just how true this is. Survive, a group for families of murder victims in New Orleans, composed mainly of indigent black women, will find little passion in the predominately white D.A.'s office to prosecute black-on-black homicides. Of the forty or so members of the group, only one or two will see the killer of their loved one brought to trial.

The U.S. Supreme Court, after being presented with irrefutable evidence from an extensive study of two thousand capital cases in Georgia,[14] admitted in *McCleskey v. Kemp* (1987) that there exists in capital sentencing "a discrepancy that appears to correlate with race." Faced with similar empirical evidence of discrimination in housing and employment, the Court upheld legislative remedies, but in the arena of capital punishment they shrugged off disparities in sentencing as "an *inevitable* part of our criminal justice system." Prisoners facing execution, unlike plaintiffs claiming job or housing discrimination, must show intentional bias, which is very difficult to demonstrate.[15]

Millard explains that because public defender offices in Louisiana can't handle the large load of cases, judges often appoint attorneys in private practice to take on capital cases, even though many of them practice only civil law. "They may never have cracked a single book on criminal law, and yet they are asked to defend a person's life and to master a highly complex body of law in a short period of time," he says. In Louisiana the only statutory requirement for an attorney to defend someone accused of capital murder is five years' practice in law — any kind of law.[16]

"They don't call Southern states the 'Death Belt' for nothing," Millard says. Four states — Louisiana, Georgia, Texas, and Florida — carry out two thirds of all U.S. executions.[17]

He explains that in Louisiana the maximum reimbursable amount indigent defenders can spend to prepare for trial is $1,000.[18] "Chicken feed," he says because one expert witness can cost that much. He says that if Pat Sonnier had lots of money, he would have gotten himself a crackerjack attorney, who would hire top-notch investigators, a ballistics expert, a psychologist to compile profiles of "desirable" jurors, "and you can be sure he wouldn't be sitting on death row today. That's why you're never going to find a rich person on death row."[19]

And often, he says, if a D.A. knows he's up against a top-notch defense attorney, he'll think twice about prosecuting for the "max" and maybe losing, and so be much more amenable to a plea bargain — reducing the charge in exchange for admission of guilt — and there won't even be a trial.

Millard says the application of the death penalty is like a lottery because such a small percentage of murderers get the death penalty — 1 or 2 percent of the thousands who commit homicide every year. And of those receiving death sentences, only a fraction are executed.[20]

"Most people think this 1 or 2 percent who go to death row must have committed the most heinous, premeditated, cold-blooded murders, but you see in many, many of these cases panic murders by defendants who have a history of child abuse or have had head injuries or who are mentally retarded or outright insane. Or kids. Some juveniles get caught in the net too."

In *Penry v. Lynaugh* the Supreme Court ruled that the "cruel and unusual punishment" provision of the Eighth Amendment does not prohibit the execution of the mentally retarded.[21]

In *Thompson v. Oklahoma* the Supreme Court ruled that sixteen-year-olds can be executed.[22]

In *Ford v. Wainwright* the Supreme Court ruled that the Eighth Amendment does prohibit the execution of the insane, but provided no criteria for determining insanity.[23] The Court held that should an insane death-row inmate be made sane through therapy or medication — a judgment rendered by the *state's* medical examiner — his or her execution would then be allowed.

Florida death-row inmate Gary Alvord, judged to have become insane while on death-row, was transferred to a mental hospital, where health-care professionals were asked to restore him to sanity so he could be killed.[24] And recently Louisiana courts had to decide whether death-row inmate Michael Owen Perry could be forcibly injected with antipsychotic drugs to make him sane enough for execution.[25]

Finally, Millard says, summing it all up, race, poverty, and geography determine who gets the death penalty — if the victim is white, if the defendant is poor, and whether or not the local D.A. is willing to plea-bargain.[26]

The public has no idea, he says, how much discretionary power the D.A. has in determining indictments. Grand juries, he adds, which state constitutions provide to guarantee that the charge matches the crime, generally go along with the indictment the D.A.

wants. At grand jury hearings only government witnesses appear, defense is excluded, and the presentation of exculpatory evidence — evidence that points to innocence — is not required.

Millard explains that in 1972 the U.S. Supreme Court in *Furman* had found the death penalty "arbitrary and capricious" in its application and hence unconstitutional. "Well," he says, "I'd like for anyone to show me how it is any less arbitrary and capricious today."

I am disturbed at what I am learning. I hardly know what to feel — except overwhelmed. Thank God, I think, that at least now Pat has someone of Millard's caliber to represent him. Maybe as Millard talks to Pat he'll uncover a big, glaring legal issue that the courts will be forced to look at.

Millard points and says, "Hey, look at that." He is seeing a sign nailed high up in a tree that I now take for granted: "Do not despair, you will soon be there."

"Somebody knows this road real, real well," he says.

We come to a sharp S-curve in the highway which means we're just about a mile from the prison.

As we go into death row Millard deposits twenty dollars into Pat's inmate account. "They need cigarettes, coffee," he says. "I think smoking is bad, but in prison cigarettes are about all inmates have to take the edge off."

Pat comes into the visiting room. As always he is shaven, his hair is combed. I have been telling him about Millard.

Millard leans over close to the screen and says, "Wish I could shake your hand, Pat, so nice to meet you." Pat knows the score, that he's facing certain death.

Millard is calm, systematic, competent. I clear everything else from my mind and take out a piece of paper and take notes as he talks to Pat. In the car on the way to the prison Millard had said that I ought to go over the trial transcripts and learn all I can about Pat's case. He's a team player. "We need everybody's eyes and mind and heart looking at this case," he had said. "Sometimes it's the nonlawyers who catch something we miss."

Millard tells Pat to think of every legal issue as a rock, and that he wants to go over his case thoroughly with him and for him not to leave out anything, even if he thinks it insignificant. "We want to load as many rocks as we can into our wagon," he says.

He explains one of the issues — the Clark issue — that they plan to litigate in the appeal. The Louisiana criminal code, he says, specifies that a person cannot be convicted of first-degree murder unless he personally possessed the intent to kill, and also that a person who is considered a principal in the crime, who aids and abets in a first-degree murder, cannot be convicted of first-degree murder unless he or she specifically intends for the victim to be killed.[27]

"But your transcript," Millard explains, "shows both the prosecutor and the judge instructing the jury that regardless of who pulled the trigger, you or Eddie, both of you were in concert and so could be held to be principals and guilty of first-degree murder. That instruction is clearly against the Louisiana criminal code because it relieves the state of its burden to prove beyond reasonable doubt that you possessed the specific intent to kill. The judge in his instruction clearly omitted this part of the code, and so this instruction made it easier for jury members to convict you of first-degree murder, especially those who might be entertaining doubts about which of you was the triggerman.[28]

"The good news for you is that this exact issue has been raised in the Clark case and he was granted a new trial by the Fifth Circuit."[29]

I am beginning to feel relieved and picture a substantial boulder being hoisted into Pat's wagon. This is new to me, that the Louisiana code requires intent to kill. I had always thought that if two people were involved in a felony that led to murder, the very fact that they were present during the crime made both equally guilty.

Millard reminds me of a surgeon.

"But the bad news," Millard says, and his voice drops, "is that your attorney, when he presented your habeas appeal to the Fifth Circuit Court, must not have known about the Clark case because he failed to raise this issue, and now we are going to have a tough time getting a rehearing. They will probably say that we're abusing the writ, that your attorney should have raised this issue earlier. We're going to argue that you should not die while Clark is allowed to live solely because of the disparity of legal skills in attorneys. We are going to appeal to their sense of fairness and reasonableness."

I know when I hear this that this rock is far from being in the wagon.

Pat brings up his confession, his and Eddie's mixed-up plan to confuse the authorities, his fear that he was going to be beaten if he didn't confess, but Millard shakes his head,

"Impossible to prove. Not a rock for the wagon."

Millard asks how often Pat's attorneys conferred with him before trial. Was there any written correspondence between them?

"Nothing written," Pat says, and then tells how he was in jail nine months before he met his trial attorney and then only once on the day before trial, and that he had gone before the judge in pretrial procedures three times without an attorney.[30] He says that at his trial his attorney called Eddie up as a witness to testify against him without having interviewed Eddie beforehand.

"I saw that in the transcript," Millard says. "I couldn't help but notice that the attorney introduced himself to Eddie there on the stand." He shakes his head, but he's staying upbeat with Pat, I can tell. He tells him that they are planning to raise ineffectiveness of counsel in the petition and "every other issue we can, the big ones and the little ones."

Pat keeps saying, "Thank you, Mr. Millard, thank you for going to all this trouble for me."

When Millard's conversation with Pat is over there isn't one rock in the wagon.

On the way home Millard clears his throat and grips the steering wheel and says to me, "I'm going to be very, very honest with you. Pat has no 'net' in the courts." Then he lays out his strategy: Edwin Edwards is soon to be inaugurated for his third term as governor. "From what I know of Edwards," he says, "I believe he is a reluctant supporter of capital punishment, and Pat will be his first confrontation with execution." He explains that what we have to do is to mobilize religious leaders and people close to Edwards to appeal to him to grant clemency, and we will need to arrange a private meeting with him — no media present — where we can talk to him about Pat as a person and appeal to his deepest moral instincts.

"No doubt about it, he has the power to save this man's life," Millard says. "He can commute the death sentence to life or he can grant a reprieve, which is only temporary, but it will keep Pat from dying."

When I get back to Hope House I sit down with Sister Lilianne Flavin, who is on staff, and ask her to come with me to visit Stanley Ott, the Catholic bishop in Baton Rouge. Lilianne — devoted to the poor — is a kindred soul.

On February 6 Lilianne and I drive to Baton Rouge to meet with Bishop Ott. He is a cordial, kind man. He will do anything he can, he tells us, to help save Pat's life. We ask him to talk to Governor Edwards. Reverend James Stovall, head of the Louisiana Interchurch Conference, also present at this meeting, commits himself as well to talk to the governor.

On February 21, Pat's thirty-fourth birthday, the U.S. Supreme Court denies his petition. On March 5 the trial judge, C. Thomas Bienvenu, Jr., issues the third date of execution: April 5, 1984.

I am visiting Pat and Eddie often these days. "Keep hope alive," Millard is telling me. "Death-row inmates look at me all the time, words unspoken, their eyes asking the question: 'Am I going to die?' Keep hope alive." And that is what I am trying to do with Pat and Eddie. I tell them in detail of all the efforts being made. I don't have to fake the hope. I believe that somehow, from somewhere, against all odds, Pat will not be executed.

On March 17 en route to the prison I stop at a little store along Highway 66 to telephone Archbishop Philip Hannan, Catholic archbishop of New Orleans. For days I have been trying to telephone him to ask him to intercede with the governor on Pat's behalf. While waiting for him to come to the phone I look at bottles of ketchup and cans of pork and beans. I am in one of these old-time country stores with rusted gas pumps out front, the ones that have the round glass tops. I notice there's dust on the necks of the ketchup bottles. The merchandise must move slowly here. A woman sits on a stool behind the counter. She has the radio on. Normal life. The way life ought to be. People at their jobs listening to the radio.

At last the archbishop comes to the phone. I make my request in simple terms. It's a short conversation, maybe five minutes. He asks a couple of questions but doesn't ask for any documentation on the case. Yes, he'll contact the governor and request clemency.

Yet, this is the same archbishop who has sent two priests to the death-penalty trial of an indigent black man, Willie Watson, to counter the testimony of a Jesuit priest, George Lundy, who urged the jury to vote for life. In other death-penalty trials preceding Watson's, Lundy and other Jesuits, quoting from the U.S. Catholic Bishops' statement in opposition to capital punishment,[31] had convinced some juries to vote for life. This had so dismayed the pro-death-penalty Catholic D.A. of New Orleans, Harry Connick, Sr., that he asked Archbishop Hannan "as official spokesman for the Catholic Church" to give his position on the death penalty in writing. The archbishop had obliged him, setting forth a pro-capital-punishment position and assuring Catholics that they "can in good conscience endorse capital punishment." In the letter, which Connick brings to first-degree murder trials and reads to jurors, the archbishop also asserts that "the position of the U.S. Catholic Bishops does not express the official position of this archdiocese."[32]

At the Watson trial, where the archbishop's representatives had countermanded Lundy's testimony, the jury returned a death verdict. Afterward the state prosecutor remarked that the archbishop's position had certainly "helped" their case. But Willie Watson's mother offered a different view: "Ain't nobody who's of God want anybody killed."[33]

Several weeks before his execution on July 24, 1987, Watson wrote a letter to Archbishop Hannan saying that it was "wrong" for him to have sent the "two old priests" to argue for the death penalty, and he asked the archbishop to urge clemency on his behalf before the Pardon Board. The archbishop sent a letter urging the Board to spare Watson's life.

Archbishop Hannan is a perplexing man.

The prospect that a person will be killed according to the policy he promulgates prompts the archbishop to urge clemency, an incomprehensible position logically. But, despite his strong views on capital punishment, he does not try to silence those who disagree with him, as some church prelates do. I respect him for that.

Millard, in preparing for the meeting with the governor, has been talking a lot these days about Brad Fisher, a clinical psychologist and an expert in prisoner classification whom Millard has recruited to evaluate Pat. It's important, Millard says, to show the governor that this man will make an ideal lifer at Angola.

Fisher's assessment of Pat's "prison adjustment potential" could not be more positive.

In his affidavit he points out how Pat in twelve years of incarceration has never had one disciplinary report; how he functions well in a structured environment; how his past work experience indicates that he will be a good worker; how, in the "thousands of cases" he has reviewed, "not a single inmate has promised to be more of a constructive element in the prison environment" than Pat Sonnier.

You can't get a more positive evaluation than that.

It gives me hope.

On Tuesday, March 27, at 2:00 P.M. we are scheduled to meet with Governor Edwin Edwards at the state capitol building. There will be about eight of us: Bishop Stanley Ott; Rose Williams, mother of Robert Wayne Williams, executed in December; Brad Fisher; Millard; Kimellen and Joe Nursey, an attorney on Millard's team; and myself.

We expect to be ushered into the governor's office for a private conversation. Instead, we are directed into a large room. There are TV cameras, bright lights, reporters, a long conference table. I take a seat almost directly opposite the governor.

Obviously the governor intends to make public his policy on executions. That must mean his mind is already made up. I sink inside.

Governor Edwards is coming to this meeting with us right after lunch with the Catholic Bishops in which he sought to clear up a "misunderstanding" about his belief in the resurrection of Jesus. He had gotten into trouble for a public statement he made which seemed to doubt Jesus' resurrection, and he begins by announcing that he and the bishops have met and "cleared up this matter of the resurrection," (the press chuckles) and an image of the governor's appointment calendar flickers across my mind: Tuesday, March 27: noon, resurrection; 2:00, execution. Inverse order exactly of the Gospels of Matthew, Mark, Luke, and John.

We each make our statements and the governor makes his.

Millard talks about Pat's inadequate legal defense and the arbitrariness of a system which gives one brother life, the other death.

Rose Williams talks about her son's execution and says that Christians should forgive, not seek revenge.

Bishop Ott says that the death penalty is a simplistic solution to a complex moral issue and that executions signal to society that violence is an acceptable way of dealing with human problems.

Brad Fisher points out Patrick's excellent disciplinary record at Angola.

And I say that Pat is a good worker and could be productive in Angola serving a life sentence, and though I in no way condone his crime, what will we accomplish by killing him?

The governor encourages us to introduce legislation to abolish the death penalty. "Now's maybe the time," he says, "because there have been two executions in recent months [Johnny Taylor followed Robert Wayne Williams] and maybe the public could be persuaded that the death penalty does not deter crime." But he stresses that we must understand, "I'm the governor and represent the state and must carry out the laws and must submerge my own personal views to carry out the expressed will of the people." He is hesitant, he says, to express his own personal views on the subject, saying he fears provoking another controversy like the one on the resurrection. And he clearly delineates his position: yes, he'll look carefully at the case, but unless there is "some clear, striking evidence for innocence and gross miscarriage of justice" he will not "interfere" in the process.

He moves to collect his papers. Television lights are being shut off. Some are already beginning to rise and move from the table.

I call to him, "Governor."

He looks up at me.

I say to him, "I am Pat Sonnier's spiritual adviser. If he dies, I will be with him. Please don't let this man die."

"Can you do that?" he asks me. "Can you watch that?"

There is concern on his face. I notice how shiny his forehead is from sweat. Maybe it's just sweat from the TV lights.

"I promised him," I say and plunge ahead. "Governor, there are two brothers involved in this case, they're indigent and had terribly ineffective legal defense, and I have real questions whether Pat is truly guilty of first-degree murder."

"I'll give the case careful consideration," he says.

I realize that the governor has found a moral niche in this process, a position from which he can make decisions and still lay his head on the pillow at night and go to sleep. He is a public official. His job is to carry out the law. He subordinates his conscience to the "will of the people." The law speaks for itself: if it is the law, it must be right, it must be true. Edwards is not "personally" responsible if he simply "does his job" within the law.

Several years later we will have a long talk, the governor and I. When we talk, he will have "presided" over thirteen executions in his third term of office, Patrick Sonnier's being the first, and he will tell me how, as governor, he tried to distance himself as much as possible: "I tried to get the legislature to remove the whole process from the governor, but I recognize that in the final analysis some one person has to have the authority to stop an execution, even though you don't have to take an affirmative action to make it happen. The whole process is in the judicial system; then, all of a sudden, in the last thirty days to have it sitting on the heart and mind and soul of one man is a very difficult position to be in."

In 1978 he transferred responsibility for signing death warrants from the governor to the sentencing judge, a task that in most other states remains with the governor.

Edwards tries to put the death process as far from himself as possible. Still, he can't escape the red telephone in the corner of the death chamber, where a call from him, even at the last minute, means life for the man being strapped in the chair and silence means death.

John Maginnis, a Louisiana political writer, calls this pardon power of the governor the last vestige of the power of kings, the last of the life-and-death choices bestowed upon individuals in a democracy.[34]

Politics plays its part. In the recent gubernatorial election campaign Edwards's Republican opponent, David Treen, had put up billboards across the state and run TV ads citing the number of pardons Edwards had granted criminals in his previous term of office. "Soft on crime," "coddler of criminals" — Treen's accusations had hit Edwards hard. Now Edwards gives serious thought to the political fallout should he commute a death sentence. Plus, he knows that behind Pat Sonnier stands a line of other condemned men. If he commutes Sonnier's sentence, what about the others? Dare he risk his political career to save the lives of a few condemned criminals? What's a governor to do?[35]

There is silence in the car as Millard, Kimellen, Joe, and I drive back to New Orleans. They will now be working around the clock to prepare for the Pardon Board hearing and to file appeals in the courts. "Let's not give up on the courts," Millard says. "We still might hit pay dirt with one of the issues." Millard is the "heart" man, always injecting hope. Joe is the "head" man. At will, he can pull from a file in his head the names and dates of court decisions of the past hundred years.

Sam Dalton, an attorney in New Orleans, has lent Millard's team the use of his office and equipment. With great care they set about preparing for the Pardon Board hearing. Kimellen quickly learns Sam's word-processing program and begins typing. Millard asks me for a picture of Pat and he gets it color-copied to go on the first page. The papers for the hearing are being put into a neat black binder with tabulated sections — Personal Background, Prison Adjustment, Facts of the Crime, Prior Legal Proceedings — and several appendixes of court records and the statement of the U.S. Catholic Bishops on the death penalty.

In obedience to Millard I cart home the seven volumes of trial manuscripts and read through them at night when the day's work is done.

The transcripts are powerful and evoke the trial vividly. Some of it is tedious. All of it is painful. I can only guess the horror that must have gripped the victims' families sitting there in the courtroom listening to the terrifying details of the abductions and murders.

There are thousands and thousands of words, and I read them all. There are a few discoveries.

I find that Eddie in his first confession had claimed that only Pat, not he, had raped the girl, but later he admitted that he had lied, that he too had sexually assaulted her. Pat's most insistent point with me has been that he did not rape the girl.

Which leads to the autopsy report. The bodies had been discovered six to eight hours after death and the autopsy was performed shortly afterward. Semen was found in the vagina of Loretta Bourque, but there was no report of semen identification.

Was the blood-matching test omitted?

Was the test lost or misplaced?

Was it suppressed?

Isn't this a serious omission in the state's prosecution of a rape/murder case?

If, in fact, semen identification had revealed that Pat had not raped the girl, would it not discredit Eddie, who claimed that Pat had raped her? And if Eddie was lying about the rape, was he also lying about the murders?

Then this discrepancy: When he confessed to the police at the scene of the crime, Pat had pointed out where he had stood while firing — some eight feet away, maybe more, from the victims — and he had said that he had shot back and forth from one victim to the other. But the pathologist testified that the small circumference of the wounds indicated that the shots had been fired at close range with the muzzle of the weapon against the skin. But how do you get wounds in such a small circumference from a gun alternating from one victim to the other and fired from eight feet away?

I examine Eddie's testimony on the stand with great care.

At times he is hard to believe.

He says that his brother had told the kids to *lie face down* so he could take their photographs for *identification* purposes. He asserts that he had seen the suffering on the boy's face after he was shot, although he has already said that the boy was lying face down. He asserts that he had heard the boy moaning "for several seconds or more" after he had been shot (the pathologist had testified that he believed death to be instantaneous).

None of this now matters legally. The opportunity for arguing evidence is long past.

At some point Millard decides that Pat should not attend the Pardon Board hearing. Several weeks ago Millard, Kimellen, and I had traveled to see Pat's mother. Millard judges that the hearing would be more than she can handle. She writes a letter appealing to the Board to spare the life of her son. Pat's sister, Marie, who lives in Tennessee, and Pat's aunt, his mother's sister, also write letters to the Board.

I am not privy to the decision that Pat should not attend the hearing, but I trust it. Brad Fisher, Millard, and I will speak at the hearing.

This will be the first clemency case for Edwards's newly appointed Pardon Board. "Our job," Millard says, "is to convince them that they do not have to kill this man. The D.A., of course, and probably members of the victims' families will try to convince them otherwise."

Bill Quigley, a local attorney from New Orleans, joins us. He is a close friend whom I met when I first came to St. Thomas. In the late seventies he and his wife Debbie had worked at Hope House, he a seminarian, she a nun. They had fallen in love and married, incorporating into their wedding vows a commitment to serve the poor. That led Bill into a legal practice, which he describes as "raising money for my family one half of the day and raising hell in the other half." Which means representing the causes of poor people – public housing residents, prisoners, the homeless, death-row inmates.

It comforts me to know he will be part of this effort. I am often a visitor in the Quigley household. Patrick, seven years old, is always eager for my stories, jokes, and the few magic tricks I have mastered. Bill and Debbie's bathroom wall is plastered with sayings from Dorothy Day and Gandhi, and behind the toilet is a Catholic prayerbook.

In Sam Dalton's office Bill tells us about a recent conversation with Patrick.

He was sitting by Patrick's bed until his son fell asleep, (a protection against "monsters") and was leafing through the materials on Patrick Sonnier's case that Millard had given him. Patrick had asked what he was reading and Bill told him, and Patrick had asked why people wanted to kill Mr. Sonnier.

"Because they say he killed people," Bill had answered.

"But, Dad," Patrick had asked, "then who is going to kill them for killing him?"

"Sign this kid up on our team," Millard says.

The Pardon Board hearing will meet in Baton Rouge on Saturday, March 31.

On the morning of Friday, March 30, Joe Nursey visits Pat in Angola. Soon afterward Pat is moved to the death house. Four more days: one more Saturday, that's March 31, then Sunday, April 1, Monday, Tuesday, Wednesday. That's it. Wednesday night just after midnight. No more Thursdays for Pat.

Millard puts his hand on my shoulder and says, "He's not going to die. I'm not sure how it will happen, but he's not going to die."

In the afternoon of March 30 we file the petition with the Pardon Board. Inside the office we meet Howard Marsellus, chairperson of the Board, who offers us a cup of coffee. He certainly is friendly enough, a black man who has had to work his way up in life, he says, and he seems extremely open to the issues we raise about the death penalty.

Millard says that in the South nine times out of ten when the death penalty is sought it's because the victim is white, even though blacks are most often the victims of violent crime. Marsellus agrees with that. And Millard says that capital punishment as practiced in the United States is a poor man's punishment and Marsellus enthusiastically agrees, adding, "You'll never see a rich person coming before this board." And Joe adds that you won't see a rich person not because rich people never commit terrible crimes but because the expert legal counsel they hire know how to "play the system." This gives Millard a chance to give a brief history of the kind of legal representation Pat has had and how, if he and his team had taken his case from the beginning, this man would never have gone to death row. Marsellus nods. I talk about who Patrick Sonnier is as a person, hoping that Marsellus can sense from my words the reality of this man, the goodness in him despite his part in such a heinous deed. He listens intently, kicked back in the chair behind his desk, looking me straight in the eyes. I tell a bit of my experience of living and working in St. Thomas and how I came to be involved in the struggle for this man's life.

We chat like this for about thirty minutes. Marsellus agrees with everything we say.

"I'll study the petition very carefully," he promises, "and I'll see that each member of the Board does the same. See you tomorrow."

We thank him and leave the building, but once back at the car we cannot contain our excitement. Marsellus could not have been more sympathetic.

"I feel so go-od" (two Georgian syllables), Millard says.

I let out a whoop.

Millard and Joe's analysis is that Edwards does not want to execute people, but he must protect himself politically, so he has appointed a pro-clemency Pardon Board, who will make recommendations to him which he will then follow, thus giving himself "cover." We are all buoyed up.

Later Marsellus will serve time in a federal prison for rigging pardons and accepting bribes while serving as chairperson of this board. When he gets out of prison, he will weep as he tells me how he betrayed his deepest ideals by trying to be a "team player" for the governor by protecting him from difficult clemency decisions.

On the morning of the thirty-first, the day of the Board hearing, I get up early to pray. I sit in the rocking chair in my room where I always begin the day. I face the crucifix and the small burning flame of an oil lamp. *Just this space, this time now, not yet in the rapids, not yet in the fire of debate, the points and counterpoints. Only me here and, you, God of truth, God of life, give me words, essential words, words to pierce the conscience, to turn the heart.*

I am awed at the power invested in these five human beings on the Board. How can they possibly assess the facts, nuances, ambiguities, testimony, countertestimony, politics, race, class, and legal arguments all bundled into the case of this man? Or, maybe their lines of decision-making are much simpler. Perhaps they do not see it as their role to question the judgment of the courts. Maybe their position will be like Edwards's: if they do not see a gross miscarriage of justice, they will go for death. They know that the law and the public mood demand this death. If anyone is opposed in principle to the death penalty, he or she is not sitting on this board.

I have spoken before in public. But I have never pleaded for someone's life.

In my journal the night before the hearing I list a few basic points:

I'll acknowledge the evil Pat has done and make very clear that I in no way condone his terrible crime, but I'll try to show that he is not a monster but a human being like the rest of us in the room: that he deserves punishment but not death.

I'll speak of mercy being stronger and more God-like than vengeance, and that this man can live the rest of his days productively at work behind the walls at Angola. He will pay for his deed and the public will be protected.

The next day I dress in my navy blue suit and white blouse and look with new meaning at my little silver crucifix before kissing the figure of the Executed Criminal and slipping the chain around my neck. I go to Mass with the Sisters in St. Alphonsus church, eat some Cheerios, and drive to Baton Rouge.

There I meet Millard and the others and we go to a little hamburger place for lunch. I find myself taking extra-deep breaths. I know I am doing all I can do and there is peace in that. I know that

62

Millard Farmer is at the helm and I trust that. I keep asking God to bring these efforts to good.

At one-thirty we head to the building on Mayflower Street where the hearing will take place. As we enter we are asked to sign a book, a kind of registry, and we must state which "side" we're on — the state's or the defendant's. People are beginning to come in, mill around, drink coffee. I see some of the Sisters from my religious community. I had called them and invited them to come, and we stand in a little cluster and talk. Sisters Kathleen Bahlinger and Lory Schaff are here — good, reliable friends who work among the poor in Baton Rouge. They will play a crucial role in events over the next five days.

Millard, I see, is over in a corner talking to Dracos Burke, the assistant district attorney who will argue for death.

By two o'clock we are all in the small, airless hearing room, and people are sitting close together in folding chairs. Some are standing near the doorway. The Pardon Board members take their seats behind a large table. They each have the black folders Millard gave them. They also have other papers from the D.A.'s office. Howard Marsellus is in the middle.

Our side will talk first. The Board will ask questions. The state will speak second. The Board again will ask its questions. Those are the rules. Marsellus in his introduction stresses the importance of order in the proceedings, both from those testifying and from those in the audience.

We begin. Brad Fisher goes first. The Board has a copy of his affidavit but he takes his time and goes over the main points with them. He is calm and reasoned. I am struck by how ordinary, how banal the procedure seems. Someone looking in through a window, not knowing what is being said, might think this is a neighborhood meeting to discuss how the tree-planting project is progressing.

Millard is up next. He points out all the legal issues not raised because of inadequate defense and why now it is difficult to get the courts to consider them. He raises the question of whether, under the law, Patrick Sonnier is guilty of first-degree murder. His voice is measured but earnest. He says that the state of Louisiana does not need to kill Pat Sonnier to protect its citizens, that this man will work and work hard for the rest of his days at Angola.

I speak last. I say all I planned to say. Coming to the end, knowing these are my last words, I raise the question about which of these brothers did the actual killing. I raise it knowing that there is no way to prove what I am saying. I raise it anyway.

Our side has had its say. Marsellus invites the state to present its case.

Dracos Burke speaks. He says that it is six years and five months since the murders have happened and that justice is "long past due." He reviews the "lengthy, thorough" court review given Mr. Sonnier — not only a trial but a retrial for sentencing, then the numerous appeals reviewed by both state and federal courts, and, finally, the successor petitions filed by Mr. Farmer, obviously a "most excellent attorney" at the service of Mr. Sonnier. He says that there has been no doubt in the courts' mind about who did the murder, that the killings were "cool and calculated," and now it's time, he says, past time, for Mr. Sonnier to pay the consequences of his deed. He passes out pictures of the slain teenagers for the Board members to see.

"If we don't carry out the death penalty in this case, what case will be appropriate?" he asks.

He calls as a witness Lloyd LeBlanc, father of David LeBlanc, who speaks for both of the victims' families. Lloyd says that Elmo Patrick Sonnier has put himself in the situation he is in today and all this talk of Sonnier being a rehabilitated man is hard to buy. "I have a son that is in the grave — that I can show you — who is the product of this 'rehabilitated man.' " He asks the Board to uphold the death sentence.

The testimonies given, a few questions asked, Marsellus announces that the Board will now retire to render their decision. They gather their materials and move from behind the long table. People are standing up, beginning to leave. Outside in the bright white sunshine, clutches of people stand about on the sidewalk just outside the building. As I step through the door I meet Lloyd LeBlanc and his wife, Eula. They're middle-aged. He's solidly built, a little thick at the middle, receding hair. My heart is pounding. I fumble for words. "I'm so sorry about your son," I say.

Leblanc says, "Sister, I'm a Catholic. How can you present Elmo Patrick Sonnier's side like this without ever having come to visit with me and my wife or the Bourques to hear our side? How can you spend all your time worrying about Sonnier and not think that maybe we needed you too?"

"I thought I would only add to your pain," I say.

I am shocked by what he is saying to me. I feel that I have made a terrible mistake and done what I was most trying to avoid — added to their pain.

He introduces me to the Bourques, who are polite enough, but I can see the hurt in their faces and the deep resentment that a representative of the Church should be devoting her energies to keep their child's murderer from the electric chair.

Lloyd LeBlanc and I walk up and down the sidewalk talking. He tells me of his wife's pain, how he has had to bring her to David's grave every morning before she can get on with her day, the days and nights and weeks and months and years of weeping. He also knows, he says, another side of Elmo Sonnier, a side, he is sure, which I have not seen, an evil man who hung around bars with thieves and "trashy" people, who spouted obscenities, who stole, and who abducted teenage kids and raped young women.

This is a Pat Sonnier that I have not met or even imagined. I have only met the man in the clean blue denim shirt, the man always so glad to see me, who writes me letters and can't thank me enough for my love and care. In retrospect I wonder how I could be so naive. I wish now that I had gone to visit the Bourques and the LeBlancs. Too late now. Their hurt and anger sting.

I look at my watch. The Board has been deliberating about an hour. Despite my failure to talk to the LeBlancs and the Bourques, I still want Pat to live. I feel I am still right to oppose capital punishment, but I had not thought seriously enough about what murder means to victims' families and to society. I had not considered how difficult the issue of capital punishment is. My response had been far too simplistic.

My instinct tells me the longer the Board deliberates, the better. The uphill battle is ours and uphill battles do not resolve quickly.

The word comes to us casually. "The Board is back."

I take leave of Lloyd LeBlanc. "Thank you for talking to me," I say, and I tell him I will be praying for him, for his wife, for his family, and again I say I am so sorry about his son. I cannot say it enough.

We shake hands. I sense in him an unmistakable friendliness and a great loneliness. He has spent the last hour talking to me despite my earlier failure to reach out to him. I decide that later I will telephone him. Somehow, across the emotional minefields and opposing views of the death penalty, we can talk to each other.

Voices drop and there is a subdued stillness and silence as Board members seat themselves once again at the long table. Marsellus announces that each is to record his or her decision on the form, which he now passes to them. I think of the Sisters handing out final exams, the silence in the classroom as the fateful papers are passed out, everyone anxiously scanning the questions, the sound

65

of scribbling pens. The Board members can see the papers and we can't, but soon now all will be revealed. My heart is racing. Die or live? There is a tight feeling in my stomach and I try to take a deep breath but it doesn't catch.

Marsellus waits as the marked papers make their way back to him in the center of the table. He looks at each of the papers. He arranges them in a neat, squared pile. He looks up and says, "It is the finding of this board that clemency be denied to Mr. Elmo Sonnier." The vote is four to one. No one states a reason except Dr. Lionel Daniels, the one vote against denial. He is bothered, he says, by questions concerning the adequacy of Mr. Sonnier's defense at the sentencing trial.

A group of us gather in the back parking lot. Millard's face is ashen and he is saying that he will get a private meeting with Edwards, he and I and Edwards — somehow he will do this.

From the back door one of the Board members, Lawrence Hand, walks over to us. He's a Catholic, has a sister who's a nun. He pats me on the arm and says, "Even Christ didn't win 'em all, Sister."

"What happened to Marsellus?" somebody says.

Millard and team will head back to New Orleans. I will stay in Baton Rouge with my mother for the night.

That night I make two phone calls. One is to Lloyd LeBlanc. I tell him that even though I am against the execution of Pat Sonnier, that does not mean that I do not care about him and his family and what happened to his son. I ask him to please not hesitate to call on me if there is anything I can do to ease his pain and his terrible loss.

He has a question.

"Are you a Communist?"

"A Communist?" I repeat.

"No, Mr. LeBlanc, I am not a Communist."

"I didn't think so," he says. "That's what some people are saying, with you defending this murderer, but I didn't think so."

Then I make my second phone call. I call Sister Kathleen Bahlinger and ask her and Sister Lory to take care of Pat's funeral arrangements. It has been one of Pat's few requests — "Please don't let me be buried here" — and I have promised that I won't let that happen. This means getting a funeral home to perform the services, a suit of clothes for him to be buried in, a plot of ground.

Kathleen and I talk about asking our religious community for one of our burial plots. We have been friends since childhood, attended the same high school. Many a night I fell asleep in the back seat of the family Oldsmobile as we came home from the Bahlinger's (in distance, exactly one rosary from their house to ours). She had plenty of brothers, too, seven of them, which always made it exciting to go to her house.

"And the prayer service, too," I add, "will you and Lory take care of it? Pat is a Catholic. Maybe Bishop Ott will be willing to celebrate the funeral Mass. He's opposed to capital punishment and he's invested quite a bit of his time urging the governor to grant clemency to Pat."

Kathleen says she'll ask him. She'll also go to Goodwill to pick out a burial suit.

"What size do you think he wears? How tall is he?" she asks.

And I say, "He's a good six feet and not thin. He's a big man."

"I'll take care of it," she says.

I am silent then.

And Kathleen says, "Perhaps we won't need any of this."

CHAPTER
4

It is good to be back at Mama's house at a time like this. Four more days until they kill Pat Sonnier. She comes into my room to sit by my bed and talk awhile and kiss me good night. I have drawn her into strange waters — murders and victims and plans for electrocution, pardon boards and governors — my face on the evening news, identified as "spiritual adviser to the convicted murderer." She gets angry phone calls about her daughter's "misplaced kindness." Mother and child. What happens to one happens to the other.

I wonder about Mrs. Sonnier. She doesn't have a telephone and won't get any threatening phone calls. But when she goes to the grocery store, if she glances over her shoulder can she see people whispering? Can she feel their eyes on her, fingers pointed toward the "mother of the murderers"? Or perhaps she doesn't leave the house these days. Perhaps she waits out the days in seclusion in her two-room apartment. When Millard and I visited with her, she told us that she had unplugged her television. During Pat's last brush with execution she had been watching television and had seen her son's face and a picture of the electric chair flash on the screen.

On Sunday, April 1, before I leave for the prison, Mama cooks up "some good, hot grits to stick to your ribs." My sister, Mary

Ann, who lives just a few houses down the street, comes over and joins us. Nobody in the family can quite grasp this situation — myself included. I cannot convince myself that Pat will be killed.

At the prison I visit with Eddie first, before going to see Pat. I see him come toward me. He's pale, and he tells me he is "holding up okay" except for his "tore-up" stomach and that it's been "hard to get to sleep." He looks around the visiting room, then quietly pulls a folded piece of paper out of his blue denim jacket and whispers, "Get this to the governor." I look at it: a letter, written in his neat handwriting in black ballpoint pen on yellow, lined legal paper. "Please, Governor," it says, "you're about to kill the wrong man . . . I'm the one who killed the teenagers . . ."

It is against prison rules for an inmate to bring written documents into the visiting room. It is against prison rules for a visitor who is not an attorney to take such documents out of the prison. But the governor *must* see this letter. Maybe if he reads these desperate words, he will ask to study the trial transcripts himself. Maybe he will meet with Millard Farmer. I rise from the table and show the letter to one of the guards. He knows about the pending execution. All the prison personnel know about the execution, and every guard in this visiting room knows that Eddie is Pat's brother. They are watching Eddie carefully these days. One of the guards had said to me this morning, as I came through the visitor center, that the Angola "grapevine" had it that the "wrong brother was getting the chair." Prison talk.

"I can't authorize your bringing this out," the guard says, and he takes the letter and telephones for the captain. I wait. Perhaps I should not have given him the letter. Better to keep it in my hands. I look over at Eddie sitting alone at the table. He is smoking a cigarette and looking down at the ashtray.

The visiting room, full of visitors, is buzzing as usual. Families sitting together talking. Children pattering over to the ice-cream concession. Over at one of the corner tables near the wall an inmate and his girl are kissing. A long kiss. If the kissing gets too passionate, a guard will walk up to the couple and tell the inmate to cool it. The captain appears and puts in a phone call to the warden and tells me the warden says it's okay to take the letter out. I take a deep breath. The captain is not unkind. There is concern in his eyes, a gentle tone to his voice. Maybe he can put himself in the place of this man, trying to save his brother from death.

If Pat is to be killed, then Eddie has visited with him for the last time. Eddie tells me how, two weeks ago, he was awakened by a guard at three-thirty in the morning and told to dress. He was not told where he was going but was directed, hands and feet shackled, into a prison vehicle and driven to the front of the prison. There, in the death-row visiting room, he had been allowed to visit Pat for two hours.

It was the second such visit of the brothers in the four years they have been at Angola. Prison rules prohibit brothers' being assigned to the same camps or visiting each other. Brothers, natural allies, might team up against other inmates or plot escape.

Ross Maggio, the warden, had given special permission for the brothers' recent visit. Shortly after receiving the April date of execution, Pat had written the warden and requested a visit with his brother. No answer. Once again he wrote, requesting the visit. No answer. Then one day when he was out of his cell for his "hour," Pat reached up and grasped one of the water pipes above his head and said to the guards, "Go tell Warden Maggio I want to talk to him about my brother, and I'm not moving from here until I see him. If any of you try to force me — see this pipe? I'll rip it loose, and you may get me but I'm going to take a lot of you with me."

The guards immediately radioed the warden. It would have been easier for them to subdue the prisoner if he had been inside his cell. They could then have used regular procedure — several guards, protected by face masks and body shields, would move in on him with tear gas, mace, and billy clubs.

In ten minutes Maggio had arrived on the scene.

Maggio was called "Cowboy" because he had come to Angola to "straighten out" a few things, and inmates are quick to acknowledge that the prison is safer because of his reforms. The most recent tale circulating about the tall, good-looking warden is of his rescue of his mother from two escaping inmates who had abducted her from his house within the prison compound. Holding a screwdriver to her throat, the inmates ordered the warden to drive them in a truck out through the front gate. But on reaching the gate, Maggio rammed the truck into an iron post, leaped out, grabbed a gun from a guard, and shot one inmate dead and wounded the other.

Now Warden Maggio had come on the tier to confront Patrick Sonnier. He told him that before they could talk, he would have to get back into his cell. If he did that, the warden promised to "be fair." Pat had complied and the two men had talked and once again Pat had asked to see his brother.

"Maggio kept his promise. I got to see Eddie," Pat told me, and he took a certain pride in having brought it off. He had also appreciated that the warden had not charged him with a disciplinary infraction. "He knew I was desperate to see my brother."

With the letter to the governor tucked into the pocket of my suit, I leave Eddie around 11:00 A.M. and head to the death house to see Pat. Eddie tells me as I am leaving, "Talk to the warden, and ask him please, please, not to put me in lock-down." He wants to stay in "population" with his friends around him and be able to go to work and stay busy. I promise him I will ask the warden.

A guard drives me in one of the prison vehicles to the death house. I talk to the driver. I always talk to the guards when I visit the prison. I ask them about their work and their families and what they do to relax. (Most fish or hunt.) Their minds, what happens to their minds, I wonder, all day long, all night long, just *watching* other people. They are not allowed to read on duty. One of the guards has told me that in their training they are discouraged from sharing their "personal" lives with inmates. Their relationship to inmates is based on distrust. They expect that inmates will try to con them. I'm thinking that must make their job doubly costly — not only boring but isolating as well.

"It's a steady paycheck," one guard said to me. His father has worked here, and his grandfather, and I soon discover that's a prevalent pattern — families working here for two, three, four generations.

I've talked to women who work in the towers located near the front gate and the main yard. Into the tower they go at five o'clock every morning. They lock the door behind them and climb the steps. The tower is glassed all around at the top. In the middle sits a toilet, unseen from the ground. A radio. A telephone. A rifle. And twelve hours to go. Watch the empty yard when inmates are at work inside, the yard stripped of all trees and bushes, with only the fence to break the horizon. Watch the inmates when they come out for recreation. Watch if any cluster together. Watch if any huddle by the fence. Watch. Watch and think, maybe listen to music on the radio. Twelve hours. Look forward to the tray of food that will come to you around eleven o'clock and then at four. Memorize the menu. Know on what day red beans come and cornbread and mustard greens and especially, fried chicken.

What saves their sanity, some women tell me, is the telephone. They call each other and talk. But this is against the rules. They have a code to alert each other about unannounced visits of supervisors.

Riding along in the van now, I refocus my mind on my destination. It is a rainy, blustery day. I see a dark line of trees on the edge of the horizon. Behind the trees is the Mississippi. The river figures prominently in escape stories told around here. Most escaping prisoners meet one of two fates: the bloodhounds sniff them out in the swamps surrounding the prison, or they drown in the river. A few have made it to the other side only to find a search posse waiting for them. Not many successful escapes from this place. On foggy days no inmates are allowed outside.

My driver stops and parks in front of a green cinder-block building, an ordinary building except for the large generator to the left. Across the front of the building in four neatly painted cans are geraniums, brilliant red. Just across the road, ducks swim in a lagoon. In front of the glass doors at the entrance sits a blue-uniformed guard with a rifle across his lap.

Before I enter the building, the guard asks me to empty my pockets. He runs the metal detector over my body, front and back. Just inside the door in a small foyer another guard sits on a metal folding chair. He has one of those fresh-scrubbed, baby faces and a .357 Magnum strapped to his side. It's unusual to see guns like this. Inside the prison you never see a firearm, except for the guards on horseback who carry rifles out in the fields, or the guards at the front gate who have Magnums holstered at their sides.

I look around to see what I can of the building. Straight ahead are two small offices: one, the major's office, with a desk and telephone and filing cabinet; the other a place where there's a coffee percolator and some cabinets and a long table and chairs. To the left is a visitor room, rather large. You can see it through the glass paneling which separates it from the foyer. In it are several tables and chairs and a drink machine. To the extreme left of the visitor room is a white metal door with no window. I know that this door is always kept locked. Behind it is the electric chair. Everything is very clean. The tile floors are highly polished. The paint on the walls looks fresh.

I turn to my right out of the foyer into a small hallway. Straight ahead through the glass exit door I can see a cement walkway and the buildings of Camp F. Brown sparrows hop on the walkway outside the door. To the right of the exit door is a white metal door with a window of heavy mesh screen that leads onto the tier. Behind it, his hands and feet shackled, sits Patrick Sonnier.

I have been calm until now, but seeing him here in this place, I feel my stomach muscles tighten.

Looking past Pat, I see a row of four cells. A guard stands at the end of the row watching Pat. His shift over, another guard will take his place. Guards will be observing Pat now until his death. There is a television set on a metal can on the floor opposite the first cell, where Pat sits on a plastic chair. Everything is painted green. The floor is unpainted cement. On the wall next to Pat's cell is a telephone. He is allowed to make collect phone calls.

"I don't want Mama or anybody from the family coming to this place," Pat tells me. "Mama couldn't stand it."

That means I'm all he's got.

I pray, *Please, God, don't let him break down.* I don't know what I will do if he starts to sob or shake or struggle against the guards. I remember in the newspaper account of his arrest that he had urinated on himself from fright.

I try to be upbeat.

I tell him about Eddie's letter to the governor and that I know a reporter at the *Times-Picayune* who might be able to get the letter published. I take him step by step through the Pardon Board hearing — what Millard said, what Brad Fisher said — but he interrupts me. He is angry about the Pardon Board hearing. "Why wasn't I there?" he asks me.

Why wasn't he there? I don't know why. He wasn't there because Millard said he shouldn't be. I have been following without question whatever recommendations Millard makes. Did he fear that Pat's being in the presence of the victims' families would produce too charged an atmosphere? Did he think that Pat would not express himself well and might sound too self-serving?

Pat has his own letter he wishes to write to the governor. His hands are shackled, so he dictates it and I write it for him:

Dear Governor Edwards,

I feel that the so-called hearing before the Pardon Board yesterday was done unjustly because I was not allowed to appear and speak for my own life. The victims' families were all there and that was bound to influence the Board, but I was deprived of being able to meet them face to face.

I ask you, as Governor of this state, to uphold my right to appear before this Board which is deciding whether I live or die.

Thank you for hearing this request.

I think: not being at your own hearing that decides whether you live or die. I can't imagine ever being so powerless. I think of Camus' description of the condemned: *everything goes on outside of him . . . He is no longer a man but a thing waiting to be handled . . .*

Such powerlessness before his executioners is one thing, but in the hands of his attorneys too? I feel terrible that I followed Millard's judgment without question. I haven't practiced blind obedience like this since the old days of convent life, when I obeyed my superiors unthinkingly.

It has begun to rain heavily outside. You can hear the water splashing on the walkway outside the glass door. The sparrows have gone. There is only the sound of the rain. Pat is smoking one cigarette after another and drinking black coffee. Visitors are not allowed food of any kind in the death house. I drink coffee, too.

Over and over in my mind I calculate the days. It is Sunday, April 1; tomorrow, Monday, April 2; then Tuesday, April 3; then Wednesday, April 4; and that night, just after midnight, death. The guard watching Pat shifts from foot to foot. Another guard comes to replace him. I am told to step away from the door while the guards change.

Around two-thirty I am told that visiting time is over. I promise Pat to come back tomorrow. "You're all I've got," he says, and manages a smile. I leave him some passages in the Bible to meditate on if he wants to. I stand at the door and put my hand against the mesh screen. He stands up too. I pray, asking God to give him courage, to strengthen his faith, to help him take each day at a time. I pray that God will give Millard and the team the wisdom they need to persuade the courts to grant a stay of execution. I pray for the governor's heart.

Once outside the prison, I use a public pay phone to call Millard in New Orleans. "We need you to come in for a strategy meeting," he tells me. It means a three-hour drive. I stop at a café near the prison for a sandwich and a coke. I eat in the car as I head to New Orleans 120 miles away.

I get to Sam Dalton's office at six o'clock. Millard and the others have been working round the clock drawing up the petitions that Bill Quigley will file in the courts tomorrow morning. They have decided to include Pat's affidavit stating the circumstances which led him to make his confessions. They are throwing everything they can think of into the petitions. This is Pat's last shot in the courts.

I show them Eddie's letter to the governor and we decide to get the letter over to James Hodge, a friend of mine at the *Times-Picayune*. At this point, Millard says, press attention can't hurt.

I tell Millard that Pat is upset that he was not allowed to be present at his hearing before the Pardon Board. Millard, I can tell, has his mind on other things. "It was a judgment call," he says. "It's hard to know what's best, you know what I mean?"

Everybody looks pretty ragged. I suspect they have been working most of the night. I am pretty tired myself, though I am not attending much to how I feel. I am developing a cough and my lungs don't feel right. I am allergic to smoke and Pat has been smoking one cigarette after another.

Early Monday morning I head back to Baton Rouge, bringing Eddie's and Pat's letters to the governor. I go to Fran Bussie's office and turn the letters over to her. She's a friend of Edwards's and had arranged for our meeting with him.

While at Fran's I call Sister Lory Schaff on the phone. She puts Kathleen on, who wants to talk about funeral arrangements, but just before she does this, she reminds me of something: "I know you're doing everything you can with the attorneys and the others to save this man from dying," she says to me, "but as his spiritual adviser you're the one who has to help him die. Don't be so absorbed in fighting for him to live that you don't help him die."

She is right, of course. I thank her for helping me to keep on course. Thank God for the sisterhood.

Kathleen tells me that the leadership of our community has met and we can probably use one of our own burial plots and she's found a funeral home willing to donate its services. She's still got to go to Goodwill to get the suit coat, but she can get a shirt and tie from one of her brothers.

That morning I drive to Angola.

As I enter the death house I can hear the television near Pat's cell. A basketball game is on. As I approach the visitor door I see that the guard stationed to watch Pat has moved down closer to the TV to catch the critical play. Pat is inside his cell. A moment, a silence, the snap of the ball, and the two men cheer. They could be two friends in somebody's den on a Saturday afternoon. But then the guard moves back to the end of the tier and assumes his position.

Pat seems to be holding up well. He is getting letters from his young pen pals and he reads parts of the letters to me. "It's a good thing we don't have hanging as a method of execution here in Louisiana, or Mark would feel bad, because look what he says in his letter: 'hang in there' " and he laughs. It's bravado, of course. "They're not going to break me," he says to me again and again. "I just pray God gives me strength to make that last walk." He says he didn't read the Bible last night. Instead, he says, he talked a long, long time with the guards on duty. Reading, he says, might make him sleepy and he's not too keen on sleeping. He's staying conscious and in control as much as he can.

I tell him that his letter to the governor has been delivered. I tell him that Bill Quigley is filing the petitions in the courts this morning, and that Millard is making his move to see the governor in private.

"Look," he says, "I appreciate all the efforts to save me, but me and God have squared things away. I'm ready to go if it comes down."

And I can see that he does have strength and resilience and this gives me courage too. I think of Kathleen lining up the burial plot, the coat from Goodwill. But with Pat I am in a circle of light and strength. I learn to stay in this space of the present moment and not to think to the future, not to think past today to Wednesday night at midnight. Today is Monday and Pat is alive and I am alive and we are here talking together.

Outside it is another rainy, gray day, the third in a row. Pat sees the stormy weather as a bad omen. And he adds another: "They've already executed two blacks — Williams and Taylor — it's time for a white; the governor is under pressure to get a white."

Captain John Rabelais comes to the door where Pat and I are visiting. He is captain of Camp F and the death house falls under his jurisdiction. He asks Pat if he wants a lunch tray. Pat shakes his head no. The rules prohibit him from offering me one. I am drinking coffee and canned drinks from the machine in the lobby. I look up at this man, Rabelais, with the long, lined, hangdog face. In his 60's I'd guess, and a paunch hangs over his belt, but unmistakably the brown eyes are friendly. He offers to get me a cup of coffee and I accept.

Later in the day, when Pat is inside his cell to use the toilet, I get a chance to talk to Rabelais.

"What's a nun doing in a place like this?" he asks. "Shouldn't you be teaching children? Do you know what this man has done, the kids he killed?"

"What he did was evil. I don't condone it," I answer. "I just don't see much sense in doing the same to him."

He looks at me and I look at him, and I am thinking that if

circumstances were different, I could be sitting at this man's kitchen table, eating jambalaya and swapping stories. I like the man.

"You know how the Bible says 'an eye for an eye,'" he says to me, but it's like a gentle pitch in softball, slow and big and easy.

"And you know," I say back to him, "that Jesus called us to go beyond that kind of vengeance, not to pay back an 'eye for an eye,' not to return hate for hate."

He smiles, puts up his hand. "I ain't gonna get into all this Bible quotin' with no nun, 'cuz I'm gonna lose."

Making my way back to Pat, I pause to talk awhile to the guard sitting inside the door. I comment on the rain and he looks outside and says, "Yup, just don't seem to want to stop." And I say something about how it must get pretty tiring just sitting here all day, and he couldn't agree with that more. "Borrrrring," he says, and he drops his voice and I bend down lower to him and he whispers, "I don't particularly want to be here, you know what I mean, doing this, being part of this, but it's part of the job. I got a wife and kids to support."

Morning has turned into afternoon. I will be leaving soon to go back to New Orleans. I ask Pat if he is interested in a prayer service tomorrow. I know he is not keen on being in the company of the old priest. Some months ago he had told me how he had confessed to the priest "you know, the heavy-duty stuff," and when he had finished the priest had asked, "Have any impure thoughts? Say any obscene words?" And it was all he could do, he says, not to hit the "old man."

"If you're there with me I'll do the prayer service with him," he says, "but not by myself."

I tell him that I'll plan it and I'll talk to the priest. There's a song I want him to hear, I tell him, called "Be Not Afraid," based on Isaiah 43, and I have my Bible there and I read the words to him. I read the words slowly so that he can take them in.

On Tuesday, April 3, I leave New Orleans for Angola at 6:45 A.M. after a sleepless night. I kept jerking awake, wondering what else might be done for Pat. Were we doing everything we could? By 3:00 A.M. I couldn't go back to sleep. Ann Barker, my close friend, a doctor, had started me on an antibiotic for a bronchial infection. I know I am running on adrenaline. I know my physical resources are running low.

I arrive at the prison at about nine o'clock and ask to see Warden Maggio. He comes immediately to the front gate. Briefly I tell him what I know about the two brothers, Pat and Eddie. I show him

Eddie's letter to the governor. I make the request for Eddie that he not be put in lock-down if Pat is executed. The warden makes no promises. "I'll see," he says, and then, referring to Eddie's letter to the governor, "I can't get into who's guilty or who's innocent. I'm here to carry out my job as warden, but I can tell you this — nobody's doing handsprings over this execution. It's not easy on anybody." Then he tells me that the head of the Department of Corrections, C. Paul Phelps, wishes to talk to me. I can come with him to his office for the call and then he'll see that I get a ride back to Camp F.

I walk into the antechamber of Maggio's office. Several armchairs line the wall and a secretary sits behind a desk. She looks very professional in her tailored suit and white blouse with the colorful bow at the neck. The office is quiet and well organized. There is the appointment calendar, the telephone, the computer. And there on the desk is a green potted plant and pictures of laughing children.

I realize that I am very, very tired. I did not eat breakfast before I left New Orleans this morning. Maybe that was a mistake. I won't be able to eat again until I leave the death house.

I telephone Phelps in Baton Rouge at the Department of Corrections. A friendly, crisp voice on the other end of the phone asks me to wait "one moment please." I shut my eyes and take a few deep breaths. A glimmer from a recent dream flashes: Pat Sonnier in a red-and-black plaid shirt, alive and smiling and sitting in my living room. I'll have to tell Pat about the dream. Maybe he'll see it as a good omen.

"Sister Prejean?" It is Phelps on the phone. As head of the Department of Corrections he is responsible, he tells me, for the "overall process," which includes approving each of the witnesses. Do I wish to witness?

"Yes."

"I would like to talk to you eyeball to eyeball," he says. "I want to make sure that each witness understands that this event is to be carried out with as much dignity and respect as possible."

I tell him that I will be in the death house all day with Pat, that I don't see when I can come and see him at his office. My first obligation, I say, is to be with Pat every minute that I can.

A pause. Then he says that I will be given a paper to sign before the execution. It states the rules witnesses agree to follow. I am to read it very, very carefully.

I tell him that I will do that.

DEAD MAN WALKING

He is calm, reasonable, organized, professional, and he's planning to kill someone two days from now.

The warden's secretary has a kind and pretty face. She asks me if I would like a cup of coffee while I am waiting for my ride to Camp F. She goes to the urn in the corner and pours coffee for me in a plastic cup. I am cold and shaky. I sip the coffee slowly. These people too, the warden, the pretty secretary, they're also getting ready to kill someone.

Before leaving the prison yesterday I had made preliminary preparations for the prayer service with one of the associate wardens and requested the presence of the Catholic priest. I had been told that the music tape would have to be approved. Music of all kinds is frowned on at a "time like this," the warden had said. "Stirs up too many emotions."

At last the rain has stopped. The sky is wide and arching and blue. The sunlight is brilliant and white and falling lavishly on everything. I ride with a guard to the death house by a different route. We drive down "B" line, where houses of prison personnel are located. There's a small store. There's a tiny post office. There's a cemetery on a hill.

As I walk into the foyer of the death house, Captain Rabelais awaits me. With him are the Catholic priest and the chief chaplain of the prison. They are assembled here to talk about the prayer service. One of the associate wardens asks for the music tape so that he can "preview" it. The priest and I are talking when everything begins to blur. I make an effort to keep speaking. I feel hands under my arms, supporting me. When I come to, I am lying on my back on the floor. Above me I see a ring of faces. I feel as if I have had a little nap. All I can think is how good it felt to sleep.

They tell me to stay lying down. (Later, Captain Rabelais tells me that everybody thought I had had a heart attack.) They have called an ambulance. I tell them that I am really okay, it's just that I haven't had much sleep, that I am taking an antibiotic, that I can't get anything to eat in the death house.

"You just stay right there, young lady," Captain Rabelais says. I close my eyes. It feels delicious to rest.

"Please tell Pat what happened, he'll be worried," I say as the ambulance drives up (did they use the siren?) and they are lifting me onto the stretcher.

They bring me to the prison hospital, where attendants quickly run an EKG. I wonder how much the medical personnel here at the prison will be involved in Pat's execution. I ask one of the nurses administering the test. "One of the doctors is a witness and declares the man dead afterwards, and then the ambulance brings the body here and we run an EKG—unfortunately," she tells me, and I think that Pat may be the next one lying on this table.

Associate Warden Roger Thomas appears and announces he's taking me to lunch. He drives me in his car to the personnel cafeteria. As we are standing in line with our trays, Thomas talks about the importance of carbohydrates. I tell Warden Thomas that it would help if they fed visitors in the death house. It's the only rule at Angola I have ever helped change.

By the time all this hoopla is over and I am driven back to the death house, it is almost one o'clock in the afternoon. Pat looks at me anxiously and asks, "Are you all right?"

I tell him I'm fine and I explain about taking the antibiotics and feeling weak and the EKG and the importance of carbohydrates.

"I thought you had a heart attack. I thought I was going to have to go through this by myself. Please, please take care of yourself," he says, and his voice is hoarse with feeling. In ordinary circumstances the whole incident would have been a great joke, but not now, not here.

"I kept asking them here what happened but they wouldn't tell me nothin'," he says, and the anger makes him punch the words. I thought surely someone would have had the sensitivity to inform him that I was okay and that I'd soon be coming back to him.

I turn all of my energies now to this man on the other side of this metal door. I give him an update on what Millard says and how he has an appointment to see the governor tomorrow at 3:00 in the afternoon (in case the courts don't grant relief) and I tell him about my request to Warden Maggio that Eddie not be put in lock-down, but I do not tell him about my conversation with Phelps. I point to the brilliant day and how blue and bright the sky is. The dark, stormy clouds are gone.

The old priest arrives around three o'clock for the prayer service. He carries a prayer book and a small, round, gold container with the communion wafers in it. He wears the stole around his neck, the symbol of priestly authority in the Catholic Church. I suggest a plan to him for the prayer service and he nods his head in agreement.

I turn on the audiotaped hymn:

If you cross the barren desert
you shall not die of thirst . . .

DEAD MAN WALKING

be not afraid, I go before you always . . .
if you stand before the fires of hell
and death is at your side . . .
be not afraid . . .

The harmony of the young Jesuits is sweet and close, a song that promises strength for difficult journeys. Pat's head is lowered, his ear cocked close to the metal door, intent on every word.

I picture the words of the song echoing from room to room within the death house, the words filling the place where the witnesses will sit, where the executioner will stand, the tender, merciful God-words, traveling across the hundred feet of tiled floor that must be walked to where the electric chair waits. I picture the words bouncing off the oak wood of the chair and wrapping themselves round it: *be not afraid*. I know the words may not stop the death that is about to take place, but the words can breathe courage and dignity into the one who must walk to this oak chair and sit in it.

The old priest says prayers in Latin and takes the communion wafer from the container and places it on Pat's tongue, then into my outstretched hand.

"The Body of Christ," he says.

"Amen."

Yes, in this place I believe that you are here, oh Christ, you, who sweat blood and who prayed "aloud and in silent tears" for your Father to remove your own "cup" of suffering.[1] This man about to die is not innocent, but he is human, and that is enough to draw you here.

The priest leaves. I feel sorry for the old man. He is performing his priestly office as he has performed it for fifty years or more. The Latin prayers said, the communion wafer given, he has nothing else to say to this man about to die. His trust is in the ritual, that it will do its work, even in a foreign language. For him, the human, personal interaction of trust and love is not part of the sacrament.

After the prayer, Pat's mood is lighter. The sunlight is flooding in everywhere — through the glass door, through the row of windows at the top of the tier. The little sparrows are loud and busy and flitting in and out of the eaves. Seeing the birds, I share something I remember from a college course about how the brains of certain animals compare with the human brain, how a bird can be flying at a fast clip, then suddenly light on a small wire or branch perfectly poised because so much of its brain is devoted to seeing. And blood-hounds can smell much better than human beings because much of a dog's head cavity contains large sinuses and corresponding brain matter for smelling. But even though we can't smell as well as a bloodhound or see as well as a bird, we can *think*. And Pat laughs and says, "Some of us." And then he tells me some of his animal stories, about deer and rabbit and coon and how you track them and how it is when it's cold out in the woods and it's just you there listening, watching, waiting, and how when he and Eddie would come back with a deer, his Mama would always cook up a pot of white beans and rice to go with it and how even the little dog, Beauty, would "lick her chops" waiting for her share.

If he were dying of cancer, it would be easier to comprehend his death. But here he is, fully alive, and it is hard to picture him fully dead. Death is thirty-three hours away and here we are talking about the brain size of birds and bloodhounds and hunting in the woods. You can only attend to death for so long before the life force sucks you right in again.

I encourage him to share his feelings and not feel he has to put up a front with me. I tell him I won't think less of him as a man if he admits he's afraid. "I'm afraid," I tell him. "Everybody's scared of dying." But he is holding down his emotions. "I can't let myself go," he says, "I'd lose control," and so he holds tight except to express love and gratitude to me. "I have never known real love," he says, "never loved women or anybody all that well myself. I gave Mama a lot of trouble and Eddie was always her 'baby.' She always loved her 'baby' and it's not that I blame her. It's a shame a man has to come to prison to find love." He looks up at me and says, "Thanks for loving me," but I feel guilty that so much love has been lavished on me. In the face of this man's utter poverty, I feel humbled.

I am getting ready to leave for the day.

He makes me promise to get to sleep early. "Take care of yourself," he says as I leave.

I promise him I will, that I won't be driving all the way back to New Orleans tonight but staying at Mama's. I tell him I'll see him tomorrow after I visit with Eddie.

As I leave the prison I see a familiar car in the parking lot. My brother and sister, Louie and Mary Ann, have come to drive me home. They have heard that I fainted. Millard had called to tell them about it after I had checked in with him earlier in the day. Ann, Louie tells me, is also coming to Mama's for the night, and plans to stay for the "duration." That's just like her to do that, good friend that she is, to drop everything to come and be near me when

I need her. She's a doctor in an inner-city clinic in New Orleans and it must not have been easy to rearrange schedules.

At Mama's I telephone Millard in New Orleans.

"Any word from the courts?" I ask.

"It's in the Fifth Circuit," he says. "They haven't rejected it out of hand, they're studying it, that's a good sign."

Then he tells me that he has an appointment to see Governor Edwards tomorrow afternoon at three o'clock. "The governor specified that I am to come alone."

I say that sounds good — the governor alone with Farmer — that might help.

"No," he says, "it means that he doesn't want *you* there. He doesn't want to face you again."

This surprises me.

Ann gives me a sleeping pill and I climb into bed thinking of the man in the death house crawling into his bunk for the last full night of his life, and I think of the Bourques and the LeBlancs and their murdered children and of Mrs. Sonnier, and how she will make it through this long night and perhaps she is being hard on herself for paying too much attention to Eddie, her "baby," perhaps she is berating herself for not loving her eldest son enough . . . and I say a prayer for all the mothers — Mrs. Sonnier and Mrs. Bourque and Mrs. LeBlanc. Then I am opening my eyes and the light is already in the windows and I know what day it is.

Ann drives me to Angola. The April day could not be more sparkling. All along the winding road the azaleas and dogwoods bloom, and the oaks and maples and cedars have new-green, sticky leaves and surely, I think, surely this is too beautiful a day for anyone to be killed, and I am filled with the hope that any moment now the courts will grant a stay of execution and this will all be remembered as a bad dream.

Ann, always organized, has worked it out that she will drive me to the prison this morning, then come back in the afternoon and wait for me in the parking lot from three-thirty on. That way, if Pat gets a stay of execution, I'll have a ride home. And if not, she'll be there when I come out, and she tells me that some of the Sisters plan to come to the front gate of the prison to protest Pat's execution.

I visit Eddie first and he seems in remarkably good shape and my own hope buoys him up. His letter to the governor has appeared on the front page of the *Times-Picayune* this morning with the headline: "Brother to Governor: you're killing the wrong man." Perhaps this kind of public knowledge will create doubt by which the governor can justify a reprieve should the courts not grant relief.

At noon I leave Eddie to go to the death house. I am holding my thoughts on a tight rein and refusing to allow myself to think ahead. It is noon on this bright April day and Pat and I are going to have a long visit. But I tense up as soon as the death building comes into sight.

Almost as soon as I'm inside, Captain Rabelais appears with a tray of food. "Eat, young lady," he says, and they serve Pat a tray of food, too — gargantuan amounts of meat loaf, corn bread, mustard greens, and cake. "Our cook here at Camp F is one of the best at Angola," Rabelais brags, and Pat says, "Sure beats what we get on the Row." I'm glad to see that Pat is eating something. I go for the carbohydrates.

Pat says he did not sleep much last night. I tell him I did, and that Ann gave me a sleeping pill. He refuses the "nerve" medicine they offer him. He wants to be fully awake, he tells me, and he doesn't trust what they might give him.

I tell Pat about my visit with Eddie. "I'm angry at him," he tells me. "I'm angry at him for shooting the kids. I'm angry at the kids for being parked out in the woods in the first place. I'm angry that Mr. Bourque and Mr. LeBlanc are coming to watch me die. I'm angry at myself for letting me and Eddie mess over those kids and for me letting Eddie blow like that.

"I'll have a chance to say my last words," he says, "and I'm going to tell Bourque and LeBlanc a thing or two, coming to watch me die. Especially Bourque. I've heard he's been telling people that he wishes he could pull the switch himself."

"Your choice," I tell him, "if you want your last words to be words of hate." And then I talk to him about how his anger at a time like this is understandable and how it would be understandable too if he chose to make his last words a curse, a hateful attack on people who have come to watch him suffer and die, and maybe if I were in his place I would want to do the same thing — at least a part of me would. "But there's another side to you too," I say, "a part of you that wants not to be shriveled up by hate, a part of you that wants to die a free and loving man. I'm not saying it's easy, but it's possible and it's up to you." And then I ask him to think about the parents of David and Loretta and how they have already suffered torments and whether he wants to add to their grief. He's hunched over in the chair, his elbows on his knees, smoking and thinking.

84

Then Nancy Goodwin comes into the death house. She had been with the Louisiana Coalition on Jails and Prisons in the mid-seventies, and had befriended Pat and Eddie after Eddie had written asking for help. The relief I feel in seeing her makes me realize how close the terror is. Now here's someone else to shoulder the afternoon and the waiting. It is just about 3:00. While Nancy visits with Pat, I go to Captain Rabelais's office and telephone Joe Nursey at Sam Dalton's office in New Orleans.

"Any word from the Fifth Circuit?" I ask.

"None yet," he says. "A good sign. They've had it a good while now and maybe that means they see something substantive in the petition."

"And Millard?" I ask.

"He just called from the mansion. He was about to go in to see the governor. He must be with him now."

I count the hours on my fingers: nine hours before midnight. Time rushes by and yet time is frozen. Funny how we get so exact about time at the end of life and at its beginning. She died at 6:08 or 3:46, we say, or the baby was born at 4:02. But in between we slosh through huge swatches of time — weeks, months, years, decades even.

I look at my watch. It is 3:15 P.M. I go to the visiting door where Nancy now sits talking to Pat.

At 5:00 she says she must leave, and my heart gives a turn. I steel myself. Before she goes, we huddle close to the door — she, Pat, and I — and pray. There is strength and comfort in her presence and she is about to leave. Just as she is walking to the front door the telephone rings. My heart stops. Is it the Fifth Circuit? Is it Millard? But we can hear the major or somebody on the phone, and the conversation drones on.

Nancy walks out of the foyer, and Pat watches until he can see her no more. When he stands up and gets close to the mesh screen he can see into the foyer just inside the front door. Just after Nancy leaves, a man walks in. "That's the electrician. Come to check out the chair," he tells me.

The front door is opening and closing often now.

A guard I haven't seen yet comes to the door. "How you doing, Sonnier?"

"That's the head of the goon squad ["Strap-down Team"]," Pat tells me.

A little later, a man in civilian clothes approaches the door. "Need anything, Sonnier?"

"Just a little more coffee," Pat says.

"That's the shrink," he whispers.

The telephone rings again. Heart-stop. Wait. See if Rabelais comes with news. I imagine the words that will make all the difference: "Sonnier, you got a stay."

I look at my watch: 5:15. I call Joe Nursey again.

"Any word from Millard?"

"He's still at the mansion," Joe says. "All he said was that he was going to stay there until everything is all right."

What can that mean, I wonder. Why is he there so long? It must not have gone well. If it had, Millard would be calling us.

There is a gush of air as the front door opens. Pat looks. "It's Wardens Maggio and Thomas," he says. I turn to look at them. They are wearing three-piece suits. Each has a shortwave radio at his side.

It is 6:00. The sun has set behind the trees. Afternoon has now turned to evening. The sparrows are silent, nested up under the eaves for the night. It is time for Pat's final meal.

Pat tells me what he has ordered: a steak, medium-well-done, potato salad, green beans, hot rolls with butter, a green salad, a Coke, and apple pie for dessert.

Warden Maggio comes to the door to tell Pat that the chef has been giving "real special attention" to his meal and will be bringing it in shortly. He is to eat it inside his cell so that his hands can be freed of the handcuffs and Maggio is granting special permission for me to join Pat inside the tier just outside his cell, where I will be served my tray.

The fluorescent lights are on now in the building. You can see the light shining on the polished tiles. I think of how comforting the orange glow of a lamp is in a window, when you come home in the evening and the darkness is closing in. But these lights are cold and greenish white. I am waiting for the telephone to ring.

It does. Just as the chef brings Pat his meal and I am served mine. I look up through the metal door and see Captain Rabelais's face. He is looking at me and shaking his head no. Warden Maggio tells Pat in a matter-of-fact voice: "Sonnier, the Fifth Circuit turned you down."

I do not give any outward sign, but inside I fall headlong down a chasm. *The Fifth Circuit turned him down.* Only Millard left now, with the governor.

Pat teases the warden. "Well, Warden, I won the last round" — in August — "and it looks like you're winning this one." He waves his spoon in the air and then points it toward his heaping plate and laughs. "At least I got me this good meal off you, and I'm sure going to enjoy every bit of it."

And I am remembering his words: "They are not going to break me." I look down at my own tray of food and know that I will not be eating one bite. There is a glass of iced tea and I sip that. I feel unreal.

Pat talks and eats and talks. He is like a man in a bar who tells stories too loudly. The telephone rings again. It's Rabelais at the door. "Sonnier, the U.S. Supreme Court turned you down."

Millard. Still no word from him.

It is dark outside.

Pat has eaten everything on his plate except some of the green salad. He eats the apple pie, then lays the spoon on the tray and says, "There, finished, and I wasn't even hungry."

Warden Maggio comes to the tier just outside Pat's cell. Pat says to him, "Warden, tell that chef, tell him for me that he did a really great job. The steak was perfect," — he makes a circle with his thumb and forefinger — "and the potato salad, and really great apple pie."

The warden assures him he will pass on his compliments to the chef. "He put himself out for you, Sonnier, he really did."

"And you tell him, Warden," Pat says again, "that I am truly, truly appreciative."

I rise from my chair and hand my tray of untouched food to Rabelais. The guards are changing shifts. I look at the face of the guard leaving the tier. Is he finished for the night? Will he be going home to his family now? Will his children ask him questions? His face is tight. I cannot tell what he is thinking.

I give Pat some moments alone in his cell. I tell him I'm going to the rest room. The building is buzzing now. Guards are everywhere, and men in three-piece suits. A secretary has arrived and has begun typing. You can hear the *click*, *click*, *click* of the typewriter. It sounds like a business office.

"What's she typing?" I whisper to Rabelais.

"Forms for the witnesses to sign," he says.

The large aluminum coffee pot is percolating a fresh batch of coffee. I see that someone has put a white tablecloth on a table and has placed ballpoint pens in the center of the table.

I go into the rest room. A few precious moments of privacy. I look at the sparkling tiled walls, the clean white fixtures, ample soap, paper towels. Everything is so clean. I keep feeling as if I'm in a hospital, the cleanliness, attendants following a protocol . . . *Oh,*

Jesus God, help me, help me, please, and I harness all my energies, I gather myself inside like someone who pulls her coat tight around her in a strong wind.

I leave the rest room and glance down at the path of tiles that leads to the white metal door at the end of the room. Rabelais comes through that door now with someone in jeans and a plaid shirt and jacket. Must be the electrician. Rabelais locks the door behind him.

I go back to the visitor door. Pat is still in his cell. The phone rings on the wall near the cell. The guard on the tier walks down and answers it and hands the phone to Pat. I can see the coiled wire of the phone along the wall until it disappears into the cell. I can hear Pat's voice rising and falling. "Thank you, Mr. Millard, thank you for what you and all the others done for me. I got you too late. If I had had you sooner . . ." Silence. "No, Mr. Millard, no you didn't fail, you didn't fail, it's the justice system in this country, it stinks. It stinks bad, Mr. Millard, no, no, no, Mr. Millard, you didn't fail . . ."

And now for the first time I know surely that he's going to die. I look at my watch. It is 8:40.

I go to Captain Rabelais and ask to make a couple of phone calls. I call the Sisters to ask them to pray, and I call my mother to let her know I am okay and to ask her to pray.

I go back to the visitor door. The guard inside is putting the shackles on Pat's hands and feet inside the cell. He opens the cell door and Pat comes over to the metal folding chair by the door. As he approaches the chair his legs sag and he drops to one knee beside the chair. He looks up at me. "Sister Helen, I'm going to die."

My soul rushes toward him. I am standing with my hands against the mesh screen, as close as I can get to him. I pray and ask God to comfort him, cushion him, wrap him round, give him courage to face death, to step across the river, to die with love. The words are pouring from me.

His moment of weakness has passed. He sits in the metal chair and calls to Rabelais for a cup of coffee. He notices as he pulls a cigarette from the pack in his shirt pocket that there are just a few left. "Ought to just about make it," he says.

He makes out his will, one single line on a piece of yellow legal paper. "I give to Sister Helen Prejean all my possessions." Rabelais has someone notarize the will.

That done, Pat composes a letter to Eddie.

"Dear Brother," he says, "don't worry about me, I'll be okay. You keep your cool, it's the only way you'll make it in this place.

When you get out someday, take care of Mama. Remember the promise you made to me. I love you. Your big brother."

The front door is opening regularly now. Pat looks up every time he hears someone coming in. He watches. He notices everything.

A guard called Slick comes through the front door. He is a big, burly man with a shiny bald head and he is carrying a small canvas bag. Rabelais comes and asks me to step out into the foyer. Slick, accompanied by two other guards, goes into the cell with Pat. I quietly walk up and down the foyer. I look down at my black leather pumps. I walk back and forth, back and forth. "Please, God, help him, please help him."

A chaplain named Penton approaches me. He is dressed in a bright green suit. I have the feeling that he has worked here for a long time. He tells me that he is here "in case the inmate might need my services at this time." Then he tells me to prepare myself for the "visual shock" of Pat's shaved head. "They must remove the hair to reduce the possibility of its catching fire," he says. I keep walking slowly up and down the foyer and he walks alongside me. I am thinking of Gandhi. I am thinking of Camus. "Resist, do not collaborate in any way with a deed which you believe is evil . . . resist . . ." In his *Reflections* Camus tells of a Russian man about to be hanged by the Tsar's executioners who repulsed the priest who came forward to offer a blessing: "*Go away and commit no sacrilege.*" (p. 224)

Camus says about Christians:

> *The unbeliever cannot keep from thinking that men who have set at the center of their faith the staggering victim of a judicial error ought at least to hesitate before committing legal murder. Believers might also be reminded that Emperor Julian, before his conversion, did not want to give official offices to Christians because they systematically refused to pronounce death sentences or to have anything to do with them. For five centuries Christians therefore believed that the strict moral teaching of their master forbade killing. (p. 224)*

I talk to Penton about a phone call I received from one of the Catholic prison chaplains several weeks ago. The priest had asked me which funeral home would pick up Pat's body if the execution were to take place. Before I got this call, Pat had told me that the old priest had approached him in his cell and said brightly, attempting humor, "Well, Sonnier, what are we gonna do with the body?" Pat had said angrily, "Don't you call my mama and ask her that. Don't you dare upset her. Call Sister Helen." And so the phone call had come to me, and I had said I had no idea who would pick up the body.

I see how easy it is for chaplains, on the payroll, to play their part in this "uncomfortable but necessary business," and I ask whether it should be the role of the chaplain to collaborate with the prison in planning the "disposal of the remains" of the person the state has killed. Penton tells me he will think about that. (He does. Later he sees to it that chaplains no longer make burial arrangements for executed prisoners.)

Rabelais comes to tell me that I can go back now to Pat.

I move to my side of the visitor door and wait for Pat to come from the cell.

Slick and crew are just coming through the door from the tier. One of the guards is carrying a towel and small broom, another a brown paper bag with Pat's curly black hair in it. Slick is zipping up his canvas shaving kit. He moves quickly. I look at Pat as he comes back to the metal chair. His head looks whitish gray and shiny. His hair is gone now, eyebrows too. He looks like a bird without feathers. I see that they have also cut his left pants leg off at the knee. "They shaved the calf of my leg," he says, and he holds out his leg for me to see. I see a tattooed number.

"What's that number?" I ask.

"That's from when I was at Angola before," he tells me. "In case anybody killed me, I wanted them to be able to identify my body."

I notice that he is wearing a clean white T-shirt.

I look at my watch and Pat looks at his. It is 10:30. Everything is ready now. All Pat needs to do now is die. He asks the guard for a pen and writes in his Bible, up in the front, where there is a special place for family history—births, marriages, deaths.

"There," he says, "I wrote it in my own hand."

The guard unlocks the door and hands me the Bible. I look at the front page. He has written loving words to me, words of thanks. Then I see under "Deaths" his name and the date, April 4, 1984.

I remember Jesus' words that we do not know the day nor the hour. But Pat knows. And in knowing he dies and then dies again.

Two guards inside the tier stand on stepladders and hang black curtains over the windows along the top.

"They don't want other inmates to see the lights dim when the switch is pulled," Pat tells me. He is smoking and talking now, his talk a torrent, a flood, all coming together now, snatches from childhood and teasing Eddie and school and the sugar-cane fields gleaming in the sun and Star, what will happen to her, and his Mama, to please see about his Mama, and Eddie, will he be able to keep his cool in this place, and if only he knew when the current first hit that he would die right away . . .

He begins to shiver. "It's cold in here," he says, and the guard gets a blue denim shirt from the cell and puts it around his shoulders, then goes back to his position at the end of the tier.

People are chatting nervously in the foyer and lobby now. The witnesses must all be inside by now, the press, all the prison officials. You can hear the hum of talk and some snatches of conversation. You can hear when someone inserts coins into one of the drink machines and the clunk of the can when it comes out.

I look around. There, standing behind me, are Bill Quigley and Millard Farmer. I rise and move toward them and have to hold myself in close check. Their presence, their love, knowing they have tried so hard to save Pat's life, makes me want to weep. But no tears now. Bill gives my hand a tight squeeze. Millard does not look into my eyes. We move to the visitor door. Guards bring two chairs for Millard and Bill. What words to say during these (I look at my watch) last fifty minutes? Pat says, "Look at the time, it's flying."

The old priest approaches us. I rise and go over to him, "Let Elmo know" — Pat hates being called Elmo — "I'm available for the last sacraments," he tells me.

I give his message to Pat.

Pat shakes his head. "No, I don't like that man. All of you, my friends who love me, you make me feel close to God. Sister Helen, when it is all over, you receive communion for both of us."

I promise that I will.

The warden approaches Millard and asks him to step into the foyer. In a few moments Millard comes back. "Pat, the governor has given permission for me to be a witness."

Thank God. It strengthens me to know that Millard will be there too.

Captain Rabelais asks the three of us to step into the foyer for a moment. Three guards go into the cell with Pat. It is 11:30. No one can say much, but Bill whispers to me that Ann, Lory, and Kathleen and some other Sisters are at the front gate.

People are all still milling around in the large room. The witnesses have not been seated yet. Mr. LeBlanc and Mr. Bourque must be here. What are they going through? Will this help heal their loss? I wonder. I hear the toilet flush in Pat's cell.

Rabelais summons us back to the door. Pat comes from his cell, his legs and hands cuffed. Anger flickers in his eyes. "A grown man, and I have to leave this world with a diaper on," he says.

"I'll be free of all this," he says, shaking his handcuffs. "No more cells, no more bars, no more life in a cage," he says.

He reaches in his pocket for a cigarette. He turns and shows the guard, "Look, the last one. It'll see me out."

Warden Maggio approaches us. He is flanked by six or seven very large guards. It must be midnight. "Time to go, Sonnier," Maggio says. One of the guards takes Bill out to the foyer, another tells Millard to follow him. I stand to the side of the door. I will walk with Pat. I am holding his Bible. I have selected the Isaiah passage to read as we walk, the words that were in the song, words that Pat has heard and the words will be there for him to hear again, if he can hear words at all, when he will be trying to put one foot in front of another, walking from here to there across these polished tiles.

"Warden," he asks, "can I ask one favor? Can Sister Helen touch my arm?"

The Warden nods his head.

I am standing behind him. Guards, a mountain of blue, surround us. I put my hand on his shoulder. He is tall. I can barely reach. It is the first time I have ever touched him.

We walk. Pat walks and the chains scrape across the floor. God has heard his prayer. His legs are holding up, he is walking.

I read Isaiah's words:

> Do not be afraid . . . I have called you by
> your name, you are mine.
> Should you pass through the sea,
> I will be with you . . .
> Should you walk through the fire,
> you will not be scorched,
> and the flames will not burn you."
> (43:2)

As we pass through the lobby the old priest raises his hand in blessing.

We stop. There is the oak chair, dark and gleaming in the bright fluorescent lights. There are the witnesses all seated behind a Plexiglas window. There is a big clock on the wall behind the chair. There is an exhaust fan, already turned on to get rid of the smell of burning flesh. Two guards have firmly taken hold of my arms and are moving me toward the witness room. I lean toward Pat and kiss him on the back.

"Pat, pray for me."

He turns around toward me and says, his voice husky and eager like a young boy's, "I will, Sister Helen, I will."

I see Millard then and I sit in the chair beside him. He reaches over and takes my hand. Mr. Bourque and Mr. LeBlanc are seated on the first row over to the right of us. Their faces are expressionless.

There is a small podium with a microphone on it and Pat is standing behind it. I can see past him to a wall of green painted plywood with a slit of a window behind which the executioner waits.

The warden is standing over in the right-hand corner next to a red telephone.

"Have any last words, Sonnier?" he asks.

"Yes, sir, I do," Pat says, and he looks at the two fathers, but addresses his words to only one of them. "Mr. LeBlanc, I don't want to leave this world with any hatred in my heart. I want to ask your forgiveness for what me and Eddie done, but Eddie done it." Mr. LeBlanc nods his head. Mr. Bourque turns to Mr. LeBlanc and asks, "What about me?"

Pat is in the chair now and guards are moving quickly, removing the leg irons and handcuffs and replacing them with the leather straps. One guard has removed his left shoe. They are strapping his trunk, his legs, his arms. He finds my face. He says, "I love you." I stretch my hand toward him. "I love you, too."

He attempts a smile (he told me he would try to smile) but manages only to twitch.

A metal cap is placed on his head and an electrode is screwed in at the top and connected to a wire that comes from a box behind the chair. An electrode is fastened to his leg. A strap placed around his chin holds his head tightly against the back of the chair. He grimaces. He cannot speak anymore. A grayish green cloth is placed over his face.

Millard says, "Father forgive them, for they know not what they do."

Only the warden remains in the room now, only the warden and the man strapped into the chair. The red telephone is silent. I close my eyes and do not see as the warden nods his head, the signal to the executioner to do his work.

I hear three clanks as the switch is pulled with pauses in between. Nineteen hundred volts, then let the body cool, then five hundred volts, pause again, then nineteen hundred volts. "Christ, be with him, have mercy on him," I pray silently.

I look up. His left hand has gripped the arm of the chair evenly but the fingers of his right hand are curled upward.

The warden says over the microphone that we will wait a few minutes for the doctor to make the "final check." Then the prison doctor, who has been sitting with the witnesses, goes to the body in the chair and lifts the mask and raises the eyelids and shines the light of a small flashlight into the eyes and raises up the clean white shirt and puts his stethoscope against the heart and listens and then says to the warden that, yes, this man is dead. Warden Maggio looks up at the clock and announces the time of death: 12:15 A.M. His eyes happen to look into mine. He lowers his eyes.

The witnesses are led from the room. As we walk through the lobby, I go over to the old priest and ask him to give me communion for "both of us," as Pat had requested. I go to where the witnesses are gathered to sign the papers. Everyone is silent. All you can hear is the papers being shuffled across the white tablecloth and the scrawling of ballpoint pens as people put their signatures on three copies of the official state papers.

As we are filing out of the room, Lloyd LeBlanc is behind me and I turn and look at him and he looks shaken and the rims of his eyes are red. I touch his arm but I have no words. It is all so overwhelming. What can I say? I am not sure why Pat addressed his last words to Lloyd LeBlanc and not to Mr. Bourque, but I suspect it's because Pat was trying to make his last words loving and he didn't trust himself to say anything to Bourque, who had been outspoken to the press about wanting to see him die. Who knows? But Pat's dead now. As dead as Loretta Bourque and David LeBlanc are dead, and I think of Gladys Sonnier waiting out the night.

A guard guides Millard and me to the van that will take us to the front gate. It is very cold outside and it is very dark. We ride past the main prison building where Eddie is and past the administration building where a press conference will soon take place in which only prison officials will speak. There will be no dissenting voices about what took place tonight.

"Look how shamefully secret this whole thing is," Millard says. "A few select witnesses brought deep inside this prison in the dead of night to watch a man be killed. If most people in Louisiana would see what the state did tonight, they would throw up."

We arrive at the front gate. There are lights and a SWAT team lined up along the front fence.

At the gate the Sisters are waiting, and here too are Joe Nursey and Kimellen. Joe has on a white Irish sweater. I put my arms around him and he sobs and I can feel his stomach muscles heaving through the thick sweater. And Kimellen, shivering in the car, takes my hand and cries and kisses my hand and cannot stop crying. I feel numb and cold. And Millard takes me by the arm and walks with me awhile around the parking lot and he is telling me not to give up, to keep on fighting, and I am not hearing many of his words but I catch their earnestness and I know that I love this man, this spark of God, who has taught me so much.

Ann and Bill Quigley will ride back with me in the car. We start out down Highway 66, but before we get too far we have to pull the car over to the side and stop because I have to vomit.

CHAPTER

5

I open the car window a little so fresh cold air can blow in my face as we drive to Baton Rouge. Bill reaches to the back seat and takes one of my hands in his and says a prayer.

Ann talks about the SWAT team along the fence as she waited in the parking lot. The weather was cold, so she had mostly stayed inside the car, getting out only for bathroom breaks. She was the only person in the parking lot, but every time she opened the car door and stepped out, the SWAT team stiffened and aimed their rifles toward the ground but in her direction; then, when she got back into the car, they once again stood at-ease. At 5:30 P.M. seven or eight state police cars drove up and the troopers went inside the visitors' building where they kept watch until the execution was over. She could see them inside, eating sandwiches and playing cards. One, with a rifle, stood watch by the window nearest the parking lot.

"That has to be the weirdest experience of my life," she says. "I felt like I was in some sort of police state. All that energy and organization and money to kill a man . . ."

It's the doctor in her talking. It's a hard struggle for her to keep the clinic for poor people open. Every year she has to do battle with city and state officials to keep the funds in place.

DEAD MAN WALKING

Arriving in Baton Rouge, we drop Bill off at his car. He'll drive back to New Orleans tonight. At about 2:00 A.M. Ann and I turn into Mama's driveway. The lamp is on in the den. The door opens and Mama's arms open wide, her rosary still in her hands. She has a fire going in the fireplace.

Ann hands me a sleeping pill with a cup of hot, sweet milk. I sleep and do not dream.

I awake to clinking dishes and voices in the kitchen and the telephone ringing.

Pat's body must be at the funeral home by now and maybe the morticians are already at work. I remember how he once told me he had watched his father being embalmed. It was such a bizarre thing to have done, but he told me about it matter-of-factly. His father had died of liver cancer in 1967 when he was not quite sixteen years old, and he knew the mortician and asked if he could watch. He said he was thinking of becoming a mortician, and he thought he'd "see how it was done."

It seems that in the blur of events outside the prison last night Kathleen had mentioned something about funeral arrangements, but I can't remember what she said.

It's Tom Dybdahl from the Coalition office on the phone. When I hear his voice I begin to cry. The shock and numbness are wearing off. I am thawing.

Tom is thanking me for being with Pat. *Thanking me.* I think of Millard, who never allows anyone to thank him for his work. "I *must* do this," he says.

Mama hands me a cup of coffee. But I have no desire for coffee. I see Pat holding up his cup, calling to Captain Rabelais. "Black. No cream, no sugar."

The phone rings throughout the morning — Millard, Kathleen and Lory, Bill. Phone calls and tears. It reminds me of Daddy's wake. Each new person that came up to me in the funeral home personalized the grief in a new way. And with each new grief, new tears.

Millard says that he and Joe and Kimellen are getting ready to drive back to Atlanta. He mentions a man's name, someone else on death row in Georgia, whom they are representing. He doesn't say much. "I will never forget you, Millard," I tell him.

Several local reporters call. They have heard that I was a witness at the execution. They interview me over the phone.

Kathleen calls. Pat's funeral will take place tomorrow morning at ten at Rabenhorst Funeral Home on Government Street, preceded by a wake beginning at nine. She has been telephoning Pat's family. Community leadership has given its approval for Pat to be buried with our Sisters at Roselawn Cemetary. Afterward, Kathleen says, the Sonniers can come to their house for a meal. Will Eddie be attending the funeral? I realize that I had better call the warden and make the request. From what I know about LSP rules, inmates are allowed to attend only the funerals of parents, not siblings.

I call Warden Maggio's office. He explains that Eddie's attendance at the funeral would require bending the rules and added expense — armed guards, a vehicle — but let him think about it and he'll call me back. And within an hour his secretary telephones and says that the warden has given his permission for Eddie to attend the funeral.

On Friday morning about thirty people gather for Pat's wake and funeral — half family members and half nuns. Kathleen asks six family members to serve as pallbearers.

Rabenhorst is the funeral home in Baton Rouge that I know best. In this very room where Pat's body is laid out I had first seen a corpse — Uncle George's body. I was ten years old. The sight of him dead like that had horrified me, and I refused to kiss the cold forehead when other family members lined up for the final farewell. And now I look down on the still face of Patrick Sonnier. The morticians have bandaged his head with gauze. He seems too big for the coffin. It's a tight fit. But, then, the people here have been good enough to donate their services and the coffin. Kathleen has found, I see, a powder blue jacket for him. It too seems tight. There is a spray of red roses on the coffin. The tag reads: "Mother and Family." Pat's mother is not here. Her sister, Joan, tells me that the funeral would be "too much" for her. The television cameras are assembled outside. No place here for private grief. I think of the Bourques and the LeBlancs. They went through this seven years ago, looking down in disbelief at their youthful, blooming children lying in cushioned coffins, murdered by the Sonnier brothers.

There is a stir at the entrance of the room and Ann whispers to me, "Eddie's here." He stands just inside the doorway with guards on either side. I walk over to him. His hands are cuffed tightly on either side of a "black box" at his waist and there is a chain on his ankles. I walk with him over to the body of his brother. He looks down and says, "Well, Brother . . ." Tears run down his face. I have my arm around his waist and I tell him how Pat loved him to the end, and he says, "Now three people are dead because of me." Ann has a Kleenex and wipes his tears and helps him blow his nose (the black box prevents him from raising his hands). Star, Pat's daughter, comes up to him and gives him a light hug. She calls him "Uncle Eddie."

Someone whispers to me that Bishop Stanley Ott has arrived. The little clutch of people gather in the first two pews for the celebration of Mass. In his homily the bishop says that Jesus has revealed God to us and that God is a God of compassion and love, not a God of retribution. He prays for Pat and for all families who have lost loved ones to violence — the Bourques, the LeBlancs, and the Sonniers.

Eddie is not allowed to go to the graveyard. The guards are about to lead him to the vehicle that will take him back to Angola. Family members line up to kiss him good-bye near the door where the hearse is waiting. Two farewells are happening here — Pat's and Eddie's. I know that most of these family members will never see Eddie again. Two brothers in two vehicles are now taking leave of each other: one going into the ground and one going into Angola for the rest of his life.

At the grave site Bishop Ott says the customary prayers for the dead. He prays for God to be merciful to Patrick Sonnier and to receive him into the heavenly kingdom. And then I say a few words to the family, especially to Star. I try through my words to show them love, respect, dignity. I can scarcely imagine how shameful it must be — and so public — for a family member to be killed by the state.

We are in the part of the cemetery, marked by a towering crucifix, where nuns and priests are buried. Pat's plot is right alongside Sister Isabel's. She was a feisty soul and quick-witted, and I can't help but wonder what her comment would be, having this *man* buried beside her — she who, when young women would come to the convent to introduce their new husbands, would whisper to the Sister near her, "I'm glad I don't have to share my bed with some *man*."

People are beginning to move toward their cars. One of the reporters pulls me aside. "Were you in love with Elmo Sonnier?" he asks. "I mean, his last words, 'I love you' — he said he loved you, didn't he?" The question surprises me and I have to smile (what a good story for the *National Enquirer*: *Nun falls in love with murderer*).

No, I tell him, I loved Pat as a sister loves a brother, as Jesus taught us to love each other; it was not a romantic relationship.

I am the last to leave. I reach out and touch the side of the coffin. Men are standing nearby with their shovels.

I am scarcely back at Mama's house after Pat's funeral when the doorbell rings and a man from United Parcel Service asks for me. He is delivering three large brown boxes. I look at the return address: Louisiana State Prison. Boxes for me? Then I remember: "I give to Sister Helen Prejean all of my possessions."

Mama, Ann, and I open the boxes. Wet towels and washcloth and wet soap are thrown in with shoes, pants, shirts, photograph album, legal folders, letters ... Everything smells like cigarette smoke. Here's a rolled up, damp T-shirt. This must be the shirt Pat wore before they shaved his head. I see some old "store" lists and look to see which items he had last ordered: coffee, barbecue corn chips, stamps, Bugler tobacco, and papers (he rolled his own cigarettes — "cheaper," he'd say, and brag how he could get thirty cigarettes from a pack).

Ann and Mama sort out the clothes and start the first batch in the washing machine. I will need to drive to St. Martinville and bring these belongings to Pat's family. He had told me that he wanted his daughter, Star, to have his photograph album. I open it and there he is in his blue denim shirt smiling, and there, in another photo, laughing. Here's the photo of me on the pony that I had sent him in my first letter, and here's Eddie and his mother. Here's Star and some of his young pen pals. The pictures are all neatly arranged under the plastic pages with names printed in black ball-point pen. Next to my picture he has written "My spiritual advisor."

Sorting through papers in manila folders, I see a stack of disciplinary reports on Eddie. Pat must have requested these. Or maybe Eddie sent them to him on his own.

The man who owned the things in the boxes is dead. I have to keep reminding myself of that. I think of the scene from George Bernard Shaw's *Saint Joan* and what Chaplain Stogumber had said after he witnessed Joan of Arc's execution. No one had been more eager than he to see her die. So eager that he had physically pushed her into the arms of the executioner and urged him to light the fire quickly. He couldn't wait to see her die. But then he had watched and in the epilogue says: "I tell my folks they must be very careful. I say to them, 'If you only saw what you think about you would think quite differently about it. It would give you a great shock. . . . I did a very cruel thing once because I did not know what cruelty was like. I had not seen it, you know. That is the great thing: you must see it. And then you are redeemed and saved . . . it was not our Lord that redeemed me, but a young woman whom I saw actually burned to death. It was dreadful: oh, most dreadful. But it saved me. I have been a different man ever since . . ."[1]

But that was when the torture was visible. Witnesses could see the flames lick the flesh. They could hear the cries of agony. But this death . . . with witnesses behind the square of Plexiglas like that, it was like a framed scene, death in the movies, death in celluloid, death under glass. There he was, saying his last words. There he was, walking to the chair. There he was, being strapped in. Three clangs of the switch. No smell of burning flesh (the Plexiglas shields witnesses from the smell). No sight of his face (the mask conceals his face, his eyes). And with his jaw strapped shut like that, he could not cry out.

Who killed this man?

Nobody.

Everybody can argue that he or she was just doing a job — the governor, the warden, the head of the Department of Corrections, the district attorney, the judge, the jury, the Pardon Board, the witnesses to the execution. Nobody feels personally responsible for the death of this man. D.A.'s are fond of saying that criminals "put themselves in the chair." Shortly before the execution in Louisiana of a convicted murderer, Tim Baldwin, on September 10, 1984, a guard in the death house whispered to him, "You gotta understand, Tim, this is nothing personal."

I think of the telephone conversation I had with head of Corrections C. Paul Phelps shortly before Pat's execution. How had he phrased it? He wanted the execution to be carried out with *dignity*. Now that Pat has been killed and I don't have to steel myself to carry on, I realize that Phelps's cool, professional tone had terrified me.

Phelps is a "good, Catholic man." So the people in Catholic circles of Baton Rouge describe him. And with a master's degree in social work, he is reputed to be one of the more humane, progressive heads of the Louisiana Department of Corrections. I've heard that he has confronted members of the Louisiana legislature and argued against their lock-'em-up-throw-away-the-key solution to crime, urging instead more intensive efforts with first-time nonviolent offenders to keep them out of prison.[2]

Yet he supervises executions.

In fact, he's the one who designed the process.

I plan to stay in Baton Rouge a few days and Phelps's office is here and I decide to talk to him. I can't say exactly why. Maybe it's to confront the cool professionalism. Maybe it's because I know he's a social worker and a "good, Catholic man."

Back at Mama's house I call Phelps and he readily grants me an appointment.

"You were the only wild card, among the witnesses, the only one I wasn't sure of," Phelps says to me as we meet in his office and begin to talk. He's in his mid-fifties, a tall man, his hair thinning. He's soft-spoken, reflective. On the bookshelf behind his desk is a photograph of his family.

"You were the only one I hadn't talked to face to face before the execution," he says, and he tells me how he had inquired about me to find out what I was like and how I might react seeing someone executed.

"I've been wondering about you, too," I say. And then I tell him what it was like to watch a man being put to death in such a premeditated, inexorable process and ask what he thinks has been accomplished by this execution.

"Zero," he says, "absolutely nothing." Nor does he think that executions prevent crime, because in his view punishment, to be effective, must be "swift, sure and fair." As he sees it, the criminal justice system produces the death penalty "when it is to the advantage of the prosecution." He explains how D.A.'s weigh a number of factors — the cost of the trial, the evidence, the expertise of the legal defense arrayed against them — and he points to a recent example in Baton Rouge in which a judge sentenced a man who had shot and killed four people to two life sentences. "The cost of the trial would have been fantastic," he says, "so the D.A. offered a plea bargain and the defendant was willing to accept two life sentences. But some people are not given a chance to choose, especially if they kill somebody important. If you kill an LSU professor or a priest or any other highly respectable citizen, you'll probably go to trial and they'll push for the death penalty, but not if the person you kill is a nobody. By its nature the criminal justice system will always be somewhat arbitrary."

"Yet you played your part," I say. "You don't seem to believe that the death penalty is morally right, but here you are lining up the witnesses, designing the protocol. Do you experience any conflict of conscience between your personal religious beliefs and what your job calls you to do? If Jesus Christ lived on earth today, would he supervise this process?"

Predictably, he explains that he didn't make the law, he's only following the law and, in fact, doing his best to make the "process" as "humane" as possible. He says that if something is required by law and is the function of a job, then it's not "optional." The personnel in the DOC, he maintains, "don't have to take any personal responsibility for what they are doing. It's their job. They are told to do it. They are told how to do it. They are told how long it's going to take and what you do when you do it. It's like a drill, like an exercise, so they have no personal responsibility."

I ask him what happens to his personal convictions in this process, and he says that when he is called on to speak in public, he never speaks from his personal convictions.

There it is again, I can't help but notice — the severance of personal values from public duty — just like Governor Edwin Edwards, who felt moral repugnance for the death penalty but who nevertheless allowed it to be carried out.

Phelps is so reasoned, so soft-spoken, so professional. My heart weighs a hundred pounds.

I ask him whether it isn't ethically dangerous to submerge personal convictions so that they have no bearing on one's work. What, I ask, if the law which a government uses to legitimize killing is itself morally wrong, as in Nazi Germany? Aren't there, I argue, some rights fundamental to human beings — such as the right not to be tortured or killed — that everyone, including governments, must respect? Doesn't the moral foundation of a society erode if its government is allowed to treat these fundamental, nonnegotiable rights as some sort of privilege, which they take on themselves to dispense for good behavior or withdraw for bad behavior? I point out that the United Nations General Assembly adopted the Universal Declaration of Human Rights, which unequivocally endorses the right of every human being not to be killed and not to be subjected to torture or to cruel and degrading punishment — and the United States signed that declaration.[3] If a policy or law is morally wrong and we know it's wrong, aren't we bound in conscience to oppose it? I ask him.

He says that if he's opposed to doing any part of his job he should quit or refuse to accept the job in the first place.

Which I know is true, and the moral complexity deepens because a caring and intelligent man like Phelps can accomplish much good in this position. The head of Corrections sets the tone and affects the polices of what goes on in the prisons; and in Louisiana, which incarcerates such a huge number of its citizens, a man like Phelps goes a long, long way.

I ask him to tell me about the execution process that he has designed, and he shows me a copy of Department Regulation Number 10–25, issued April 6, 1981. I glance at the document and notice headings: Purpose, Responsibility, Legal Authority, Incarceration Prior to Execution, Media Access, Time and Place of Execution . . .

"From a personal standpoint it is very, very bizarre to design a process like this," he says, "because you find yourself approaching an execution the same way you approach putting on a rodeo or any other special event." Before designing the process, he says, he made field trips to talk to corrections officials in other states that use the electric chair, and he engaged the services of an electrical engineer — "he worked for free, he refused to be paid" — to devote his attention to "the technical aspects of the apparatus."

Inwardly I translate the terms, *technical aspects of the apparatus*, and I think of how silent it was there in the room as the guard screwed the rubber-coated wire to the top of the metal cap on Pat's shaved head.

Setting up the "process," Phelps explains, involved hiring an executioner.

"We hired a man, an electrician, who filled out a civil service application for the job. Frank Blackburn, the warden at Angola at the time, interviewed the prospective candidate for the job in some depth because we obviously wanted somebody who was screwed down pretty tight and very, very firm in his convictions, not just someone with a morbid interest. We were looking for — this may sound strange — somebody professional. We didn't want a mafia-type executioner." Blackburn, he says, gave him a name, "Sam Jones," to preserve his anonymity. (Sam Jones had been governor in Louisiana in 1941 when the method of execution changed from hanging to electrocution). He agreed to be paid $400 per execution. It was a verbal agreement, not written.

I make a mental note of the anonymity of the executioner and the reluctance to sign a contract specifying fee for service. I log it alongside something that Phelps mentioned earlier: that the electrician who wired the chair refused to be paid — the intuitive recognition that this is "blood money," this is "death for hire."

The fact that anonymity is granted to the executioner intrigues me. I've heard that in Utah, when Gary Gilmore was executed by a firing squad, blanks were inserted into one of the rifles so that those firing the guns would not know for certain if they killed the man. No doubt, the uncertainty helps diffuse responsibility.

Phelps says that for him, the most "troublesome" aspect of the "process" has been the selection of witnesses. With the resumption of executions, some victims' families asked if they might witness, and he says he "pondered" this a long time but "couldn't think of a reason why they shouldn't. Our position in the D.O.C. is that I am not the 'keeper of the morals' but merely the enforcer of the law, and if there is no legal reason barring a victim's family, I see no reason to deny them."

Phelps says that he emphasizes to all witnesses — victims' families included — that during an execution there must be "no emotional outbursts, no obscenities uttered, no undignified behavior of any kind." They have designed a process, he says, that "protects everyone's rights," including those of the one being executed. "They have a family too. A circus atmosphere is not in anyone's interest."

I am listening to all this and I keep picturing Pat's dead body in the chair, the fingers of his right hand curling upward, the doctor's light shining into vacant eyes.

I say that I disagree that the rights of the man being killed are protected because the witnesses to his death are expected to be polite.

"Pat Sonnier was tortured, Mr. Phelps," I say. "I'm not sure what he felt physically when the nineteen hundred volts hit him, but certainly he agonized emotionally and psychologically — preparing to die, anticipating it, dreaming about it. Amnesty International defines torture as an extreme physical and mental assault on a person who has been rendered defenseless. That is what happened to Patrick Sonnier, isn't it, Mr. Phelps?

Phelps nods. "People these days want revenge, and that's what revenge is — 'eye for an eye,' pain for pain, torture for torture."

I can tell he doesn't agree with this bent toward revenge. I know that at heart he's a social worker.

"Will you attend an execution and witness for yourself the end result of this process?" I ask.

"Never in a million years," he says.

Which doesn't surprise me. I have a hunch that if this man were to remove the bureaucratic gauze and see with his own eyes this killing laid bare, he'd quit this job.

I rise to leave and reach out to take his hand. I thank him for his time. Outwardly I'm poised but inwardly I'm devastated. It's the fact that a man as obviously good as this is participating in this process that is most disturbing. Phelps is the fourth public official I have met — before him the governor, the warden, the chairperson of the Pardon Board — who, despite his personal reservations about the moral rightness of state executions, nevertheless plays his part in carrying them out. It all seems so intractable. I tell myself that I had simply better accept the fact that the death penalty is here to stay in our society, at least for a while, and there is nothing I can do about it. Maybe, in time — after how many executions? — people will come to realize the futility of randomly selecting a few people to die each year. In time, perhaps, people will realize that executions do not deter violent crime.

Pat is dead now, I tell myself, and I know that I did everything I could for him, and there is peace in that. But for me there will be no more involvement with death-row inmates. The end. No more death-row pen pals. No more visits. Except Eddie. I'm the only steady, caring lifeline that he's got. I can see his life solidifying. In the prison welding shop he's becoming a productive worker, and his disciplinary write-ups have ceased.

My sister, Mary Ann, has agreed to go with me to St. Martinville to see the Sonniers and to deliver Pat's possessions. The clothes are all washed and dried and smelling clean and folded neatly in the boxes — gray sweat pants and white T-shirts, jeans, socks, underwear. It's about a two-hour drive to St. Martinville from Baton Rouge. We leave in late morning and stop for a sandwich in a little snack shop once we get there. Pat has been dead for four days now.

We drive up to Gladys Sonnier's little project apartment. It's a small one-story red brick building. It has a small yard. The grass has been cut recently. She grows a few vegetables. There's a heavy, sweet smell in the air. Must be ligustrum bushes nearby. I take a deep breath. The last time I was here I was with Millard and Pat was still alive. Houses, when you look at them, always look different when you know someone associated with them has died. This little red brick house looks different now.

When I greet Gladys Sonnier, she hugs me briefly, then turns away, wiping her eyes. There are deep circles under her eyes and her body seems leaden, sagging. She's barely sixty but she looks very, very old.

In her kitchen Gladys has brewed a fresh pot of coffee for us. Her hands shake as she hands me my cup. She asks us to serve ourselves. Marie, her daughter, is here, and Joan, her sister, and Glenda Ann, Joan's daughter.

Glenda and Marie express their distress about how the press

"misrepresented" their family. Glenda tells me that one story said the family had "refused" Pat's body and so the body had to be "turned over to the nuns." Marie says another story said Pat's family was "too poor" to bury him. "We would have found a way to bury him if he had only asked us," she says. And Glenda says that the media said there was no one from the family with him at Angola at the end, "but they don't say that we weren't there because Pat wanted it that way." And she tells how she had written Pat and offered to come and be with him in the death house and so had her mother, but he had refused, saying he didn't want to "put us through it." And Marie says that one newspaper article said that the flowers on Pat's coffin had been donated by the funeral home, but it was the family who had bought the wreath. "And one account mentioned Eddie as the only family member present at the funeral Mass. They didn't even mention that there were fifteen of us there and it was all family members who were the pallbearers," says Marie.

"Will you write a letter to the editor and present our side?" Marie asks me.

I promise them that I will, right away, and I'll send them a copy.

I tell Mrs. Sonnier about Pat's last moments and how strongly he had urged me to convey his love to her. I tell her how Bishop Ott had remembered her in his prayers at the funeral Mass. I am very brief. I know she can't take very much. Then I talk about Eddie. I suggest that if she wants to visit Eddie, I could drive her to Angola. Transportation is a problem for her. Mrs. Sonnier shuts her eyes tight and shakes her head from side to side and says that she doesn't know if she can ever "set foot inside that place again." Maybe, after some time has passed, perhaps we can talk about it again, I suggest.

The boxes of Pat's things have been sitting on the floor and I mention them now, but Mrs. Sonnier turns away from the boxes, and Marie offers to sort through the clothes to see who might be able to use them.

On the morning after the execution, Mrs. Sonnier tells us, she had found a dismembered cat on her front porch.

"People are so cruel," she says.

I think of the Bourques and the LeBlancs. Lloyd LeBlanc, I hear, cannot sit behind teenagers in church because he cannot bear to look at the back of their heads.

Back now in Baton Rouge I pack my things. It is time to return to Hope House. Sister Lilianne has been carrying a double load, covering for me at the Adult Learning Center. Time to head back.

Am I the same person I was before? I had learned as a child from my Catholic catechism that some sacraments like baptism leave an "indelible" mark on the soul, a mark that can never be erased. Does witnessing an execution also leave an "indelible" mark?

The thought of working with students appeals immensely to me. I picture the large classroom at Hope House and how the breeze ruffles the curtains as it comes through the tall windows, the mimosa trees blooming outside. It will be good to be in the flow of normal life again. I am glad to step out of this surreal landscape. I figure I will never be going to death row or an execution chamber again.

Back in St. Thomas a stack of newspaper clippings and letters is waiting for me on my bed. Sister Lilianne says, as she helps me unpack, that the letters to the editor about Pat's funeral in the *Times-Picayune* have been running "hot and heavy." The *Picayune* had run the AP story on Pat's burial with the headline: "Executed Killer Blessed with Burial for the Elite," and the article had said that this executed murderer "received in death what few Catholics ever achieve — a funeral Mass conducted by a bishop and burial within the shadow of graves of other bishops." There is no mistaking the thrust of the article — Pat Sonnier was buried as a hero.

Over the next six weeks that becomes a theme of outrage in the letters to the editor of the *Picayune* and the *Daily Iberian* and in personal letters sent to me:

> My husband and I have supported the church all our lives, sent our children to Catholic schools, and what happens? We see a criminal getting buried in the place reserved for nuns and bishops!

> . . . have you witnessed the VICTIM being raped, stabbed, shot, not to mention the agony of the family left behind? You only think of the killer's plight, who will not be tortured or suffer, just instant death.

> So the state finally executed this poor murderer. Terrible. Why didn't you hold his beautiful hand with the blood on it when they executed him? May God send him to hell for all eternity!

> Your professed Christianity leaves a lot to be desired when one learns that in all of your misguided attempts to make Elmo your martyr of the Catholic Church, you failed to communicate even the smallest gesture of com-

passion, kindness, or comfort to the innocent, life-long Catholic families who did nothing to deserve the horrifying brutality inflicted on them . . . you are not the first wolf to hide in sheep's clothing . . .

I have before me a copy of the Vatican City report banning priests and nuns from engaging in political activities . . . I suppose [Sister Prejean] would use the trite phrase "violation of human rights" in reference to the death sentence . . . But what else can you expect from a bunch of naive, frustrated women who know nothing of the real world . . . ?

I let the outrage come. I have no desire to write a letter to the editor to defend my actions. I regret that so many people do not understand, but I know that they have not watched the state imitate the violence they so abhor. Only one criticism causes me anguish — that I did not reach out to the Bourques and the LeBlancs when I first began visiting Pat. But there are, I decide, a couple of steps I can take on their behalf. I call Bishop Gerald Frey's office in Lafayette, the diocese in which the Bourques and LeBlancs live, and urge him to visit them. Perhaps his visit can help heal their hurt. He promises to see them soon and he keeps his promise. I also talk to Nancy Goodwin and encourage her to pursue her plan to engage the Catholic community in victim advocacy. With Nancy's help over the next several months the Catholic Diocesan Office of Lafayette will inaugurate a special Mass, with the bishop officiating, to be celebrated every year for victims of violent crime. The diocese also helps to organize a support group for victims of violent crimes.[4]

One day I receive two letters. One is from Patrick Sonnier. It's an Easter card, the kind the prison chaplains give to inmates. It must have been in limbo for a while on some chaplain's desk. On the front of the card is a bouquet of flowers and inside is a quote from the Gospel of St. John about eternal life. Pat had written: "I can't begin to express how much your friendship means to me. But I thank the good Lord above for sending you into my life."

The other piece of mail is an article published in the *Picayune* on May 2, less than a month after Pat's execution. Father Joseph Doss, an Episcopalian priest, has sent the article to me with the comment: "Amazingly similar to the Sonnier crime."

The article describes the abduction at gunpoint of a teenage couple from a shopping center near Hammond, Louisiana, on April

21 (about two weeks after Pat Sonnier's execution) by a man who forced the couple to drive down a rural road where he then robbed them and shot them in the back. The boy had died at the scene. The young woman was described as being in "serious but stable condition" in a nearby hospital. The article also mentions two other recent robbery abductions of young people at gunpoint.

It would be difficult to prove, I realize, that media coverage of the Sonnier crime, which was extensive (Hammond is near New Orleans and Baton Rouge), had triggered a "copycat" abduction-murder, but, it's clear that Pat Sonnier's execution did not deter the perpetrator of a similar crime. And the incident makes me wonder if state executions — which legitimize killing — incite violence rather than deter it. Some studies show an increase in homicides immediately after publicized executions, although as yet the evidence of such "brutalization" is inconclusive.[5]

But evidence that executions do not deter crime *is* conclusive. In the U.S. the murder rate is no higher in states that do not have the death penalty than in those that do.[6] In Canada, the homicide rate peaked in 1975, the year *before* the death penalty was abolished, and continued to decline for ten years afterward. And the first major report on capital punishment prepared for the United Nations in 1962 concluded: "All the information available appears to confirm that such a removal [of the death penalty] has, in fact, never been followed by a notable rise in the incidence of the crime no longer punishable by death."[7]

In the fall of 1987, immediately after the state of Louisiana executed eight people in eight and a half weeks, the murder rate in New Orleans rose 16.39 percent.[8]

A 1991 CNN/Gallup Poll shows that only a small percentage of Americans — 13 percent — believe that capital punishment deters future criminals, in contrast to 59 percent in 1977.[9] Nor do the majority of Americans now seem to think that increasing the number of executions is the way to reduce crime.[10]

A week after arriving back at Hope House I get a telephone call from Joseph Larose, the editor of the *Clarion Herald*, the New Orleans Catholic newspaper. He tells me he's been reading the "mean" letters to the editor about me and he'd like to send out one of his reporters — Liz Scott — so I can express "my side."

"Sure," I say, and the next afternoon Liz comes to Hope House and we sit on the front porch on the green, wooden bench and begin what will prove to be a lasting friendship. Later, Liz will confess to me that she had come to the interview highly suspicious of me, figuring I must be "some kind of nut" to get myself involved with murderers on death row.

Liz is pretty. She's funny. She writes a humor column for *New Orleans Magazine*. She went to a Catholic high school, "Celibacy Academy," as she calls it in her humor column. She has six children, but they're mostly grown and so she can pursue her writing. Her husband, Art, is a dentist, but she always wanted to be a writer and she couldn't be just a dentist's wife, she says, dressing up like a giant tooth to visit kindergarten classes, as some wives of dentists do.

I hadn't known that some dentists' wives paraded around like giant teeth. I have to laugh.

I tell her the story of how I came to St. Thomas, how I came to know Pat, and what I've learned about the death penalty and victims' families. She has a tape recorder and takes careful notes. I am thinking how pleasant it is to be sitting here on this bench and talking. It is May and the air is drenched with the sweetness of the pink mimosa blossoms and there is a cool breeze coming off the river. On the sidewalk in front of us gaggles of chattering children meander home from school, and I know that one of the gifts I have now, after the death house, is to know how precious life is and how I want to savor it and taste it and use my powers to the fullest and not niggle them away.

Liz's article about me appears soon after the interview. The headline reads: "Controversial Nun Takes Christ's Directive Literally." Controversy was one of the things Liz and I had talked about. It is proving to be one of my main surprises: get involved with poor people and controversy follows you like a hungry dog. (If you work for social change, you're *political*, but if you acquiesce and go along with the status quo, you're *above* politics.)

Back into the stream of events at Hope House, I am working with students and publishing a newsletter and a book of residents' poetry. The image of the death house with its polished tiles and gleaming oak chair is fading. I turn my attention to where life is. Although I have decided that I will not be going to death row again, I cannot bear to think that there are some men there now who are facing death alone with no spiritual adviser to befriend them. I also now know that inadequate legal representation can get a man killed and so, somehow, whatever it takes, I must see that every death-row inmate has a decent attorney for his appeals.

What I'll do, I decide, is talk with Tom Dybdahl in the Prison Coalition office to see whether we could conduct a training session for people interested in becoming spiritual advisers to death-row inmates. We'll have to recruit them, of course, but I know some people to invite and Tom knows some people, too.

And so I sit down with Tom and we hatch some plans.

I telephone Millard Farmer in Atlanta and tell him about our proposed training session and ask him if he will give a presentation on the legal system. I have not talked to him since Pat died. And here he is with that gravelly Georgian voice, saying once again that he'll "hep" us. He asks me how I'm doing and he says, "I heard a little rumor that you are taking on another guy on death row as his spiritual adviser."

"Unh-unh, Millard, you heard wrong," I say, and punch *wrong*.

The training session goes well. Tom, who knows all the death-row inmates, matches volunteers with inmates.

After the training session Millard, Tom, and I sit down at the table in the Hope House kitchen and talk about legal representation for death-row inmates. Poor Tom is tired. For two years now he's been ministering to the needs of *all* prisoners in Louisiana, an impossible job in itself, not to mention all the needs of death-row inmates. The executions have drained him. What we need, Tom says to Millard and me, is a legal office just for death-row inmate appeals. Millard has some suggestions: recruit an attorney who has a "passion for this issue," someone willing to work for $12,000 a year for two years, maybe someone just getting out of law school, raise about $25,000, and we're in business. "Our office will work with the attorney and give our expertise," Millard says.

This plan of Millard's is exactly what we do. Tom and I enlist Martha Kegel, director of the Louisiana branch of the American Civil Liberties Union, and Bill Quigley, and some folks who have money, and we put the office into operation in September 1984. [11]

It's time to make my yearly retreat — a time to sit on the riverbank and take a look at where I've been and where I'm going. Time to get in touch with the "soul of my soul."

I pack my suitcase and go to our motherhouse in New Orleans for a week. All I need is a room, some food, silence. The silence I both long for and resist. I have made enough retreats to know that silence almost always entails at least one soul-sized wrestling match. The writers of the Christian Gospels talk about Jesus being led into the desert of solitude to be "tempted" by the devil. Not all sweetness and light, this silence.

The first few days of retreat are all calmness and soft light. No blinding flashes. Quiet waters. I float. I sleep. But one afternoon, several days into the retreat, I come into my bedroom and find a newspaper clipping on my bed placed there by one of the Sisters. I see Bishop Ott's picture, taken as he appeared before the Criminal Justice Committee of the Louisiana legislature to speak in favor of a bill to abolish the death penalty. The accompanying article recounts how the bill was defeated in committee: thirteen to two. I see that Dracos Burke, the assistant D.A. who prosecuted Pat's case, is there to speak against the bill. Noting that opponents of capital punishment are saying that executing criminals may not deter crime, Burke says, "If it doesn't, all we've lost is the life of a convicted criminal."

As if some among us — not-as-human-as-you-and-I — are disposable. And who selects and eliminates the *disposable* ones?

Government.

For the last year or so I've been reading and studying Amnesty International's investigation into the death penalty as it is practiced by governments around the world. Amnesty has found that ten countries — China, Iran, Malaysia, Nigeria, Pakistan, Saudi Arabia, Somalia, South Africa,* the former USSR, and the United States — account for eight out of ten executions worldwide. And six countries — Iran, Iraq, Bangladesh, Barbados, Pakistan, and the United States — have, for the last decade, led other countries in juvenile executions despite a worldwide trend setting eighteen as the minimum age for execution.[12]

The Amnesty reports include photographs: in China two young men atop a flatbed truck en route to their deaths by firing squad, their crimes — "thief," "rapist" — on signs above their heads; in Nigeria an elderly father touching the face of his son, tied to a post, about to be shot by firing squad for armed robbery; in Egypt, a woman, her face contorted with fright, about to be hanged for murdering her husband; in Saudi Arabia two decapitated bodies in a public square, people huddled, staring.

Amnesty's investigation into the judicial processes of the hundred or so governments that impose the death sentence (the United States and Turkey are the only NATO countries that continue to execute)[13] has revealed that without exception, the penalty of death is disproportionately meted out to "the poor, the powerless, the marginalized or those whom repressive governments deem it expedient to eliminate."[14]

No government gets it right.

Most of the governments that execute, Amnesty points out, do

---

*Since February 1990, executions in South Africa have been suspended.

not deny that imposing death is cruel; they simply argue that executions are necessary.

But the U.S. Supreme Court denies the cruelty.

In *Furman v. Georgia* in 1972 the Court found the practice of the death penalty to be constitutionally unacceptable, not because it considered killing criminals inherently cruel, but because it thought the penalty too "arbitrary" and "capricious" in its implementation. The Court found that, lacking specific guidance, the imposition of the death penalty by juries was frequently based on race or random luck. The court also found the infrequency of the punishment problematic. "When a country of more than 200 million people inflicts an unusually severe punishment no more than 50 times a year, the inference is strong that the punishment is not being regularly and fairly applied," wrote Justice William Brennan, concurring in the majority opinion.[15]

In response to *Furman*, state legislatures quickly set about redrafting capital statutes that were supposed to provide specific trial guidelines so that juries might apply the death penalty more even-handedly.

In *Gregg v. Georgia*, (1976) the high court ruled that Georgia's "guided discretion" laws for capital sentencing effectively removed the randomness from death sentencing. Other state legislatures, using Georgia's reformed statutes as a model, passed legislation reinstating the death penalty.[16]

The Court in *Gregg*[17] expressed its satisfaction that such reformed guidelines, coupled with "meaningful appellate review," would effectively eliminate capriciousness in death sentencing: " . . . no longer can a jury wantonly and freakishly impose the death sentence."

So, the Court reasoned: death *evenly handed out* to criminals was not cruel. Then it gave further arguments why killing criminals was not in violation of the "cruel and unusual punishment" provision of the Eighth Amendment:

- "The imposition of death for the crime of murder has a long history of acceptance . . . It is apparent from the text of the Constitution itself that the existence of capital punishment was accepted by the Framers . . ."
- A large proportion of American society consider the death penalty "appropriate and necessary."
- The death penalty is an "expression of society's outrage at particularly offensive conduct."

- The death penalty is justified even though its deterrent effects are "inconclusive."
- Even if it could be demonstrated that life imprisonment as punishment for murder is as effective as the death penalty in deterring crime, capital punishment is, nevertheless, justified. Quoting *Furman*, the Court said, " . . . we cannot 'invalidate a category of penalties (death) because we deem less severe penalties (life imprisonment) adequate to serve the ends of penology."

Pressing its argument further, the Court ruled that in some instances death as a punishment not only is allowed, it is demanded:

> *Indeed, the decision that capital punishment may be the appropriate sanction in extreme cases is an expression of the community's belief that certain crimes are themselves so grievous an affront to humanity that the* only *adequate response may be the penalty of death* [emphasis mine].

At the heart of the Eighth Amendment is the concept that human beings are not to be subjected to cruelty and torture because they possess an inherent dignity. But in *Gregg* the Court reaffirmed what *Furman* had determined: retribution — even in its most extreme form, killing, is not "inconsistent with our respect for the dignity of men."

Given such a moral climate in the judiciary, Dracos Burke is not ethically far afield when he argues before the Criminal Justice Committee of the Louisiana legislature that the loss of life of a "convicted criminal" is no loss at all.

Burke's words ignite me into action. I realize that I cannot stand by silently as my government executes its citizens. If I do not speak out and resist, I am an accomplice. Here I see Bishop Ott calling for abolition, standing up for what he believes. Here he is and here I am and what am I going to do?

After retreat, I call Bill Quigley and he invites me to a meeting in New Orleans of attorneys, civil rights leaders, and religious leaders. At the meeting about eight of us sit around a table in Julian Murray's office. (Julian is an attorney representing Earnest Knighton, a Louisiana inmate facing imminent execution.)

Bill says that he believes it's time to take the issue of the death penalty directly to the people. All other avenues of recourse, he points out — the governor, the legislature, the courts — are closed.

It is time, he says, for public witness, public education, a grass-roots campaign.

Barbara Major, a black woman who knows about marches and their role in history, says, "Let's walk. Let's walk big-time. From here to Baton Rouge." And it's a spark and it catches and everybody starts throwing in pieces of kindling and a little fire sputters and builds.

We open up calendars and set a date: October 26 to 28. Bill, Barbara, and I will serve as steering committee. Everybody commits to raising fifty dollars. There are flyers to be printed. Invitations to be sent across the state. Permits to be secured for marching on state highways and city streets. Food, lodging, and transportation to be solicited. A whole swarm of things to be done.

We know that this public action is only the first step, that the task of informing people in schools, churches, and civic groups is the real work. There will need to be brochures printed, speakers trained, educational videos produced.

We know we have our work cut out for us, aware as we are that the vast majority of U.S. citizens say they favor capital punishment. A 1966 Gallup Poll showed 42 percent of the population in favor of the death penalty; a 1991 CNN/Gallup Poll showed support at 76 percent.[18] Clearly, the public's fear of escalating violent crime has fueled the recent ferver for capital punishment. Between 1960 and 1976, the number of reported murders in the United States more than doubled — from 9,060 to 18,780 — and between 1960 and 1980 the rate of "index crimes"* listed by the Federal Bureau of Investigation rose by more than 230 percent.[19]

Despite high pro-death-penalty sentiment, however, public support seems stronger in the abstract than in the concrete. Most juries, for example, faced with actually imposing death in capital trials, choose life imprisonment, even in "Death Belt" states;[20] and a growing number of public opinion surveys show that it is protection from criminals rather than executions that most citizens want. A 1986 Gallup Poll reveals that while 70 percent say they favor the death penalty, if they are given new data that show that capital punishment does not deter crime and are offered the alternative of life imprisonment without parole, support for executions drops to 43 percent.[21]

*"Index crimes" are eight offenses used by the Uniform Crime Reporting Program of the FBI to measure U.S. crime rates: murder, aggravated assault, rape, robbery, burglary, larceny, auto theft, and arson.

In *Furman*, Justice Thurgood Marshall argued that "informed public opinion" about the death penalty was, in fact, anything but informed: " . . . the American people are largely unaware of the information critical to a judgment on the morality of the death penalty . . . if they were better informed they would consider it shocking, unjust and unacceptable."

In 1975 Austin Sarat and Neil Vidmar, fellows at Yale Law School, empirically tested the "Marshall hypothesis" and found it to be correct. Their study found most subjects ignorant of the way the death penalty was imposed and of its effects and less inclined to favor it once they received even minimal information about it.[22]

Soon after the meeting in Julian Murray's office I find myself looking around the room at a Hope House staff meeting. There are about sixteen people on the staff now, many engaged in adult education. But no one in the entire state of Louisiana is working full-time to talk to the public about the death penalty.[23]

I will do this.

The decision unfolds like a rose.

I ask to meet with the regional coordinator of my congregation. If I am to devote myself to this work, I need the confirmation of my religious community. They readily give their blessing.

My decision to work for abolition of the death penalty does *not* include offering myself as spiritual adviser to another death-row inmate. But one day in October, six months after Pat Sonnier's execution, Millard Farmer comes over for lunch and asks for my help. He says he is representing two death-row inmates in Louisiana and he would like me to become their spiritual adviser.

"Why me?" I ask.

"Because they are facing death and your care will make a great difference to them."

It takes only a moment to answer. I cannot protect myself by refusing to go back to the horror of death row when here before me is this man going back again and again, and he is not thinking of protecting himself.

"I'll do it," I say to Millard. "But only one person at a time. I couldn't handle two. Who needs me first?"

"His name is Robert Lee Willie," Millard tells me.

CHAPTER

6

Millard fills me in on Robert Willie's crime. On May 28, 1980, he and Joseph Vaccaro killed eighteen-year-old Faith Hathaway. The young victim's mother and stepfather live nearby in Covington. The stepfather is named Vernon Harvey.

My heart sinks. I have heard of Vernon Harvey. Many people in the New Orleans area know of him. In recent months he has given interviews to the press, saying that he can't wait to see Robert Willie "fry," that he can't wait to see the "smoke fly off his body." He has said that he and his family and friends will go to the gates of the prison on the night of the execution to show support for capital punishment. Not visiting the Bourques and the LeBlancs had been a grave mistake, one I am determined not to make again, and I know I must reach out to victims' families even if they reject my offer, and that includes Vernon Harvey. I shudder. It's frightening to picture how Harvey might respond to someone who opposes Willie's execution. Who knows if such an encounter might push him over an emotional edge? What if he gets violent?

Millard explains that Willie's case is far along in the courts. There may not be much time. I decide I'd better write Robert right away. But I think, maybe he won't want a spiritual adviser, maybe he'll turn down my offer. Now, there's a thought . . . which, I readily

118

admit, brings a feeling of relief. I had reached out to Pat Sonnier not knowing what to expect. Now I know.

Millard tells me about the crime. It sounds straight out of Truman Capote's *In Cold Blood.*

Willie and Vaccaro had gone on an eight-day rampage that left Faith Hathaway dead, another teenage girl raped, and her boyfriend paralyzed. Shortly after the killing of Faith Hathaway, Willie and Vaccaro had kidnapped a teenage couple and taken turns raping the young woman in the back seat of the car as they drove across several states. The eighteen-year-old Hathaway girl had been brutally raped and stabbed and left to die in the woods.

Prior to these crimes, Willie had been involved in two other murders: the drowning death in 1978 of Dennis Buford Hemby of Missouri in a scuffle over drugs, and the shooting death in 1979 of Louisiana Parish Deputy Sergeant Louis Wagner II. In the Wagner murder, Willie had been a participant with several others in a robbery which occasioned the confrontation with the young deputy, although even the law enforcement officials agreed that Willie had not fired the fatal shot.

"Robert's had a long, long history of run-ins with the law from an early age," Millard says. "Plenty of drug and alcohol abuse, you know what I mean? He takes pride in being tough. He even smart-mouthed the judge at his trial."

Millard explains that after they were arrested for the kidnapping of the young couple, Willie and Vaccaro pled guilty in federal court and were each sentenced to three consecutive life sentences. However, Louisiana authorities, concerned that federal jurisdiction would preempt state jurisdiction and allow Willie and Vaccaro to serve life sentences in a federal prison, thereby escaping Louisiana's electric chair, had prevailed in getting Willie and Vaccaro to stand trial in state court.

"The two were tried in the same courthouse at the same time, on separate floors," Millard says. "Robert got death and Vaccaro got life. Both had indigent defenders."

Mentally I'm doing a body count while Millard is talking. Three people dead, one paralyzed, a young girl traumatized by abduction and rape . . . No wonder Vernon Harvey is outraged. How could he not be? My heart freezes at the prospect of a relationship with someone who sounds as if he might be criminally insane.

Millard, reading my face, says, "I know. These are terrible crimes, and God knows I don't condone them, but you'll see when you meet him — there's a child sitting inside this tough, macho dude."

The next day I write to Robert Lee Willie. I tell him not to feel under pressure to say yes, but if he would like me to be his spiritual adviser I'm here for him. It is a sober, contained letter. No picture of me on a pony. No friendly enthusiasms.

"Sure, come on," Willie's pert letter says in reply just one week later. "Never been inclined much to church and religion but I wouldn't at all mind the visits." His handwriting is a tender scrawl and some of the words are misspelled.

But I find out from Bill Quigley, who has recently met Frank C. Blackburn, the new warden under the Edwards administration, that some "pretty bad things" are being said about me at the prison — that I was "emotionally involved" with Pat Sonnier and that I had caused "a lot of trouble" with the "fainting episode." Bill suggests that I go to see Blackburn to talk things over.

"The way things stand now," Bill says, "I think he'll oppose your visit with any inmate."

My heart tightens. I have never been accused of anything like this before. My defensive juices rise. I feel my neck redden. It makes me yearn for earlier, *simpler* ministries when I taught children, coached the eighth-grade volleyball team, conducted Bible classes, counseled novices. I hate conflict. True, I have my principles. But while part of me raises the lance and charges into the fray, another part frantically looks for shelter. E. M. Forster's observation, uttered when he was a child, says it for me exactly: "I'd rather be a coward than brave. People hurt you when you're brave." I am *not* looking forward to confronting this warden.

Bill tells me that prisoners have a constitutional right to the spiritual adviser of their choice. It's a good thing to know, because it soon becomes evident that the prison wants to block women from serving as spiritual advisers to death-row inmates. Sister Lilianne Flavin, my friend and coworker, has recently been denied her request to counsel a death-row inmate. I find out that the two Catholic priest chaplains at Angola are the ones seeking to block me and other women from death-row prisoners. One of them has reportedly said that I was so "naive" and "emotionally involved" with Sonnier that I was "blind" to the fact that Pat may have "lost his soul" because he had not received the last rites of the Church during the final hours of his life. Women, they are saying, are just too "emotional" to relate to death-row inmates.

I recall very clearly Pat's response in the last hours, when I reminded him that the priest was there for him if he wished to receive the last rites. He said that Millard and Bill and I were there with him — we who had shown him love and fought hard to save his life. Our love, he said, was his "sacrament." And he said that he had already confessed his sins and received communion, and he didn't see the point of "doing it all over again."

I run the fingers of my conscience along the fabric of this accusation and feel for the hard knots and tears that guilt brings. Had I been blind, naive? Had I jeopardized a man's spiritual well-being?

No. The fabric feels smooth and whole and sound.

I find myself searching for an explanation for the chaplains' antagonistic behavior. Maybe they feel threatened because Pat had asked me and not them to be with him at the end. The movies always show a "man of the cloth" raising his hand in blessing to the man on the scaffold. Maybe they feel that if they allow me in, others will follow and they will be displaced.

I call the prison and make an appointment to see the warden.

Driving to the prison, I picture once again the warden's office. I remember its quiet businesslike atmosphere. Now, with a change in governors, Maggio has been replaced by Edwards's appointee, Frank C. Blackburn. Tom Dybdahl at the Prison Coalition has told me that Blackburn seems to be a decent man. He's a psychologist and lay minister in the Methodist Church and has come out of retirement to take on the job of warden.

Blackburn rises from behind his large desk to greet me as I come into the office. He is short, stocky, in his early sixties with a square face and a thick gray mustache. He is smoking a cigar. I sit in one of the brown leather chairs opposite him and he sits behind his desk. He starts right in: "I've been hearing some disturbing things about you."

"That I was emotionally involved with Patrick Sonnier and so did not fulfill my function as spiritual adviser?"

"That's right. And so emotionally distraught that you fainted in the death house and caused a lot of commotion for the personnel."

I'm ready for this, sure of my moral ground. I let the warden say what's on his mind.

He has a heavy responsibility as warden, he explains to me, and doesn't "relish" having to carry out executions, but it "comes with the job," and one responsibility which he takes "very, very seriously" is that condemned inmates get good spiritual counsel and a chance to "get straight with God" before they die. In fact, on becoming warden he initiated a seminar for death-row inmates to be conducted by "a top-notch Christian preacher." Naturally, he explains, no inmates are forced to attend, but the opportunity is there for them if they want it.

I say that the way I understand it, the Constitution provides a prisoner with the right to a spiritual adviser of his choice. Blackburn agrees with me, adding, "The only way we can bar a spiritual adviser from the prison is if we deem them a threat to prison security."

I'm relieved that we see the constitutional right of inmates the same way.

I say, "I am, as you know, completely opposed to the death penalty, and when I leave this prison I work for its abolition, but inside this prison I abide by your rules. I never bring contraband in or take contraband out. I am not a threat to prison security."

I am saying all this and he is looking at me and listening and taking long, slow puffs on his cigar. He seems a reasonable man. He does not interrupt when I speak.

I tell him that, yes, I cared for Patrick Sonnier. Despite his terrible crime, he was a human being and deserved to be treated with dignity and, yes, I was emotionally distraught watching him die. "Who wouldn't be," I ask him, "watching someone killed in such a cold, calculated way right in front of your eyes? You and the others are part of a process that shields you from natural, human emotions. The raw truth is that you're killing a fellow human being whose hands and feet are tied, and who wants to admit he's doing that?"

There is silence for a short moment, and then Blackburn says, "We can't let feelings dominate our actions or we couldn't carry out our responsibilities. I keep close tabs on the guards who work on death row because they have the closest daily contact with the inmates. There have been a few who have let this thing get next to them. When this happens, I offer them an assignment in another part of the prison."

I challenge him: "But you're a Christian, a minister in your church, a man who professes to follow the way of life that Jesus taught. Yet you are the one who, with a nod of your head, signals the executioner to kill a man. Do you really believe that Jesus, who taught us not to return hate for hate and evil for evil and whose dying words were, 'Father, forgive them,' would participate in these executions? Would Jesus pull the switch?"

The blue-gray smoke from the cigar is intensifying around Blackburn in a cloud. I am beginning to feel as if I'm talking to the Wizard of Oz.

"Nope," he says, "I don't experience any contradiction with my

122

Christianity. Never thought about it too much, really. Executions are the law, and Christians are supposed to observe the law, and that's that." And then he adds, "My wife, she's a good Christian woman, and she supports the death penalty, and believe me, you can't find a better Christian woman than my wife."

How is it, I wonder, that the mandate and example of Jesus, so clearly urging compassion and nonviolence, could so quickly become *accommodated*? Over the centuries "lawful authorities" — supposedly in God's name and with God's blessing — have hanged, shot, guillotined, drawn and quartered, burned, gassed, electrocuted, lethally injected — criminals. Over the years the crimes meriting death might change, but, for the most part, the blessing of God on retaliatory punishment has been unquestioned. Of course, those who justify retaliation can cite as authority numerous passages in the Bible, where divine vengeance is meted out to guilty and innocent alike: the Great Flood, the destruction of Sodom and Gomorrah, the slaying of the firstborn sons of the Egyptians (God's "lesson" to a recalcitrant Pharoah), to mention just a few examples. Even the Pauline injunction "Vengeance is mine, says the Lord, I will repay" can be interpreted as a command and a promise — the command to restrain individual impulses toward revenge in exchange for the assurance that God will be only too pleased to handle the grievance — in spades. That God wants to "get even" like the rest of us does not seem to be in question.[1]

One intractable problem, however, is that divine vengeance, (barring natural disasters, so-called acts of God) can only be interpreted and exacted by human beings. *Very* human beings.

I can't accept that.

First, I can't accept that God has fits of rage and goes about trucking in retaliation. Second, I can't accept that any group of human beings is trustworthy enough to mete out so ultimate and irreversible a punishment as death. And, third, I can't accept that it's permissible to kill people provided you "prepare" them with good spiritual counsel to "meet their Maker." Camus had argued that for people who believe in life after death, capital punishment is more easily rationalized, since death is a mere "temporary" punishment (only eternal life is considered final). But there is, Camus maintained, one, firm, unbreachable solidarity that human beings have — solidarity against death and suffering. On this common ground, he believed, all human beings — religious or atheist — must unite (pp. 222–225).

The swath of violence cut by Christians across the centuries is long and wide and bloodstained: inquisitions, crusades, witch burnings, persecutions of Jewish "Christ-killers." Now, in the last decade of the twentieth century, U.S. government officials kill citizens with dispatch with scarcely a murmur of resistance from the Christian citizenry. In fact, surveys of public opinion show that those who profess Christianity tend to favor capital punishment slightly more than the overall population — Catholics more than Protestants.[2] True, in recent years leadership bodies of most Christian denominations have issued formal statements denouncing the death penalty,[3] but generally that opposition has yet to be translated into aggressive pastoral initiatives to educate clergy and membership on capital punishment. And the U.S. Catholic Bishops in their "Statement on Capital Punishment," while strongly condemning the death penalty because of the "unfair and discriminatory" manner in which it is imposed, its continuance of the "cycle of violence," and its fundamental disregard for the "unique worth and dignity of each person," nevertheless uphold the "right" of the state to kill.[4] But if we are to have a society which protects its citizens from torture and murder, then torture and murder must be off-limits to *everyone*. No one, for any reason, may be permitted to torture and kill — and that includes government. Before prisons existed, executions might have been justified as society's only means of defense against crazed, violent killers. But today in the United States, following the example of other modern industrialized countries, we can incapacitate violent criminals through long-term imprisonment.

Recently this point was succinctly argued by convicted murderer Willie Leroy Jones. On September 15, 1992, just before the state of Virginia electrocuted him, he said, "Killing me is not the answer. There's a place called prison."

I look at Warden Blackburn and he is looking intently at me. He is ready to move the discussion to another front.

"What about this fainting episode you had?" he asks.

"I fainted because I was hungry," I tell him. And I remind him of the prison rule forbidding visitors from bringing food into the prison and how the rule had forced me to fast for long periods of time once inside the prison.

"You know, Warden," I say, "if it were emotional stress that caused me to faint, I would have fainted when I witnessed Pat's execution, not two days earlier when I was planning a prayer service with the chaplains."

I want to handle this fainting episode carefully. What he calls "a lot of commotion for prison personnel," if stretched a bit, could be interpreted as a threat to prison security if it were judged to involve an "inordinate" diversion of attention to my well-being instead of to inmates.

He nods his head, rests his cigar on the ashtray, and says to me, "We understand each other. We're going to do all right."

Those matters settled, I tell him that I wish to become Robert Willie's spiritual adviser and I need him to speed up the process of my approval because there may not be much time for Willie. He says he'll take care of it.

We rise and shake hands.

"I think the two priest chaplains here are pretty upset with me," I tell him. He nods his head vigorously.

I say, "It seems they're trying to block women from visiting death row."

"I'll see that it's straightened out," he says.

And he does. A couple of weeks after my meeting with him, Sister Lilianne receives approval to serve as spiritual adviser to a death-row inmate.

Organizing efforts for the October walk from New Orleans to Baton Rouge are gaining momentum. The steering committee is meeting every week now. Participants are signing up.

I have decided to move into a house near the Quigleys with two other nuns, Ann Barker and Leigh Scardina. We are drawn together by our concern for the poor and our desire to translate faith into social action. Once a week we gather with Bill and Debbie to talk, pray, and share a meal. We also participate in the pot-luck dinners in the Quigleys' spacious back yard, where a refreshing cross-section of people gather — lawyers, project residents, ex-offenders, teachers, professors. I am glad to be part of an effort that draws together black and white, rich and poor — an antidote, I believe, to what I see as an endemic national malady, the isolation of socio-economic classes and races from each other.

For me, the costliest part of being a member of the new community is moving my residence out of St. Thomas. I hate to lose touch with the residents there. But I realize that the focus of my work now extends across the state, and it seems a matter of justice not to occupy valuable apartment space if I am not devoting myself primarily to the people who live there. There is a list five miles long of people waiting to get project apartments.

I also realize that by changing residence I am not changing my commitment to stand with the poor and work for justice. Plus, I will continue to have contact with the people of St. Thomas because

Pilgrimage for Life, the Louisiana abolitionist group, is housed at Hope House, and I continue to attend weekly staff meetings there.

Meanwhile, there's Eddie Sonnier. Since Pat's execution I have continued to visit him and driven his mother, sister, and aunt to visit him. He seems calmer. Something in him has settled. He has found some footing, some niche of workable peace. Once he said to me, "Pat's dead now and there's nothing I can do to bring him back. Every night before I go to sleep, I read the last letter he wrote to me." He has taken to calling me "Sis." It fits. I know I'm family to him.

Within a week after getting approval from the warden, I go to visit Robert Willie. It's October 1984, six months after Pat Sonnier's execution. With Pat time had a slower, more open-ended feel. But now time is an undertow.

Here are the same red block letters over the green metal door. Here's the same eerie feeling coming back. There is no getting used to this place. I half expect Pat to show up behind the heavy mesh screen in the visiting room. But this is no Pat Sonnier coming into the cubicle. A slight young man in his mid-twenties peers through the screen to get a glimpse of me. He has dark blond hair brushed back in front, but long in the back, down to his collar. He has one of those intricate beards, an inverted V mustache above his lips coming down in two thin lines around his lips to his chin. The middle of his chin is clean-shaven but just under his bottom lip there's a little tuft of hair. He's fair-skinned and has pale blue eyes. He looks showered and neat in a blue denim jacket over a white T-shirt tucked into his jeans. Very thin waist.

I look at this man who has left such destruction in his wake. I can't get over how small he is and how delicate his features are — nose, chin, lips — almost feminine, except for the beard. The process that has brought me to him is mysterious, but here I am and here he is.

"Thanks for coming to see me, ma'am. Never thought I'd be visitin' with no nun," Robert Willie says and laughs softly. I'm surprised at how deep his voice is — the slight body led me to expect a higher pitch. He speaks in a slow, even-toned drawl. His tone is polite and I can tell he's trying to be friendly. He bends his head down low to take a drag from the cigarette in his hand cuffed to his waist. Very self-possessed. Like a cowboy.

I take the lead in the conversation. I let him float along and come into it when he feels like it. I want him to know who I am, what I think, how I feel. I do not expect much personal revelation from him here in the beginning of our relationship. I tell him about going to the St. Thomas Project and working at Hope House. I tell him about my opposition to the death penalty and the walk we're planning from New Orleans to Baton Rouge. I tell him that after Pat's execution, I thought I'd never be coming back to death row again, but how Millard had come over for lunch and — here I am. I tell him some of the "Millard stories" (of these, there are an abundance). I tell him about my family and childhood. I tell him about becoming a nun.

He stops me there.

"Don't you miss having a man? Don't you want to get married?" He is simple and direct. I'm simple and direct back.

I tell him that even as a young woman I didn't want to marry one man and have one family, I always wanted a wider arena for my love. But intimacy means a lot to me, I tell him. "I have close friends — men and women. I couldn't make it without intimacy."

"Yeah?" he says.

"Yeah," I say. "But there's a costly side to celibacy, too, a deep loneliness sometimes. There are moments, especially on Sunday afternoons, when I smell the smoke in the neighborhood from family barbecues, and feel like a fool not to have pursued a 'normal' life. But, then, I've figured out that loneliness is part of everyone's life, part of being human — the private, solitary part of us that no one else can touch."

"What I miss most being here," he says, and I notice he blows the cigarette smoke downward so that it does not drift into my face, "are the women and just bein' in the bars and listenin' to the music and dancin' 'til three or four in the morning. And I'm not goin' to lie to you, ma'am, I believed in *doing it*. Me and my lady friends, we'd get us a blanket and a bottle or a little weed and go into the woods and do it," and he gives a slight smile.

"Well, Robert," I say, "let's face it. If I had a husband and family, chances are I'd be there with them this afternoon, instead of visiting with you."

"True," he says. "Glad you're here, ma'am."

He's primed now and he talks about his case in the courts. He's aware that "time's gettin' short" and says how he's been reading and studying every law book he can get his hands on. "When you're in a place like this, you learn the law fast," he says. "Let's just say you have special motivation," and he smiles. He speaks softly. At times I have to press near the screen to hear him.

Bill Quigley is one of the attorneys pressing a class-action suit on behalf of death-row prisoners, and I've heard him mention Robert Willie as one of the plaintiffs. The suit aims at securing better conditions on death row: more phone calls, access to a legal library, "contact" visits, better health care. Not many inmates are willing to put their names to such a suit. Facing death in the electric chair leaves them "stuck out" enough, they figure. Better to keep a low profile.

But Robert Willie says, "Hell ("hay-ull," said in two syllables), let's face it, we're all up against the ultimate, anyway. Ain't nothin' more ultimate than death, is there? I say, let's join forces and make a stand. Together we stand; divided we fall." I'm not surprised when he tells me that he subscribes to *Soldier of Fortune* magazine.

Driving home I think of the man I have just met. I had expected a wild-eyed, crazed, paranoid type, but met instead this polite, soft-spoken, obviously intelligent young man. From the terror he'd wreaked I'd expected a huge brute, but he's so small, so slight. I notice that he didn't mention his crimes; he didn't show any re-morse. While I was talking to him, I kept thinking about Faith Hathaway, and I was conscious of her there, silent, in the room. I am defending Robert Willie's right not to be executed and I am affirming his dignity as a human being, but I can never for one moment forget what he did. I decide that as soon as our New Orleans to Baton Rouge trek is over I will visit the Harveys.

On Friday morning, October 26, a group of us — about 40 peo-ple — gather on the outskirts of New Orleans to begin walking the 80 miles to Baton Rouge.

Several TV and radio stations and newspaper reporters show up. "What do you hope to achieve by doing this?" they ask. I am one of the marchers assigned to speak to the media. I say that this march is the beginning of a statewide information campaign about the death penalty.

We know that one of the key issues we must address is the fear of crime which fuels the death penalty. Actually, the public (not by accident) has an exaggerated perception of the risk of felony-type murders (murders which occur in the course of another felony which may be punishable by death). The risk varies, of course, according to one's neighborhood — inner-city residents have *good* reason to fear felony-type murders — but nationwide, according to 1989 statis-tics, a very small percentage, 2.0 persons per 100,000, die of felony-type murders each year, roughly the same percentage as those who die from drowning or accidental poisoning. In contrast, the proba-bility of dying in an automobile accident is 47.9 per 100,000, and the probability of dying from heart disease is 765.5 per 100,000.[5] But the public's view of crime is largely shaped by the media, which are prone to emphasize death from violence while downplaying more prevalent and commonplace threats to life. In one study, for example, some respondents thought that homicides cause more deaths than strokes, when in fact strokes cause eleven times more deaths.[6]

Along with media, politicians also distort public perception of crime. Politicians in dramatic thirty-second campaign ads purporting to address the "crime problem" tend to emphasize the most violent crimes, which they then propose to counter by use of the death penalty. "Tough problems call for tough solutions," they say — as if executing a few people a year has anything to do with *real management* of crime.

The truth is that the death penalty is potentially relevant to only a very small pool of the 14 million–plus "index crimes" committed in this country every year. Supreme Court decisions and resulting legislation have restricted the use of the death penalty to certain forms of aggravated homicide — about 1 of every 2,986 "index crimes" and only 1 of every 345 violent crimes.[7] Such constricted use makes the death penalty, in fact, only a relatively minor criminal-justice policy. Dealing with the real crime problem in this nation involves a far more comprehensive approach in areas of employment, drug prevention, police security, and education — not easily packaged in thirty-second, bang-for-the-buck T.V. campaign ads.

Along the road from New Orleans to Baton Rouge, I use every media opportunity to provide facts about the death penalty. I point out that in Louisiana, since the legislative reforms of 1977, life sentences for first-degree murder have become *real* life sentences, so we can protect ourselves from dangerous criminals without killing them.

I also point out that execution of a prisoner costs more than life imprisonment. That's because capital trials require more expert witnesses and more investigators, a longer jury-selection process (those who oppose the death penalty must be screened out), the expenses of sequestering a jury, not one but two trials because of the required separate sentencing trial, and appeals in state and federal courts. When a D.A. decides not to go for the death penalty, there may in fact be no trial at all, but whenever the death penalty is sought, almost always there is a trial and all it entails. In Florida, which may be typical, each death sentence is estimated to cost approximately $3.18 million, compared to the cost of life imprisonment (40 years) of about \$516,000.[8] Another reason for swollen costs is the added expense of incarcerating prisoners on death row. Most states segregate death-row prisoners in maximum security units and must hire additional security personnel. Nor are most death-row prisoners allowed to work, which prevents them from helping to pay for their upkeep.

Besides the expense there is also a "distortion cost" which capital trials and appellate proceedings impose on the court system. State supreme court judges in some death-penalty jurisdictions report that they spend a disproportionate amount of their judging time tending to capital punishment business.[9]

To these utilitarian arguments I add others in these media interviews — that the death penalty is too selective and capricious to serve as a deterrent, that it is racially biased — but the argument I always save for last is this one: if we believe that murder is wrong and not admissable in our society, then it has to be wrong for everyone, not just individuals but governments as well. And I end by challenging people to ask themselves whether we can continue to allow the government, subject as it is to every imaginable form of inefficiency and corruption, to have such power to kill. "It's not a marginal issue," I say. "It involves all of us. We're all complicit. Government can only continue killing if we give it the power. It's time to take that power back."

It's my first time meeting people in the media. I notice how friendly many of them are. After the interviews I always shake hands and thank them for coming out, the reporters and the camera people too; and before the walk is over I have quite a collection of their personal cards, which I file so I can call on them in the future. Reflecting back after ten years, I realize now, even more than I did then, just how crucial the media are to public education on this issue, and I am struck by how many reporters and journalists become sympathetic to the cause of abolition once they become knowledgeable about the issue.

We walk in the sunshine. It's October, one of Louisiana's clearest, driest months. The sky is cobalt blue. The trees and grass are still mostly green, but the swamp maples have turned orange-red. It feels good to be walking out on the open road. Bill Quigley is at the head of the line, setting the pace. We'll do twenty-five miles each day. When people drop behind the crowd (people such as me, with short legs), a van picks us up and brings us to the front. That way we keep a brisk pace. Everybody's full of chatter. Some sing. One young fellow plays a kazoo. We're an interesting assortment:

black and white, ex-cons and nuns, secretaries and teachers, housewives, students, a carpenter, lawyers, a woman whose sister was murdered but who opposes capital punishment, some family members with sons on death row, a Vietnam vet.

Many people, barreling along the highway, energetically signal their response to our cause: they put thumbs down; they flip us the middle finger; they shout "Fry the bastards"; they call us "bleeding-heart liberals"; they call us "commies." But every now and then we hear a horn and see a thumb up, and we all wave and cheer.

Then as the sun climbs in the sky and shoes rub and legs and hip joints ache, we fall silent, and all you can hear is the thud and scrape of feet moving and the whine and roar of cars and trucks on the highway.

For three days we walk.

We arrive in Baton Rouge as the sun is setting. The darkness is fast descending and streetlights have come on and give a furry amber glow. As we approach the capitol steps we spot a small group holding up posterboard signs. Supporters coming to join us for the rally? Getting closer, we can make out what the signs say: "What about the victims?" "Justice, *even* for victims." It's a counterdemonstration group. How will we deal with them? Ignore them? Talk to them? The steering committee huddles. We decide to send a couple of people on a "peacekeeping" mission.

We hold the rally. The press gives us good coverage. The "peacekeeping" mission is successful, and we are not interrupted by the counterdemonstrators. We can all go home now, and my thoughts are turning toward the free and airy bus ride home, *sitting*, not walking, and knowing I'm not responsible any longer for all these people and the myriad details of organizing.

A full moon has come out and is shining its white metallic light on the capitol steps. People are drifting down the steps toward waiting yellow school buses and cars.

A young man, one of the marchers, touches my arm and points to the bottom of the steps where the counterdemonstrators are and says that a man says to tell me "to watch out or someone is going to hurt you." The man down there wants to talk to me. He says his name is Vernon Harvey. My heart tightens. Oh, God, not here, not now. "Someone wants to hurt me?" What does that mean?

I look down the wide rows of white steps — forty-eight steps, to be exact, each engraved with the name of a state and the date it achieved statehood. At the age of ten with my Girl Scout troop, my green skirt swishing across my bony knees, I had skipped and run up and down these steps, saying the name of each state in singsong. Now I am all too glad to have forty-eight states between me and Vernon Harvey.

I don't *have* to respond to the invitation, I reason with myself. With the crowd milling about, I could pretend the message never reached me. Besides, maybe another time less confrontational than this would be better for our first meeting. *Any time* would be better than this.

The young man delivering the message looks at me expectantly. I know it would be cowardly not to respond to the invitation. I thank him for the message, my heart racing, and walk down the long, white steps to Vernon Harvey.

I introduce myself. He's a short guy with close-cropped gray hair, black-rimmed glasses. I brace myself for attack. He says he's heard I visit with death-row inmates and that I'd better watch myself with those "scum." "They'll just as soon slit your throat as look at you," he says. He's not shouting and he looks at me when he talks.

Relief. I was prepared for apoplectic rage, and here he is expressing concern about my safety.

We must have executions, he tells me, because it's the only way we can be sure these "mad dogs" don't kill again. He ticks off his favorite pro-death-penalty arguments, just as I tick off mine for abolition. I have to respect that he's out here at the foot of these capitol steps because he believes in his cause as strongly as I believe in mine. Maybe even more. I haven't had anyone close to me murdered. I tell him that I'm terribly sorry about his stepdaughter and ask if I may come to visit him and his wife. "Sure, come on over," he says, and he writes his telephone number for me on a piece of paper.

The next week I call him and get directions to his house in Covington, a small town on the north side of Lake Pontchartrain. I go in early November on a Sunday afternoon. The first feel of fall is in the air. I bring a sweater along. I don't know how long I'll be, probably late, and the evenings are getting cool. This is one visit that can't be rushed.

I turn into the driveway of a cozy-looking little house surrounded by tall trees. There is a swing on the front porch. A happy enough looking house, I think, as I climb the front steps and reach for the doorbell. As a child, riding in the family car through neighborhoods, I used to play a secret game of looking at houses and trying to guess from the outside appearance whether or not the people inside were happy. Bright, cheery houses: happy people inside. Sad, bedraggled houses: sad people inside.

Great as the sea is thy sorrow. Words well up from a prayer to Mary, mother of Jesus, who watched her son dying on a cross.

Vernon comes to the door and invites me in, asking good-naturedly if we're planning to do any more walks against the death penalty any time soon because he'd sure like to be there at the end of it to welcome us. Elizabeth, his wife, comes into the living room and introduces herself. She's younger than Vernon and more reserved, not the tease that he is. Faith's graduation picture hangs on the living room wall. A pretty girl with some of Elizabeth's features. Same facial structure, same nose, same eyes. In her blue graduation gown she looks happy, her eyes gazing past the camera into her bright, young future.

We sit in comfortable chairs in the front living room. I sit where I can see their faces and ask them to tell me about their daughter. They seem to want to talk. Maybe it's cathartic for them.

Tragedies have a date and time. Tragedy in the Harvey family happened on May 28, 1980.

Faith, eighteen years old, had graduated from Mandeville High School in early May and planned to join the Army on May 28. She wanted to study a foreign language. She hoped to be stationed overseas.

"With me having a long career in the military," Vernon says, "I had told her about the travel, the educational opportunities plus — this is a big thing with me — patriotism; it's good to give a few years of service to your country, even if you don't plan to make it a life career."

Elizabeth, calm, her voice without emotion as though she is describing someone else's tragedy, tells how on May 28 a recruiting sergeant was to meet Faith at her apartment to drive her to New Orleans for induction. (At the time, the Harveys lived in an apartment complex that Elizabeth managed and Faith had her own apartment in the complex.) A few days earlier Elizabeth had taken her shopping to get things she would be needing. "You know, practical things," Elizabeth says, "new bras with plenty of support, a case for her contact lenses, medicine for menstrual cramps."

The recruiting sergeant would not be coming until early afternoon, so Elizabeth had planned to go over to Faith's apartment to help her with last-minute packing in the morning.

On May 27 at five o'clock in the evening, Faith headed hurriedly out the door of her parents' apartment on her way to Bossier's Restaurant, where she waitressed. After work she planned to visit with friends to say good-bye and to celebrate the beginning of her new career. As Faith was leaving, Elizabeth had noticed her sandals — the one on the right foot was torn — and had suggested that she ought to change them, but Faith had been in a hurry and said she'd be late for work.

The next time Elizabeth would see the sandals they would be in a cellophane bag as state's exhibit number 10 at the trial of her daughter's murderer, and she would identify them along with other objects: a purse, a blue skirt, a blue blouse, a driver's license, a ring, a medallion, a Timex watch with a blue face.

"You don't know when you see your child leave through a door that you are never going to see her alive again," Elizabeth says. "If I had known, I would have told her how much I loved her. My last words to her — the last she ever heard from me — were about sandals."

On the morning of Wednesday, May 28, Elizabeth and Vernon waited for Faith to come through the front door. The big day had finally arrived. After today they would have to rely on letters and an occasional phone call. Letting Faith have her own apartment had been one step toward independence, but today would be the really big venture. Faith had promised to write.

"She would've, too," says Elizabeth. "We had a close relationship. She'd always talk things over with me. And she and Vern were close. Faith was four when Vern and I met, seven when we got married. He wasn't just a stepfather; he loved her every bit as much as I did." And I look over at Vernon and see his head down, tears rolling down his cheeks. It's been four years since Faith's death and he still cries when he talks about her. I wish I could take away some of his pain. I feel helpless, overwhelmed. All I can do is listen.

But Faith was late that May 28th morning. Elizabeth called her apartment. No answer. She waited and called again. No answer. No footsteps at the door. No telephone call to say that she was a little late but on her way. No Faith.

Concerned, Elizabeth and Vernon had gone over to her apartment, but it was empty, the bed still neatly made. Elizabeth describes how she held the terror at bay, thinking of possible scenarios: maybe she had overdone the drinking a little and gone home with a friend to sleep it off; maybe it had been late when the partying had ended and she had decided to spend the night with one of her girlfriends . . .

"But it was strange that she did not call me," Elizabeth says. "She would always telephone me and tell me where she was. I kept telephoning her friends one by one. I just couldn't accept that I didn't know where she was."

When Faith did not appear by 3:00 P.M., Elizabeth called the recruiting sergeant, who was supposed to drive Faith to New Orleans. He said he had already been by her apartment twice. Vernon then went to the Mandeville Police Department.

"I told them our daughter was missing," he said, "but they said someone had to be missing at least forty-eight hours before they could do anything."

Later the same evening Vernon drove to the St. Tammany Parish Sheriff's Office to file a report on their missing child.

Thursday, May 29, and Friday, May 30, passed. The sheriff's office formed a search party. Vernon joined. It was a formidable undertaking to search in this expansive countryside with its massive patches of wilderness areas full of underbrush, thickets, and gulleys.

On Sunday, June 1, a family picnicking near Fricke's Cave in a remote wilderness area south of Franklinton found a purse, clothes, and a wallet and turned them over to the Franklinton Sheriff's Department. Someone called the Harveys to tell them they had heard that some of Faith's things had been found.

"We got that information from our own resources, not from the police," Elizabeth says. "They never called us. We called them."

On Monday, June 2, Elizabeth continues, the search party from the sheriff's office went out to comb the area where the clothing had been discovered, but they found nothing. Vernon says how he had noticed "a real bad smell" in the area where they were searching, and thought there must be some kind of garbage dump or dead animal nearby.

On Wednesday, June 4, eight days after Faith's disappearance, two investigators from the district attorney's office found her body behind a log in the vicinity of Fricke's Cave. She had been stabbed seventeen times in the neck and upper chest.

Vernon is crying. Elizabeth, recounting the gruesome details, does not cry. Somehow she's found a way to leach out the horror. Their daughter's badly decomposed body was nude, supine, legs spread-eagled.

Vernon says, "Faith didn't know the animals she was dealing with when Willie and Vaccaro offered her a ride home. She had been with friends all night. You know, young people, they think everybody's their friend. We think somebody must have slipped something into her drink. The coroner's report said her vagina was all tore up. The electric chair is too good for Robert Willie and Joseph Vaccaro."

He can't stop crying. He says a couple of sentences and cries, says some more and cries again. Listening and knowing he is reliving it all over again, I want to tell him, "Stop. Please stop." I want him to be oblivious, to forget, to let all the horrible details fade. I can't find any words. I am crying too.

"At first they couldn't find the graduation medallion around her neck because it was embedded so deep from the stabbing," Elizabeth says. "She had been so proud of that medallion. She wore it all the time. It said: "Class of '80, Dawn of a New Decade."

The police would not let Vernon and Elizabeth come to the morgue to identify the body, explaining that it would be too traumatic for them. But Elizabeth says that she could not bear for the body to be buried forever without being "absolutely, positively sure without a doubt" that it was Faith they had found. "What if, because of the decomposition and the circumstantial evidence of the clothes nearby, they only thought it was Faith? I had to be sure."

So she had telephoned her brother in Richmond, Virginia, a dentist, who had done some dental work for Faith in April. On the evening before the funeral he had gone to the funeral home and made a positive identification from the dental restorations.

Vernon says, "Elizabeth's brother was pretty tore up when he came back from the funeral home. Before he reached his hand into that bag with all the lime in it and fished out Faith's jaw, he said he had always been against the death penalty. But, boy, after that, he was for it."

"I knew it had to be Faith, that's what my mind told me, but I just had to be sure," Elizabeth says.

Young Lizabeth, the fourteen-year-old-daughter of Vernon and Elizabeth, dashes into the living room. She leans close to her mother and whispers something. Elizabeth introduces me and she turns toward me and says politely, "How do you do." I calculate that she was ten years old when Faith was killed. Her life here in this room is tangible. She is pretty and whole and unharmed. I'm glad that Vernon and Elizabeth have her. Maybe she is what keeps them going. Perhaps for her sake they have not allowed themselves to dissolve in grief. Lizabeth bounds out of the room as quickly as she came in.

Vernon recounts the scene and the murder. Both Willie and

Vaccaro, he says, gave basically the same account in their confessions, except that each blamed the other for the stabbing.

Sometime in the early-morning hours of May 28 the two men met Faith outside a bar and offered her a ride home. Instead, they drove her down gravel roads to a remote place, made her take off all her clothes, blindfolded her, and led her down a ravine where they forced her to lie down and raped her. Then one of them stabbed her to death while the other held her hands. Some fingers of her right hand were missing where the knife had cut as she raised her hand to protect herself.

"The SOB, Vaccaro, got a life sentence," Vernon says, and he is crying again, "and it's been four years and they haven't fried Willie's ass yet. We've been waiting and waiting for justice to be done. I can't rest until justice is done. All you hear about these days is the rights of the criminal. What about our rights? Don't we have a right to see this chapter closed?"

I wonder how Vernon and Elizabeth would have fared emotionally if Robert Willie, like Vaccaro, had been sentenced to life imprisonment. He would have slipped into anonymity behind Angola's walls, his fate sealed, his crime punished, and maybe these grieving parents could, over time, have laid down their grief and carried on with their lives. But now they are like two deer paralyzed by headlights in the road. All they can think, all they know, all they want is the death of their child's murderer that the state has promised them. So they follow the case in the courts. They hold their breath each time there's a new appeal. They wait and wait, reliving their daughter's murder again and again. And the hope is that when Willie's death does come, it will ease their pain and their loss. At last, they will have *justice*.

The pale October sun has been sliding steadily downward and through the window I can see the trees turning into dark purple silhouettes. Inside, darkness has been slowly seeping into the room. Elizabeth gets up and turns on a lamp. I know I have to drive back across the lake, but time is standing still. In the presence of such suffering, it doesn't matter how late I get home.

"Let's go to the kitchen and I'll make us some coffee," Elizabeth says. As we walk to the kitchen, Vernon keeps talking, "Willie and I met face to face in the hallway during his trial. He was cocky. He said he'd never go to the chair. I told him I'd see his ass fry."

Then he picked up on the point he had made to me when I met him on the capitol steps — that the only way to be sure we get rid of someone like Willie is to kill him. Elizabeth agrees. "That's the only way we can be sure that he'll never kill again," she says. "In prison he could kill a guard or another inmate. Someone like Willie can escape from prison."

I disagree with these arguments, but the intensity of all the sorrow silences me. I do not offer counterarguments. I just let all the torrents of rage and loss and sorrow tumble over me.

"He's a mad dog, that's what he is," Vernon says, and he tells how Willie and Vaccaro, after killing Faith, had continued their reign of terror, kidnapping a teenage couple, raping the girl, tying the boy to a tree, stabbing him, shooting him, and leaving him for dead. "Miraculously he lived," Vernon says, "but he's partially paralyzed from the waist down."

Vernon has stopped crying. It's his anger talking now, which I welcome. At least he's not dissolving in grief and loss. I want him to survive this terrible sorrow. I want him to make it.

"Before their rampage was over," Vernon says, "Willie and Vaccaro drove through five states, stole four cars, robbing, raping, and killing all the way. The law had a bulletin out on 'em for the kidnapping, and that's what they first arrested them for. They had turned the young Madisonville girl loose, and she had gone to the police and described them. When the law arrested the two of them in Arkansas for the kidnapping," he says, "they didn't yet know they had killed Faith. That only came out as they confessed to the kidnapping."

I think of the young man I have just visited with the neatly combed hair and the quiet voice. I think of how he exhaled his smoke downward so that it didn't blow into my face.

"I am going to be Robert Willie's spiritual adviser," I tell them quietly. I have to say it. I have to let them know. We have made our way to the kitchen and now sit at the small table there. Elizabeth is pouring the coffee into our cups.

"He needs all the spiritual advisers he can get," Vernon says. "He's an animal. No, I take that back. Animals don't rape ·and kill their own kind. Robert Willie is God's mistake. Frying in the electric chair is the least of the frying he's about to do when God sends him to hell where he belongs," and he jabs his finger downward.

On two occasions, Vernon says, he almost "took Willie out." One was during a recess at the trial. In the small courtroom Vernon was standing close to Willie and within inches of a deputy's unstrapped, holstered pistol. "In three seconds I could have slipped that gun out and blown Willie away," Vernon says, "but there was the deputy there and other people. I might have hurt somebody else, so I didn't do it."

The second opportunity came, he says, when he was driving to New Orleans on the Lake Pontchartrain Causeway and saw federal marshalls in a vehicle driving Willie to New Orleans. Vernon had rammed down the accelerator and raced after them. "Willie turned and saw me, he knew who it was on their tail," he says, "and he must have said something to the driver. I saw the driver eyeballing me through his rearview mirror and he was gunning that Pontiac for all it was worth, but I had my Oldsmobile Cutlass Supreme, and his pedal was to the floor and I was still gaining on them. I could hear them over the C.B. radio. They were scared. They knew that if I rammed them at that speed they wouldn't be able to control their car, they'd go into the lake."

But then, again, Vernon says, he had refrained and fallen back. They were officers of the law doing their job. He didn't want to hurt them. "Besides," he adds, "they would have put my ass in jail and I couldn't be here for Elizabeth and Dale" (his pet name for Lizabeth).

I am amazed at these stories. I have only seen high-speed car chases in the movies. Poor Vernon. What does he do with all this rage he feels? My heart goes out to him and to Elizabeth. These are good, decent, nice people. Here they are, inviting me into their home, offering me coffee, sharing with me the most intimate, terrible pain of their lives.

"And do you know," Vernon continues, "that we almost didn't get the son-of-a-bitch, Willie, to face the electric chair here in Louisiana because the feds already had him serving a bunch of life sentences in Marion*? Willie figured he'd beat the chair here in Louisiana because he thought that as long as the feds had him, the state couldn't touch him. And I was talking to people — lawyers and a bunch of other folks — and that's what they were all telling me, that Willie had to serve his federal term before the state could get their hands on him.

"No way was that going to happen," says Vernon, and he tells how he told his congressman, Bob Livingston, about his problem and Livingston told him to write a letter to President Reagan and he would put it in the President's hand.

"Well, Livingston must have gotten through," Vernon says, because several weeks later the phone rang and a woman's voice said

---

*A maximum-security federal prison in Illinois.

to hold please for the President. "Hell, I didn't know which president the lady was talking about, the Kiwanis Club or whatever. But when I heard the voice, I knew what president it was, all right. I'd know Ronald Reagan's voice anywhere. He told me — these were his words — 'As soon as the U.S. Supreme Court turns Willie down, which won't be long, he'll be sent back to Louisiana to stand trial for your daughter's murder, you can depend on that.' And I liked the way he put it — "as soon as the Court turns him down, which won't be long" — that's just the words he used, and I told him that I appreciated that."

But I can tell Vernon's talking to the President of the United States didn't impress him. Only the satisfaction of getting Robert Willie really mattered, and if that took the President himself, so be it. The rage of his pain and the agony of his loss eclipse everything else.

It's time to leave. I get up and move toward the car. Vernon and Elizabeth walk out with me and he says, "You know, even Willie's own father, who has spent twenty-six years of his life at Angola for everything from cattle rustlin' to murder, says his son ought to get the chair."

I start the motor. I thank the Harveys for letting me visit. I promise to pray for them. I promise to come back to see them again sometime.

"We're like different baseball teams," Vernon says. "Different points of view, but we respect each other."

It's been a friendly exchange. Vernon and Elizabeth hadn't batted an eye when I told them I was Willie's spiritual adviser. I can tell they're grateful for my visit. Friends, it seems, have dropped away since the tragedy.

A month or so later the friendliness between us will be shattered. I will meet the Harveys at Robert Willie's Pardon Board hearing. They will be there to see that he dies, and because of my visit and the sympathy I have shown them, they expect that I also want to see him die.

CHAPTER
7

Driving back to New Orleans after my visit with the Harveys, I stop and pay my dollar at the entrance of the twenty-six-mile causeway. Here at these toll booths is where Vernon Harvey said he spotted Robert Willie in a federal vehicle and began his high-speed chase. Night has taken hold of the sky and the lake. All I can see as I drive are the shafts of light from the headlights and red flicks of tailights in front of me. I can't get my mind off Faith Hathaway.

She had been celebrating. No doubt the liquor had lowered her defenses. At what point did the chilling realization seize her that she was in danger, *real danger*, there in the front seat of a truck, wedged between two strangers — men, maybe with guns, whose remarks were becoming more and more sinister and who were taking her farther and farther away from the safe moorings of home and parents and friends — and help. As panic mounted, had she tried shutting her eyes tight, fighting to throw off the sluggish effects of the alcohol? It was a time when a woman needed her sharpest wits about her, a time to think clearly and keenly about escape. Or perhaps it was better that her wits were not so sharp. Better, maybe, for the anesthesia of the alcohol to dull the pain and horror soon to be hers.

Poor Vernon and Elizabeth. No matter that Faith was killed four years ago. Every time the terror is told, she suffers and cries out and dies again. *She suffered alone and in great terror and no one was there to comfort her.* Who can blame them for wanting to see her murderer executed? Maybe they feel that not to demand death, the harshest punishment possible, would be a betrayal of their daughter's memory.

Great as the sea is thy sorrow.

I wonder what will ever be able to heal the Harveys' pain and bring them peace. No, there is no replacing the unique universe of Faith Hathaway. Even if Robert Willie is destroyed, the aching void can never be filled.

I understand the Harveys' desire for retribution. Their lives have been violated by Robert Willie and they want to see him punished. They want to see him made accountable for his actions. They want to see him pay for what he did. So do I. In an ideal world, there would be no need for retribution. But in real societies, punishing the guilty is as integral to the function of law as exonerating the innocent and preventing crime.

Susan Jacoby, in her insightful book *Wild Justice: The Evolution of Revenge*, says:

> *Establishment of . . . the restraint that enables people to live with one another and the ineradicable impulse to retaliate when harm is inflicted has always been one of the essential tasks of civilization. The attainment of such a balance depends in large measure on the confidence of the victimized that someone else will act on their behalf against the victimizers . . . Stripped of moralizing, law exists not only to restrain retribution but to mete it out . . . A society that is unable to convince individuals of its ability to exact atonement for injury is a society that runs a constant risk of having its members revert to the wilder forms of [vigilante] justice . . .* [1]

But Jacoby maintains, and I agree, that the retribution which society metes out should be *measured.* Her objection to capital punishment is that such "eye-for-an-eye" retribution is as excessive as the original crime it punishes. But she also finds it excessive that those convicted of so heinous and irrevocable a crime as murder should be made to serve only a few short years in prison. The Bureau of Justice Statistics reveals that in 1986 the average amount of time served on a life sentence in the United States was six years, nine months.[2]

Jacoby holds that the public's desire to see serious punishment consistently meted out for serious crimes is legitimate and that to ignore it encourages "the boundless outrage that generates demands for boundless retribution."[3] But she says that punishment should be tempered: "There is, or ought to be, a vast middle ground between belief in the death penalty and acceptance of a system that allows too many killers to 'pay' with only a few years of their own lives — or to escape retribution altogether through legal and psychiatric loopholes — for a life they have taken from another."[4]

Such measured retribution is attained, I believe, by sentencing which requires *nonnegotiable* long-term imprisonment for first-degree murder (also termed *aggravated* or *capital* murder). At least forty states in recent years have revised criminal codes to require life without parole or lengthy mandatory minimum years served for convictions they deem most serious.[5] In a growing number of states — twenty-five as of 1992, including Louisiana — life-without-parole sentences are *true* life sentences. The only way prisoners serving such sentences can be released is by commutation of sentence by the governor, and because of the unpopularity of such commutations, governors now grant them rarely.

Most other states have taken extra precautions to assure that felony-type murderers are not released from prison after a few years served. They do this by legislating a statutory minimum time which a convicted murderer must serve before being eligible for parole. The Arizona criminal sentencing code, for example, demands that convicted first-degree murderers serve twenty-five years before eligibility for parole. Colorado demands forty years; New Jersey, thirty; Ohio, twenty; Indiana, thirty.[6] The Kansas legislature, which in 1987 balked at reinstituting the death penalty because of its costliness,* in 1990 enacted a "Hard 40" statute, which stipulates that a perpetrator more than eighteen years of age who is guilty of premeditated murder must serve forty years' imprisonment before becoming eligible for parole.[8] A South Carolina statute specifies

---

*For eight years the Kansas legislature passed death-penalty bills only to have them vetoed by an anti-death-penalty governor. With a new pro-death-penalty governor in the statehouse in 1987, the legislature had its green light. But at a time when the financially strapped state was cutting some services 10 percent, the senate balked at the death-penalty process, which would cost an estimated $10 million the first year alone and $50 million before the first execution could be carried out.[7]

that if the governor commutes a death sentence, he or she must sentence the prisoner to life without eligibility for parole.[9]

As indicated earlier, public opinion surveys in a number of states show that support for the death penalty drops significantly when the public is assured that murderers will remain behind bars for life.[10] And support for the death penalty also drops dramatically — well below the majority — when the alternative is presented of long-term imprisonment (at least twenty-five years) for offenders plus restitution by the offender to the victim's family.[11]

This evening's encounter with the Harveys has to count as one of the most painful of my life. Never have I met such unrequited grief. What, I wonder, can I possibly do to ease their pain? I am out of my depth. Driving across these dark waters of Lake Pontchartrain, I realize how vulnerable we all are. Faith Hathaway — dead. Loretta Bourque — dead. David LeBlanc — dead. Children snatched from their parents in the night. I think of my sister, Mary Ann. I think of Mama. I think of Mary Ann and Charlie's five children, especially Helen, my namesake. I think of Julie and Marcy, my brother Louie's little girls. When I get home I will telephone Mama. I want to hear that everyone is safe.

This Robert Willie, who is he? I recoil at the thought of him. How dare he calmly read law books and concoct arguments in his defense? He should fall on his knees, weeping, begging forgiveness from these parents. He should spend every moment of his life repenting his heinous deed. But, judging from my first visit, he seems to be in a world of his own, oblivious to the pain he has caused others. Remorse presupposes enough self-forgetfulness to feel the pain of others. Can Robert Willie do that? I doubt it and wonder whether his death sentence makes his own repentance even more difficult. *Someone is trying to kill him*, and this must rivet his energies on his own survival, not the pain of others.

The tragedy for the Harveys will be compounded because the murderer of their daughter, about to undergo a dramatic death at the hands of the state, is certain to draw media attention, which will carefully note what the condemned man eats at his last meal and his farewell words to the world — far more attention than his victim received. We remember the names of the executed — Gary Gilmore, John Spenkelink, Ted Bundy. Who remembers the names of their victims? Meanwhile, human rights advocates will protest the execution (in Louisiana before an execution, scores of protest letters from

Canadian and European Amnesty International members pour into the governor's office) — another kind of attention for the murderer, which to a victim's family is almost certain to seem misguided and unfair.

My hope for the Harveys is that eventually they will be able to overcome their terrible grief and once again live positive lives. How I can help them I am not sure, but I want to try. And Robert Willie? What can I possibly do for him? I will do what Millard Farmer asked me to do — accompany him, treat him with dignity — but I will also challenge him to take responsibility for his crime and to ask forgiveness of the Harveys.

Emotionally it's confusing to think of the Harveys and their needs alongside Robert Willie and his. Hearing the details of Faith's vicious murder, I find myself sucked into the Harveys' rage. But then I think of the death the state has in store for Robert Willie.

A few days after visiting the Harveys I visit Robert for the second time. I have a notebook on the front seat of the car. I'm not allowed to take it into the prison (only attorneys and news reporters can bring writing materials inside), but afterward I'll jot down notes from our conversation. I'm much more alert now than I was with Pat Sonnier. When the Pardon Board hearing comes up, facts about Robert's family life and background will be important. I feel that there isn't much time.

Robert comes into the visiting room. He is wearing a black knitted hat. He walks with a little bounce, poising momentarily on the balls of his feet. I dispense with preliminaries.

"I went to visit the Harveys," I say. "They told me about Faith's death. Robert, you raped and stabbed that girl and left her to rot in the woods. Why?"

"All right," he says, and he lights a cigarette. "I'm telling you what, ma'am, I'm real, real sorry that girl got killed, but like I told the police when they was questioning me, I didn't stab and kill that girl. Joe went crazy and started stabbin' her. I told them that when I gave my statement, and I offered to take a lie detector test then and there on the spot, but they wouldn't let me. I told them I don't kill women. I don't. But when Joe started stabbin' her, her hands went up and he told me to hold her hands and I did. But it was more instinct than anything, and with him slashing with that knife, there was blood everywhere, I was scared. I just did what he said, and afterwards we was runnin' around in those woods lost, goin' through brambles and mud and couldn't find the truck and I was some scared."

I groan inside. The truth. What's the truth? Not another one of those situations where two perpetrators each accuse the other and it's so difficult to ferret out the facts. He admits that he held Faith's hands. He did not come to her defense. Even if he's telling the truth and did not stab her himself, he is responsible for her death. Does he know what he did? And if he does, how can he live with himself?

"Robert," I say, "Vernon Harvey tells me that you taunted him in the courtroom. You said you'd never fry, is that true?"

"He said he'd see me fry and I said, 'The hell you will,'" Robert says. "I'd never show my inner feelin's out there in the courtroom, in public like that. Ever since I was a little boy I ain't ever showed my real feelin's. See, my daddy went to Angola when I was a baby. People would point to me and say, 'That's John Willie's kid,' and wham, there I am in a fight. My mama had her hands full in her own life, much less trying to take care of me. I don't blame her none for what's happened. She separated from my daddy when I was real young and married again, and me and my stepfather never got on too good. I'd stay with my grandmother sometime, my aunt and uncle sometime, my mother and stepfather sometime. By the time I was in seventh grade I was sniffin' glue, paint, gasoline, you name it. Me and Joe were loaded on Valium, acid, and booze when this happened with Faith Hathaway. I had this light airy feelin' inside. I hadn't slept in two nights."

I say, "Robert, drugs don't explain violence like this. Thousands of people take drugs and don't slash and rape and kill people. The Harveys told me about that young boy, Mark Brewster, and his girlfriend whom you and Joe kidnapped after you killed Faith. They say you raped the girl and stabbed the boy and shot him and tied him to a tree and left him to die. The boy's paralyzed now for the rest of his life and God knows about the emotional scars on the girl. Did you do that?"

I am keeping my voice low, but it's an effort. I am quivering inside.

He pauses. He always speaks in a measured way and softly. "Yeah," he says, "I let Joe Vaccaro call all the shots and I went along. I wasn't thinkin' straight.

"The only other time I was involved in hurting somebody bad, where they died, was when me and my cousin struggled in the woods with this drug dealer for a big hunk of money — $10,000. We was all three fighting in the river and me and my cousin held his head under the water and then dragged him out and left him on the bank. We thought he was just unconscious, but he ended up dead.

146

"But with that couple we kidnapped, Vaccaro told me to kill the boy and I took out my knife, which was pretty dull, and I cut him across the neck and punched it into his side, but not hard or deep 'cause I really didn't want to kill him, and I said to Joe, 'He won't die,' and then Joe came up and shot him in the head."

He shakes his head. "I was stupid to let myself get messed up with Joe Vaccaro. He was supposed to be such a tough dude. He had been to Angola and so I was saying, 'Hey, man, he's been to Angola.' All that week when we were doin' all this, I knew it was wrong. This voice kept going off in my head, 'This is wrong. This is wrong.' I was a damn fool."

"Have you ever told the Harveys that you're sorry?" I ask him.

"Well, ma'am that's hard to do because Vernon Harvey keeps holding these press conferences, mouthin' off about how he can't wait to see me fry. Personally, I think the guy is his own worst enemy. He just needs to let it go, man. The girl's dead now, and there's nothin' he can do to bring her back. Even watchin' me fry ain't gonna bring her back, but he won't let it go and he's just makin himself miserable, in my opinion."

"Robert," I say, "you understand, don't you, that you are the *last* person in the world with the right to say that to Vernon Harvey?"

"I guess you're right," he says, but he doesn't seem terribly convinced.

"Hell," Robert says, "it's hard, ma'am, to be having much sympathy for *them* when, here, they're tryin' to kill *me*. When somebody's after your hide, it kind of tends to occupy your mind, if you know what I mean."

"But look what these parents are going through," I say. "Their daughter raped and stabbed and left to die in the woods. What if someone did that to your mother? What would you want to do to them?"

"Kill 'em," he says. "I sure as hell would want to kill 'em."

I'm quiet then for a while.

I'm hoping he can take in his own words so he can feel the Harveys' pain. The quiet does not last long. He says, "I'm gonna be honest with you, ma'am, I believe in the death penalty in some instances, like for people who rape and torture little children. Messin' over adults is one thing, but little innocent kids? I'd pull the switch on them myself."

I have heard that prisoners are hardest on child molesters. I guess everybody's got a code of evil, a line beyond which they consider redemption impossible. But the irony jolts me. Here's a man condemned to death by the state and here he is defending the death penalty — not for himself, of course, only for *truly heinous* killers. And I think of what Camus said, that every murderer, when he kills, feels innocent, that he always feels excused by his particular circumstances (p. 191).[12]

I tell him that I think the state shouldn't have the power to kill anybody and that if the state is allowed to kill those who torture children, then why not those who kill old people, the mentally retarded, teenagers (close to home, but he doesn't get it), public officials, policemen? Where would it stop, I ask him, and who would decide?

He says he'll think about it, but he doesn't cede the point.

"Have you ever been close to death before?" I ask.

"Had someone shooting at me once," he says. "I was hiding behind a tractor in a barn and ping, ping, ping the pellets were hitting the metal on the tractor. That was a close call. My heart was racin' in my chest."

"Why was somebody shooting at you?"

"Well," he says, "he was the husband whose wife I was in bed with. He was supposed to be at work, but he walked in on us in their house one day, straight into the bedroom, and there we were. Me, I jumped up, grabbin' my pants and boots in my hand, and ran like hell for the barn, and there I am behind that tractor pullin' on my pants with one boot on and struggling to get the other boot on and *bam*, *bam*, those pellets were comin'.''

And Robert Willie moves into a warm stream of memories now, telling of a woman seven years his senior who was "mature" and how he could have a *real* conversation with her. "Those younger ones, they couldn't sit still, they were too active, you just couldn't sit and talk." He admits that in the beginning he was partly drawn to "the adventure of loving a married woman."

"We'd go to the woods with a bottle and a blanket. She liked what I offered her. I used to come and see her when her old man would be at work and she'd cook for me, you know, a romantic meal, and we'd sit there for hours and eat and talk. She had a lot of real good thoughts about things and she drew 'em out of me, plus my real feelin's about things, I could share them with her and she was the only one."

He tells me how one night she and her "old man" were at one of the lounges and he was there too. "I went up to their table casual-like, not even looking at her directly, talking to her brother-in-law, when I feel this foot under the table touchin' my leg and here she is askin' me if I want to dance. Well, I plumb liked to fell out. I was nervous. We danced. Her old man was mad as hell.

"I left town for a spell to work on some barges and when I got back my friends told me, 'Your woman moved out of state.' Well, I tracked her down. I got her address and me and my cousin drove two days and arrived at her house at 6:00 A.M. and there was her truck parked in front, but we didn't know if her old man was in there with her. My cousin, he was nervous, and he said we'd better *back* our car into the driveway so we could get the hell out of there if her old man showed up."

He chuckles and he is taking his time telling me all this, like someone who has some rare coins in a box and who opens the box and takes each coin and holds it in his hand and turns it over and looks at it and then clinks it back into the box. I don't rush him. I let him have his moment.

"So we checked out the scene and didn't see the guy and went in and she fed us, and my cousin fell asleep, and I was hoping she and I could have us a good, long hunk of time, and the phone rang and it was her old man and he was in jail, and I breathed easy and knew we had some time. Now that is one real good feeling, to know you've got a good-sized chunk of time with somebody you love. You're kind of like on this little island all by yourselves and nobody can get to you. I never experienced love with anyone like I did with her. It was when she moved away and I didn't have her to talk to anymore that I really started goin' heavy into drugs. I guess I was trying to fill the gap she left. I phoned her collect when I was in the federal pen in Marion a couple of years ago and she accepted the charges and we talked. I just wanted to hear her voice again. I had heard she was living with another man. I told her I just wanted her to be happy."

When he finishes I tell him that I don't know how much time we will have together but I want to make the most of it and share my best with him and that I am going to do my level best to invite him past some lines he's drawn — like not apologizing to the Harveys.

"If you do die," I say, "as your friend, I want to help you to die with integrity, and you can't do that, the way I see it, if you don't squarely own up to the part you played in Faith's death."

He is looking straight into my eyes. He is no whiner, and I appreciate that. Not much time. Have to talk straight and true.

I ask him if he has a Bible and if he ever reads it.

He says *yes* he has one and *yes* he reads it.

"Like W. C. Fields read his Bible?" I ask.

"Who?"

I explain that Fields was a famous comedian who claimed he read his Bible every day. When a skeptical friend asked, "Every day, Bill?" Fields said, "Yep, looking for loopholes."

He gives a little smile and says, no, it's more than loopholes he's after and that he reads his Bible late at night "when things settle down." He admits he never "got much religion" when he was growing up, but says he believes that Jesus died for him on the cross and will "take care" of him when he appears before the judgment seat of God.

I recognize the theology of "atonement" he uses: Jesus, by suffering and dying on the cross, "appeased" an angry God's demand for "justice." I know the theology because it once shaped my own belief, but I shed it when I discovered that its driving force was fear that made love impossible. What kind of God demands "payment" in human suffering?

But I figure now's not the time. Later, Robert and I can sort out theology.

To be truthful. To accept responsibility. Is this possible for Robert Lee Willie? I see at least one promising sign: he is pressing for better conditions for death-row inmates even though he'll probably be dead by the time the changes come about. I don't doubt that his motives are mixed. It's not pure altruism at work in him here. He likes to defy authority and the suit gives him new turf to "take 'em on."

I say, "You may want to check out some words of Jesus that might have special meaning for you: 'You shall know the truth and the truth will make you free.' It's in the Gospel of John, chapter 8."

"I'll do that. I'll check it out," he says.

Then he says, "I have a whole lot of stuff about my case — transcripts of my trials and newspaper clippings and legal papers — and maybe they would help you get a hold of things about me and my case faster."

I tell him I appreciate the trust.

"I tell you what, ma'am, I sure as hell don't trust nobody around this place — and that includes the chaplains who get their paychecks from the state just like other employees — but I do trust you. You're a fighter. I can't stand people that act like victims. That's why I don't much like niggers. They're always actin' like somebody owes 'em somethin.' Not just niggers. Chinks and spics, too."

Niggers? Chinks? Spics? We've got a long way to go, Robert and I. But I file it away for another day, another time. Not now. I am

150

standing up to leave. He stands, too. I see that he has tattoos: L-O-V-E on his fingers and a string of skulls across his wrist.

"Appreciate your visit, ma'am," he says.

I put my hand up to the mesh screen and he raises his handcuffed hands toward the screen but he can't quite reach. He's much smaller than Pat.

Several days later I get several hefty manila envelopes in the mail from Robert, and I start to sift and sort through trial transcripts and newspaper clippings. This man's organized, that's certain. File folders are neat and tagged. Newspaper articles are arranged chronologically. Here is a whole set of papers on the inmate suit to improve conditions on death row. I wade in.

The complaint is carefully typed. The grammar and spelling aren't perfect, but decent. Plaintiffs in the "Complaint for Declaratory and Injunctive Relief" declare themselves — three death-row inmates, Robert Willie among them — versus the defendants — the secretary of the Department of Corrections and the warden. It's a class-action suit and lists, in part, these grievances:

- Confinement in a six-by-eight-foot cell twenty-three hours a day.
- Inadequate lighting; in each cell there are no light fixtures; all light must come from lights on the tier.
- Telephone calls limited to one five-minute personal phone call per month.
- Inadequate heating and ventilation (in summer, one fan is turned on at the end of a hundred-yard tier with no cross-ventilation; the heat index in Louisiana can reach 115 degrees in July and August).

Bill Quigley, as it turns out, will be the attorney to see the suit settled for the inmates, eight years or so after Willie's initial filing. By the time the suit is settled the original plaintiffs (Robert Willie among them) will have been executed and the improvements gained will be modest: contact visits with attorneys and increased use of the telephone, plus a few other minor changes.

Once, when talking to Millard on the telephone, I mention the lawsuit to improve death-row conditions, and he says, "The prison officials consider these guys dead meat, anyway, know what I mean? Why worry about someone going to the dentist or having fresh ventilation or adequate recreation when they're planning to kill him anyway?"

Robert has told me that in Marion, the federal penitentiary, he had an excellent law library and he was "always in there digging into those books." Looking at the work he did on the suit, I can see — maybe for the first time in his life — he is honing his mind and his organizational abilities. Freed of drugs, he can read books, reflect, articulate his thoughts and opinions. True, there's self-interest in it, but maybe something more. Maybe for the first time in his life he has acquired knowledge and gained some authority and, perhaps, the satisfaction of being of service to others. He tells me how other inmates, out on the tier for their "hour," wend their way to his cell, asking him about legal issues in their "case" or how to go about getting their trial transcripts or how to use the Freedom of Information Act.

Then I read the newspaper articles.

Enter Robert Lee Willie, who addresses the judge as "Cap," smirks when the jury finds him guilty of murder, tells his mother to "dry up" when she weeps during his sentencing trial, and draws his hand menacingly like a knife across his throat when Mark Brewster appears in the courtroom. When Brewster's girlfriend appears, a young woman Robert raped, he winks and blows her a kiss.

And here are photographs: Robert when first arrested, with wild, long tangled hair; Robert, head shaved, hands and feet cuffed, looking at Vaccaro and grinning as they walk into the courthouse; Robert with a bandana on his head, caught close up by the camera, sneering.

Some incidents draw my attention:

> An officer had to write Vaccaro's confession because he could neither read nor write.
>
> Vaccaro, after first claiming Robert had shot Brewster, admitted in a second confession to shooting Brewster himself because he "wanted to put him out of his misery."

One file marked "Juvenile Record"[13] has a thick stack of papers in it. I leaf through and watch Robert Lee Willie go from boy to outlaw.

> When he's fourteen he shoplifts a bottle of wine from a convenience store.
>
> A few months later he and his cousin steal two horses.
>
> Then he's picked up for truancy, and there is this account: "While on patrol Sergeant Chatellier found RLW on the

Tchefuncte Bridge. He took him to his aunt's house but he got smart with Sgt. C. and he brought him to the station. While Robert was sitting in the office, he stated he wanted to go to jail and told me he didn't care where his mother was and didn't want to go back."

Then, at the Tasty Donut Shop at two o'clock in the morning, Robert, now sixteen years old, is picked up by police for threatening bodily harm with a broken Coke bottle to his uncle, who was telling him he ought to be home.

He serves five months in the Louisiana Training Institute, the juvenile correctional facility.

He returns and the offenses mount: theft of a checkbook; burglaries of Jim's Chickentown, United Utilities, a neighbor's summer home; unauthorized use of "moveables" (a neighbor's truck); carrying a concealed weapon; driving while intoxicated; aggravated assault on a police officer . . .

He's in and out of jail. When he's twenty years old, he gets a suspended sentence of three years' hard labor for burglary and serves six months in the St. Tammany Parish Jail. He escapes by jumping from a third-story window. Shortly afterward he turns himself in to authorities. The report reads:

> Subject was in the woods behind Wymers Store. Subject came out to the store and called the sheriff's office and said he would like to give his self up, that he was at the store and would wait for the deputies. Deputies arrived and arrested the subject . . . subject was transported to Charity Hospital in New Orleans because he could not walk on his feet [he had jumped three stories] and had cuts and scratches on his feet and arms.

Between 1972 and 1979, when he was twenty-one years old, Robert Willie was arrested thirty times. His last year of schooling is ninth grade. A tattoo of "Pam" appears when he's sixteen, "Peggy" at seventeen, and at nineteen, a skull and crossbones. One of the reports gives his name as "Little John Willie." During one of his stints in the St. Tammany Parish Jail he meets Joseph Vaccaro.

I review Robert's trial transcripts and other legal documents. I see that Robert had been awarded a new capital sentencing trial by the Louisiana Supreme Court on grounds of improper arguments by Assistant District Attorney, Herbert R. Alexander.[14] Urging the jury away from a life sentence, Alexander had argued that later in time a governor, who would "not know the facts of this case," might release Robert from prison. He also argued that if the jury decided on death, the final responsibility, in fact, was not theirs because there would be numerous appeals and reviews of the case by state and federal courts. "So the buck really don't stop with you. The buck starts with you."[15]

I read the appeal petition to the Federal Fifth Circuit Court, filed by Ronald J. Tabak, an attorney whose Wall Street firm has volunteered to collaborate with Millard on Robert's appeal. I am struck by the substance, the thoroughness of the arguments. It's a thick document, 170 pages, bound with a blue cardboard cover. On the front page in large black letters is stamped "Pauper Case."

In the brief Tabak puts forth fourteen arguments on Robert's behalf.[16] I don't understand some of the fine-tuned legal points, but several of the claims seem startling and obvious.

One is that pretrial publicity before Robert's second sentencing trial was so prejudicial that it required a change of venue. (Robert's second sentencing trial was held in the same parish courthouse as the first.) Tabak recounts the intense media coverage surrounding the first trial. The media had referred to the case as "the worst crime in the history of Washington Parish ... the trial of the decade." The district attorney was quoted as having referred to Willie and Vaccaro as "animals." Some newspaper articles reported that Willie had "confessed" to having raped and killed Faith Hathaway and included reports of prior arrests and the fact that his father, who had previously killed another man, was in jail for attempted murder. After trial and sentencing, the media repeatedly referred to the fact that Vaccaro had received life and Willie death, "leaving the impression," Tabak points out, "that Willie was more culpable than Vaccaro."

At voir dire for the second sentencing trial forty-seven of the fifty-two prospective jurors admitted to hearing of the case. In an affidavit, a jury expert brought in by Tabak's firm to study the possibility of bias on Robert's jury testified that people, convinced of the defendant's guilt, might lie at the voir dire out of a feeling that they could "get justice" by getting on the jury. She then cited cases of two such jurors, who first admitted to having an opinion on the case but within a few hours denied they had an opinion. There was one pool of jurors for both Robert and Vaccaro; and jurors who had been struck from one trial presented themselves for the other.

Tabak argues that the Louisiana Supreme Court, which reviewed the case and agreed that no change of venue was warranted, did not have the benefit of the jury expert's findings about biased jurors because she had been hired only after Tabak's firm — with financial resources to hire experts — took on the case.

But perhaps the most telling instance of impropriety during jury selection was this: "At least four members (one third of the jury) that convicted Petitioner were present when the attorney for Joseph Vaccaro stated [during Vaccaro's jury-selection process] that Robert Willie had killed Faith Hathaway. These assertions were made in the upstairs courtroom in which Vaccaro was being tried, only minutes before these jurors were sent to the downstairs courtroom to participate as jurors in [Willie's] trial."

Tabak argues that this statement was "far more devastating than any evidence used against Willie at trial and completely inconsistent with his defense. But neither Willie, his trial attorney, nor the trial judge knew that these highly prejudicial statements had been heard by four of the jurors."

Again, Tabak says, the Louisiana Supreme Court had been unaware that these jurors were exposed to such prejudicial statements because the defense attorney had not himself known of them.

Tabak ends the petition by citing claims of ineffectiveness of counsel, especially the defense counsel's admitted lack of preparation for both the sentencing trials (several days before both trials the defense counsel had informed the judge that he was not prepared). In the petition Tabak argues:

> The only mitigation witness called at the first trial was Robert's mother and at the second, an aunt, and even she was not prepared for the testimony. Five close family members said that they would have been glad to testify but were not contacted. Each would have brought out about Robert's unsettled childhood bereft of adult guidance, his long-standing drug habit, his troubled mental state.

By contrast, Tabak, points out, Vaccaro's attorney had amply documented his client's troubled childhood and drug-abuse history and his client had received a life sentence.[17]

In August 1984, the Fifth Circuit Court of Appeals denied the petition and a request for rehearing, and on November 12, the U.S. Supreme Court refused to hear the case. Now it is mid-November, and all that stands between Robert Lee Willie and the electric chair is the Pardon Board and the governor.[18]

I can hear the words San Quentin guards used to yell when a death-row inmate was let out of his cell: "Dead man walking."

CHAPTER
8

"*We've got to get Robert off this political prisoner kick,*" *John Craft* says to me as I walk into his office. He is preparing for Robert's Pardon Board hearing scheduled for November 19, one week away, and he tells me that Robert seems determined to expose the "politics" in his death sentence. John shakes his head "A surefire strategy for defeat with a Pardon Board, if ever I heard one."

Millard Farmer has recruited John to serve as local counsel in Robert's case, which means representing him at the Pardon Board hearing. Marcia Blum, the attorney director of the newly formed Louisiana Capital Defense Project, has been helping John prepare for the hearing, and Millard has been offering advice over the phone.

I sit opposite John in a spacious room in his new French Quarter office. French doors, flagstone floors, eggshell-colored walls. Not much furniture yet, only his desk at one end of the room and his partner's desk stuck casually in the center. There are piles of legal folders stacked in heaps along the walls, file cases, no secretary in sight. John's been busy preparing for the hearing and hasn't had much time to settle into the new place.

He's soft-spoken, serious, but not officious. Mid to late thirties, I figure. Dark-rimmed glasses, balding, a black close-cropped beard. I like his sober, reasoned energy.

157

I feel my stomach muscles tighten as we begin to talk about the hearing. The Harveys will be there with their grief and loss and their terrible need to see Robert Willie die. And there's the personality of Robert himself — defiant, remorseless. I'm afraid that Robert might smart-mouth Vernon Harvey or one of the Board members.

John tells me he'll speak first and present the legal issues, then Robert's mother, then me.

I'm dreading it. It will be the same board that took only an hour to uphold Pat Sonnier's sentence. Since Pat's execution, two other condemned prisoners have stood before them — Timothy Baldwin, executed in September, and Earnest Knighton, executed just a week ago.

Theoretically, pardon boards are supposed to have wide latitude to dispense mercy. They are not bound by previous legal rulings of the courts and may give full sway to whatever heart or conscience dictates. But, being appointees of the governor (and subject to removal at his discretion), they can hardly ignore the wishes of their patron. There are no special qualifications required by law for the job, so Board positions are natural slots for political appointments.[1] It would be two years before Howard Marsellus, chairperson of the Board, would be sentenced for taking bribes.

Joe Doss, an Episcopalian priest and cocounsel for Earnest Knighton, told me that when he was preparing for Knighton's Pardon Board hearing, someone close to the governor had said that the present board — sympathetic to Edwards's personal aversion to the death penalty — avoids putting "pressure" on Edwards in death-penalty cases. Now, as we prepare for Robert's hearing, I wonder what not putting "pressure" on the governor means.

"What do you think about the politics in Robert's case?" I ask John.

John tells me that the St. Tammany Parish D.A., Marion Farmer (not related to Millard), who is prosecuting the case against Robert, had been up against stiff opposition in his bid for reelection at the time of the Hathaway murder. Shortly after Willie and Vaccaro's arrest, Farmer publicly stated that he would seek the death penalty.

A murder case which Marion Farmer prosecuted in 1978 had sparked much of the criticism against him in his reelection bid. Two ex-offenders from New York, John DeGirolama and Vincent Pellicci, had kidnapped a teenage couple at gunpoint and brought them into a wooded area in Farmer's district. There, after holding them captive for several hours, they fired four shots into their victims, killing eighteen-year-old Rachelle Rees and injuring her boyfriend. The parish grand jury indicted the men for first-degree murder, but Farmer, wanting to avoid the cost and risk of a trial (he might not get a death-penalty verdict) and the lengthy appeals of a capital case, had let both men plead guilty to second-degree murder, which carries a life sentence.

Rachelle Rees's parents had petitioned a state court to force Farmer to seek the death penalty, protesting that his decisions for indictment were based on "whim and caprice." But their petition failed.[2]

"No doubt about the politics in Robert's case," John says to me, "but the Pardon Board hearing isn't the place to bring it up."

"I'll talk to Robert about it," I tell John. Straight from this meeting I'm going to Angola to visit Robert.

The Louisiana countryside, usually so vibrantly, verdantly green, is taking on a brownish hue. With the trees going bare I can see deep into the swamps, which cover the first fifteen miles or so out of New Orleans. The furry cypress needles have turned to rust. They're still holding on, but not for long.

Pat had died in spring when the flowers and trees and grass were exploding with life. If Robert dies, he will die in winter.

Faith Hathaway had also died in the spring.

I imagine her coming from beyond the grave to speak at this Pardon Board hearing.

I picture her speaking of love swallowing up hate and all she knows is love now and that she hopes her mother and stepfather can move on with their lives and not worry about avenging her death because she's past all that, she's past all that is negative and downward and hurtful and she occupies another kind of universe and she hopes they can occupy this universe too.

Yes, I can picture her saying that.

I can also picture her pointing to Robert Willie and saying that because of all she has suffered, this man, her killer, should be made to suffer and die and the angry desire to avenge her death is righteous and noble and holy as God is holy.

I know which of these speeches Vernon and Elizabeth are likely to hear.

I've passed the sign: "Do not despair, you will soon be there"; and now I see open sky ahead and Angola.

I get my pass from the visitor center and walk over to death row. I'm bringing a little money for Robert so he can buy coffee. During the last visit I had asked him if he needed anything and he had said, "Nah," and when I asked him how much he had in his account, he said, "About two dollars and forty cents."

He steps into the visiting booth with his black knitted cap on his head. He likes that cap.

"Glad you're here, ma'am" he says. "Thanks for the coffee money."

I tell him about the ride up and the way November is settling into the swamps and he says he can see the trees turning there on the hill near the tier and we talk a bit about seasons and how Louisiana really doesn't experience dramatic change, not like up North — small talk, but not for long. The Pardon Board hearing looms large.

He's brought a copy of his presentation — neatly typed, four pages.

It begins: "There are a few things that I would like to say, considering this will be my last time before the Courts and the Judicial System." I listen as he reads. I am standing up, my head close to the screen (tired of sitting after the three-hour drive). I think of my past students giving oral reports at Cabrini Elementary — lanky seventh- and eighth-grade boys, shifting from foot to foot, stumbling and mumbling the words, shy about standing there in front of me, their black-robed mentor, and their classmates, especially the girls. Now I hear this twenty-six-year-old man read the words of what undoubtedly will be the most important "oral report" of his life. And from what I know about his schooling — or lack of it — chances are he has never made a presentation before a group before.

He reads evenly, without any sort of inflection. Understatement, every bit of it, these words to win grace, to save his life. But his words are stamped with his pride. He begins by saying that he did not kill Faith Hathaway and that he's not going to "beg" for his life, and then he says, "This whole case was politically motivated from the first beginning," and tells how D.A. Marion Farmer "had got himself into the hot seat by letting them New York murderers cop a plea which then led Mr. Farmer to tighten up and come down hard on my case, using me as a stepping stone in his political career. Before the election Mr. Farmer stated publicly that I would go to my death before the first of the year."

As he reads on I find out why, after his arrest, he had changed his mind and given a statement to officials about the Hathaway murder without an attorney present.

"The District Attorney investigator [Assistant District Attorney

160

William Alford, Jr.] told me that at the present time my mother and stepfather were being arrested [for driving Robert and Vaccaro to Mississippi, helping them to evade arrest] and he was going to make sure that my Mother got the maximum sentence if I didn't tell him my involvement in this crime. After I gave them the statement I asked the District Attorney investigator if he would help my Mother, and he said he couldn't promise me anything but he would put in a word for her."[3]

Robert argues that his court-appointed counsel was ineffective. "After I received the federal prison terms of life my state attorney told me that he didn't really have to prepare for my charge in the state [capital murder] because I would never be turned over to Louisiana. He said that he would go through the usual procedure and put on what defense we had, which was nothing.

"He came to see me in New Orleans and brought me over a hundred news clippings of my case. On the same day he visited me he said somebody had dumped his garbage cans full of garbage all over his yard and he said he didn't know if he was making a mistake by taking my case or not."

He ends by saying:

"If I would have had a proper defense without all the pre-trial publicity and an attorney that wanted to put forth an effort to really give me the due process of law, which the Constitution of the United States of America says that I'm entitled to, I know I wouldn't have been found guilty and sentenced to death because I would have been given the opportunity to probably plead guilty to a lesser offense.

"I know the death of Miss Hathaway has caused a lot of pain and sorrow for her family members and I truly regret everything that has happened. But my death is not going to bring Miss Hathaway back to this earth. Thank you for listening to me."

I tell him I agree that politics did play a role in his case, but I tell him why the hearing is not the place to raise the issue.

He listens intently, smoking and looking down and taking in everything I say, and he says he's going to have to think about it.

"Your poor Mama," I say, thinking of her terrible conflict — caught between the law which forbade her to assist escaping law-breakers and her maternal instinct to help her son.

"She did six months in jail," Robert says, "and you *know* I'm mad about that. They double-dealed me. I gave them the statement without a lawyer there, which my better judgment told me not to because I couldn't see my mother going to jail. She's not strong anyways." And he says that his mother has had "a real hard life" (he always says this) and has worked hard all her life — as a cook, a maid, a waitress. "She didn't have a criminal record," he says. "They could've given her a suspended sentence. They were mad at me and took it out on her."

He says he's not so sure he wants her to come to the Pardon Board hearing. "She's just going to bust out cryin' and won't be able to say nothin' 'cause she's gonna be so tore up. It's just not worth it to put her through all that. And she's gonna have to sit there and hear the Harveys and the D.A."

I try to think of Mama in a situation like this, having to plead for the life of my brother, Louie, in such a public setting before such an unresponsive group.

But I can't get the picture. It's just too far-fetched to imagine. It's hard to know what Robert's mother must be experiencing. She must feel that she's walking around in a place where trees grow with their roots in the air and birds fly upside down. She must feel that she can't get out of a nightmare.

I find myself now saying to Robert some of the same words I had said to Pat, words drawn from some force that taps deep and runs strong, and I tell him that despite his crime, despite the terrible pain he has caused, he is a human being and he has a dignity that no one can take from him, that he is a son of God.

"Ain't nobody ever called me no son of God before," he says, and smiles. "I've been called a son-of-a-you-know-what lots of times but never no son of God."

He doesn't have a chance with the Pardon Board, I know that, and I think he must know it, too. I'm starting to count the weeks left in his life — four weeks? six weeks?

I glance at my watch. It's almost time to go.

"Okay, I'll let the political stuff go," he says. "I see what you're sayin' that it won't help my case even though it's all of it true. I mean, this whole death penalty ain't nothin' but politics. The Pardon Board, they're all a bunch of political appointees who do whatever the governor wants. But I'll take my ballpoint pen and scratch out those parts."

"You may want to think about your mother," I say. "I know it's bound to be upsetting for her to be part of this hearing, and you'd like to save her from it, but if you die, after you're gone, it may be bad for her if she didn't have the chance to speak for you. Maybe she will always wonder if she had been there for you, maybe it would have made a difference."

"Yeah," he says, he'll think about that. It's an angle he hadn't thought of.

I freeze with dread at the thought of the hearing. But he seems resigned. Maybe he's found a way to steel himself not to expect anything.

I put my hand up to the screen to tell him good-bye.

"See you at the hearing, Robert," I say.

"I want you to know I got my pride. I'm not grovelin' in front of those people. I don't grovel to nobody," he says.

It feels odd going through the visitor center at Angola on a Monday. Usually visitors are not allowed on Mondays and Tuesdays. Guards ask each of us coming for the Pardon Board hearing to state our names so they can check them off a typed list. When the inmate is to be present, I find out, the hearing is held here at Angola. Which gives my heart a turn when I remember that Pat did not attend his hearing.

Visitor rules are relaxed today. No pat searches, just metal detectors, and women are allowed purses and men don't have to empty their pockets for inspection. Anyone desiring to attend the hearing has had to contact the Department of Corrections beforehand and give his or her name.

Marcia Blum and Liz Scott, my writer friend, have driven to the prison with me. Liz is at work on an article for *New Orleans Magazine*.[4] Next week she plans to interview Robert Willie and the Harveys.

Through the window of the visitor center I see a yellow Cadillac driving up to the front gate. Marcia whispers to me that the people in the car are Pardon Board members.

I have my plea for Robert typed out and I feel ready. No, not ready. I feel cold and tight. I keep telling myself that we are going to do our best, we are going to make the best presentation we can and the Board is summarily going to approve this killing. I have spent hours and hours trying to get the right words. I prayed, I wrote, I scratched out words and wrote new ones in the margins, I consulted with Bill Quigley and some of the Sisters, then prayed again. Preparing for Pat's hearing seems simple compared to this. Then I had hope that the right words could matter.

The hearing is being held in the big meeting room at the main prison, the same room where Eddie and I visit. At the far end of the room there is a long table where the Board will be seated.

Marcia, Liz, and I sign the book on the "defendant's" side. I remember this from Pat's hearing, how each person must declare for the defendant or the state. Inside the rooms chairs are divided by an aisle down the middle. Blue chairs for the state's "side" are on the left, and I see the Harveys there. Red chairs to the right for Robert Lee Willie's "side." There's a group with the Harveys, maybe fifteen people. On Robert's "side" there's his mother, John Craft, Marcia, Liz and me. John is already sitting at the defendant's table, sorting through papers.

I look into the face of Elizabeth, Robert's mother, middle-aged, in blue polyester pants and a white sweater. Her hair is short and sitting rather flat on her head. She has deep circles under her eyes. I had met her briefly a few days ago when Marcia and I helped her prepare for this hearing. I put my arms around her. She says, her voice quivering, "I don't know what I'm going to say. I just don't know what I can say to these people." Marcia and I sit on either side of her. "Don't worry about the words," I tell her. "You're here. You're his mother and you're here, that's everything." But the words don't seem to help much. She smokes one cigarette after another. Her hands are trembling.

I leave Marcia and Liz with her and make my way over to the Harveys. "So, we meet again," I say to Vernon as I shake his hand. Elizabeth looks pretty in her long-sleeved blouse and skirt. Vernon has on a tan polyester suit, a white shirt and a dark tie. I go with small talk — the drive, the weather. Vernon points slyly toward the Board members (there are three black members of the board and two whites) and says, "*They* outnumber us, but maybe we'll still win." He lowers his voice when he says this, using that confidential tone that people use with a trusted friend.

Remembering Marsellus, the black chairperson, and the way he had voted with the others to uphold Pat's death sentence, I tell Vernon that I don't think the race of the board members will make a difference.

I see Robert, legs and hands cuffed, coming into the room with guards on either side. His hair is nicely combed. No black knitted hat. Even with the leg irons scraping across the tile floor, he has that cocky spring in his walk. He is smiling. I tell Vernon maybe I'll get to see them afterward, and I move back to Robert's "side."

The guards escort Robert up to the defense table and remove his handcuffs. They remain standing nearby. For the moment, John has stepped away and Robert is at the table alone. I go up to him and greet him and ask if he'd like a cup of coffee. He nods and says, "Thank you, ma'am," and I bring the coffee in a Styrofoam cup.

The prosecution takes its place at its table; two men, District Attorney Marion Farmer and Assistant William Alford, Jr.

The Board members begin taking their places at the front table. Two television cameras from local stations are mounted on rolling tripods on the side aisles. Chairperson Marsellus announces the procedures and rules. He says that there is no need to give lengthy speeches because the Board has received copies of the presentations and has already studied them. He encourages everyone to be brief and to the point.

John Craft goes first. He says that despite the court proceedings, "serious issues remain unsolved, which cast doubt upon the constitutionality and fairness of the proceedings" which have sentenced Robert Willie to death. And then he ticks them off, every one of them I've read and studied in the writs and appeals: the inept attorney, the prejudicial pretrial publicity, the failure of the defense to present documentation of Robert's substance abuse during his sentencing trials. He adds that to his knowledge he knows of no other prisoner who has been turned over by federal authorities for state execution. He ends with a quote from Dostoyevsky, that famous quote about how a society is judged not by how it treats its upstanding citizens, but by how it treats its criminals.

Robert's mother is called to testify. She comes to the table and sits by her son and does not look at him. He doesn't look at her either; nor does she touch him. They both look at a spot on the table in front of them. The television moves in. Cameras flash. Anyone with an eye for drama knows this is a special moment: the mother pleading for her son. But Elizabeth can only blurt out a few words. She says that Robert had had a hard life, that . . . She stops and her eyes fill with tears and she puts her head down into her hands and tries to continue, "but he was a good boy," and bursts into irretrievable sobs. Her head is down and Robert's head is down, and John Craft gets up and takes Robert's mother by the arm and leads her out of the room. I know that John needs to be with Robert, so I get up and go out to be with Elizabeth. All I can do is hold her in my arms and let her sob. She keeps saying, "I'm sorry. I'm sorry. I'm sorry," and I try to comfort her, saying that I am sure her tears are a far more eloquent testimony for her son than any words could ever be.

When I return to the room, Robert is already into his statement.

He is sticking strictly to what he has prepared. His voice is calm and clear. His arms lie alongside either side of his typed pages. Sometimes he looks up toward the faces of the Board, but mostly he looks down at his typed pages.

Listening to Robert, I struggle to stave off fierce feelings of futility. Maybe by some miracle the Board will vote to spare Robert's life. *Please, God, help me*, I pray. My heart is pounding in my ears. I am the last from the "red chairs" to speak.

I sit next to Robert and put my hand on his blue-denimed arm stretched out on the table. I bring the microphone close. The same feeling of strength and calmness that I had in the death house with Pat comes upon me now. I take a deep breath and look up at the five faces. One day, I feel sure, all the death instruments in this country — electric chairs and gas chambers and lethal injection needles — will be housed behind velvet ropes in museums. But not now.

"I come before this Board of Pardons today to plead for the life of Robert Willie. You've met me before. I was spiritual adviser to Elmo Patrick Sonnier, and I came before you last spring to plead for his life. He is dead now, executed on April 5, 1984."

I speak in a quiet, steady stream.

I tell them about Pat's death in the electric chair, the result of a decision made like this one today. I tell them of his funeral and his devastated family. I tell them of the guards in the death house who pulled me aside to say that they didn't want to be part of the killing but it was part of their job and they had families to support.

I tell them about my visit to the Harveys and how they have shared their terrible pain with me, a pain and a loss that no parent should have to bear, and that in no way do I condone or excuse the violence that has been done to Faith Hathaway and her parents.

I tell them that yes, Robert Willie is responsible for his actions and needs to pay society for his deed, and that he should live in a restricted prison environment so that he cannot hurt other people again.

I know, I say, that when the prosecuting attorney stands before them he will say that the courts of appeal have scrutinized Robert's case and found no evidence of ineffective counsel, but, if we are honest, we must admit that in our courts there are two systems of justice — one for the rich, who can afford expert counsel, and one for people like Robert Willie — and that is why only poor people will ever appear before this board. I ask them to consider that if their own son or daughter had received the kind of defense Robert received, would they not protest strenuously? Will you dare, I ask, to condemn the unfairness inherent in the judicial system which metes out one brand of justice for the rich and one for the poor? Or (and I know this is the heart), as a body whose mandate is to dispense compassion, will you simply stand behind the court's decision and approve this man's death? I trace for them the bureaucratic process designed to distance them from the killing about to take place, and I call on them to take personal responsibility for the role they are playing in the killing of this man if they uphold his death sentence.

When I finish speaking, Mr. Marsellus says that I have to understand that the Board members have not made the death-penalty law, nor do they enforce it. They only offer a recommendation to the governor and in no way can they be held personally responsible for anyone's execution.

"What would happen, Mr. Marsellus," I ask, "if each time a condemned man appeared before you, the members of this board began recommending life, not death? What if you shared with the governor that you find the death penalty so morally troubling that you cannot bring yourself any longer to give your vote of approval to these executions? What would happen then, Mr. Marsellus?"

Some members of the Board look fidgety. There is the rustling of papers. Marsellus declares a short break before the state presents its case.

I rise from the table to go back to my place.

"Thank you, ma'am, for what you said," Robert says, looking up at me.

The prosecution's presentation is much shorter than ours. Very short. Very effective. And in part, very true — that Robert lacks remorse and tends to blame everybody but himself.

Marion Farmer reviews the heinous details of Faith Hathaway's murder. He shows the Board the pictures of her nude, decomposed body and the results of the autopsy report. He says that Robert Willie has done many, many horrible things but that he always blames his accomplice or his lawyers. He says that Robert is arrogant and has shown no remorse, and that even here today he is still arrogant, saying that he is not here to beg for his life. He enumerates all of the courts that have reviewed Robert's case and points out that he had not one but two sentencing trials, and that both times the juries saw fit to sentence him to death. He asks the Board to give Robert the same consideration that he gave Faith Hathaway when he and Vaccaro led her nude into a cave and raped her and stabbed her seventeen times in the throat and then let her bleed to death and rot in the woods. "Robert Willie has basically given up his right to live on this earth," Farmer says. "He did these things. He should point the finger to himself. It was his own choice."

Then Vernon and Elizabeth Harvey speak. Vernon says that all the chances Robert Willie has been given in the past have been futile, that he deserves to die for what he did, not only to Faith, but to . . . and he begins to cry. Elizabeth tells the Board that it has been a long, hard four years, waiting on the endless court proceedings and appeals. It's been, she says, a long wait for justice, but now, finally, if the Board offers no interference, now at last, justice can be done. Her daughter's life was cut off while she was still young and she never really got much of a chance to live it, never got the chance to join the Army, which she had planned to do because she loved her country and felt she had a debt to pay for the freedoms and way of life she enjoyed here. She concludes by saying, "Please don't let him live to take another life because even after taking Faith's life, he tried again. There is really only one way we can be absolutely sure that he will never kill again. I wish my daughter was here to further enjoy her life, but she isn't. I would like Mr. Robert Lee Willie's life to end here."

The hearing has lasted about two hours. Marsellus announces that the Board will retire to make its decision.

I know it won't take them long.

After twenty minutes of deliberation Marsellus announces the decision to Robert: "The Pardon Board unanimously recommends to the governor that your sentence stand."

Robert gives a cocky smile when he hears the verdict. The guards come up right away to put the handcuffs on, ready to take him back to his cell. When I go up to him, he says in a whisper, "I think it was Mrs. Harvey's patriotic speech about America there at the end that did me in. I think I was winnin' before that little part of her speech."

I am amazed at his naïveté. He thought he had a chance.

When he leaves the room to return to his cell, he looks around and smiles and walks with his jaunty little walk.

His mother sits in a heap in the chair.

I look across the room to the Harveys. Friends are patting them on the back, hugging them.

I talk with Elizabeth, Robert's mother, for a while and confer with John Craft about next steps, and when I turn to leave, I see that the Harveys have already gone.

A Conversation with Howard Marsellus

On September 12, 1991, I finally get a telephone call through to the home of Howard Marsellus in Rowlett, Texas. It has taken some doing to find him. I had heard that he had moved to Texas, but I wasn't sure where, and the only leads I had were not panning out. But I read an article about Marsellus in the prison magazine, *The Angolite*,[5] and through it I have been able to locate him. I ask him what he thinks now, in retrospect, of his role on the Louisiana Pardon Board. He seems eager to talk.

A little more than a year ago he was released from the federal correctional institution in Fort Worth, where he served eighteen months for accepting bribes while serving as chairperson of the Louisiana Pardon Board.[6]

In 1986 a state undercover agent had caught him accepting a five-thousand-dollar payoff for an Angola inmate's pardon. The *Angolite*'s article recounts how he is trying to reconstruct his life and get back into public-school education, where he had worked for twenty-eight years (successfully, I hear) before his appointment as chair of the Pardon Board by Governor Edwin Edwards. It's hard now, he says, to get a job. It's been a little more than a year since his incarceration and he still hasn't gotten work. "So, I'm still paying for what I did," he says. "When people hear I've been to prison, they get scared off, especially education supervisors and administrators."

I think of the Board members in the sleek pale-yellow Cadillac pulling up to the entrance of the penitentiary before Robert Willie's hearing. I think of the conversation that Millard Farmer, Joe Nursey, and I had with Marsellus before Pat Sonnier's hearing and how he had so readily agreed with us that the death penalty was biased against poor people and people of color and then voted to uphold Pat's death sentence. (During Marsellus's term on the Board every request for clemency of condemned murderers was denied.)

I think of the last words I heard this man say to me at the end of my testimony at Robert Willie's hearing: that the members of the Board hadn't made the law and they were not personally responsible for this man, or any man, dying in the electric chair.

Marsellus now talks about how good it is to sleep at night with a clean conscience, how blessed he is to have a wife and two daughters who love him, and how glad he is to be out of all the politics, all the corruption.

"I did it. I was wrong. I confessed to my crime and I paid for it," he says.

The *Angolite* article told how in 1984 Marsellus had been considering a bid for the state legislature when a "high-ranking" politician in the Edwards administration had offered him a deal: if he would agree not to run for the legislative seat, he would be appointed chairman of a top administrative board. It was well understood, he explains to me, that accepting chairmanship of the Pardon Board required something in return from him. That something was "loyalty." He said he had promised that he would be a "team player."

I tell him that I had heard that while on the Board he had once asked to witness an execution. Was that true?

"Yes," he says "Tim Baldwin. I asked to witness his execution [September 10, 1984]. I wanted to *see* what we as a board were voting to uphold, and I had grave misgivings about Baldwin's guilt."

Bill Quigley had presented Baldwin's case before the Board. I had been at that hearing and watched Bill ask a number of questions about Baldwin's case that pointed to his innocence. Bill had listed each argument in neat black letters on large white charts (he is a teacher as well as an attorney), and after presenting each argument, he would say, "No court, no jury except you has ever heard this information."

Baldwin had been convicted of bludgeoning to death Mary James Peters, his child's eighty-five-year-old godmother, while robbing her home. He had protested his innocence, even when offered a chance for a life sentence in return for a guilty plea.

There were two crucial but conflicting pieces of evidence at the center of the case. One was Baldwin's alibi that he could not have committed the murder because he was at a motel some distance away and could not have made the drive from the motel to the scene of the murder in the time proposed by the prosecutor. The second was the testimony of his girlfriend and codefendant, Marilyn Hampton, that he had committed the murder. Hampton received a life sentence for her involvement in the crime.

"I tended to believe Baldwin's alibi and not his girlfriend," Marsellus says, "but the D.A. claimed he had sent an investigator to make the drive from the motel to the scene of the crime and Baldwin could, in fact, have made the drive and committed the murder. But the D.A.'s version didn't satisfy me. I've seen — you wouldn't believe — the games that some of these D.A.'s play. But

DEAD MAN WALKING

I'll tell you about this loyalty thing and what it exacted from me and how I let it compromise the deepest moral values I had. When we left the hearing and went behind closed doors to decide Baldwin's fate, I just couldn't convince myself that the man was really guilty and deserved to die, and right there from the room where we were meeting I called the governor's office. His chief legal counsel, Bill Roberts, came to the phone, and when I told him about the case — I was upset, I was crying — I said that if our job was to dispense mercy, that this seemed as clear a case for mercy that I had yet seen, but Roberts told me that I knew the governor did not like to be confronted with these cases and wanted us to handle it."

" 'Handle it' — what does that mean?" I ask.

"That's the loyalty bit. That's the team player bit. Roberts told me, 'Why do you think we appointed you, Howard? This is why you're chair of this committee. If you can't hack it, we'll just have to replace you with someone who can.' He wasn't saying this in a mean or nasty way, he was just reminding me of the loyalty required of me when I took the job."

I want to make sure I understand.

"Are you saying that if the Pardon Board recommends the death sentence, then the governor has something to stand behind and can say that he's only following the recommendation of the Board, and that way he doesn't have to face the political fallout of commuting a sentence? Is that the way it worked?"

"You got it right," Marsellus says.

After the telephone conversation with Roberts, Marsellus says, he knew what he had to do. The Board rendered its decision to uphold Baldwin's death sentence.

Marsellus says that a couple days after the Baldwin hearing, C. Paul Phelps, head of the Department of Corrections, came into his office to expedite the "deal" that had been worked out between the governor and Baldwin's girlfriend. Her sentence was to be cut to time served, and Marsellus was to see that her case was "expedited" by the Board.

"The way things went down," Marsellus says, "Baldwin was executed, and his girlfriend was let out of prison. She's out today. You can check it out.* But listen to this — and it was Phelps (then secretary of the Department of Corrections) who told me about this — he was there at these meetings between Edwards and Baldwin's girl-

---

*I checked. Marilyn Hampton, Baldwin's girlfriend, sentenced on October 18, 1978, to life imprisonment for first-degree murder, was released from prison on June 9, 1986.[7]

friend that I'm telling you about now. See, you have to understand that, after Baldwin's Board hearing, the press had been badgering the governor about Baldwin's possible innocence and whether he was going to let him be executed. Under this pressure Edwards decided to double-check the testimony of Baldwin's girlfriend.

"The governor went in his helicopter to the women's prison in St. Gabriel to meet Baldwin's girlfriend, but when he met her, she had her lawyer sitting there at her side, and the lawyer told the governor to come back the next day because her client needed time to consult with her.

"You understand, of course, the implications of that, don't you?" Marsellus says. "The lawyer wanted to negotiate a reduced sentence for her client in exchange for the testimony she would give. So, the governor flew back to the Governor's Mansion and then flew back the next day to talk with the woman again — Phelps was there both times — and this time she testified, as she had at the trial, that yes, Baldwin had committed the murder. Her testimony helped salve Edwards's conscience. It's what he wanted to hear — that the man about to die was guilty. But Edwards had to have known what was really going on and that in all probability the woman was lying to save her own skin, to get out of prison. To have the governor of the state come and this woman says to him, 'I'll see you tomorrow'? 'Come back tomorrow'? Why would she need to prepare overnight to answer a question she had already publicly stated under oath was the truth?"

I tell Marsellus that once, when I had talked to Governor Edwards, we had talked about Baldwin's case, and Edwards said that he was convinced Baldwin was guilty.

Marsellus is angry. "No way. No way. Edwards knew. He knew the real score. He may have said that to you to save face, but he was the one who worked out the deal with the woman. These deals were going on all the time."

He then explains to me the workings of the bribes-for-pardons scheme that went on until the time of his arrest.

He says that when the Pardon Board met, there would usually be several applicants' files marked "Expedite," which meant a "deal" had been cut. The payments varied, Marsellus says, — "sometimes a few thousand, sometimes way up at $100,000 or more."

I ask who got the money, and Marsellus says, "Lawyers, state legislators. You figure it out. Only the governor can grant a pardon. Who do you think got the money?"

He explains how the scheme worked. "Here's a mother who

wants her boy out of prison, so she goes to an attorney (who is also a legislator) and asks what it will cost and he tells her, say, twenty thousand dollars. Then, the legislator, not wearing his attorney's hat now but his legislative hat, goes to the governor and presents the request for the pardon and the governor gets in return from him his commitment to pieces of legislation that the governor wants passed. The legislator gets his pardon and the governor gets endorsement for his legislative bills. That's the deal.

"Then, before our Board hearings, I'd get the word from the governor's office about which deals would go down when the Board met. 'The governor wants this one or that one,' that's what they'd say. Then at the Board hearing the legislator/attorney, representing his client — as an attorney now, not a legislator, so he couldn't be accused of conflict of interest — would present the inmate's case for pardon. Of course, it had already been worked out with the governor."

Marsellus says that there would be cases sometimes, where an especially heinous crime had been committed and some of the Board members would balk at giving the pardon, and he'd have to pull them aside and tell them the governor had already committed to the pardon and their task was to put it through.

Driving home after Baldwin's execution, Marsellus says, "down that dark, curvy road, my hands were shaking and the tears were running down my face and I said to my wife, 'Why did I ever get out of education? How have I let myself get involved in all this horror?" But then, he says, he had come back to the required loyalty. If he wanted to remain in his position, he would have to continue being a "team player."

I feel sorry for Marsellus. His boat got caught in a current and he went along. It must have been a terrible ordeal to know all the wheeling and dealing going on and yet sit there, time after time, and look into the faces of people about to die and then turn down their request for clemency. I ask him about this, about how he feels now, knowing he did this.

He is crying, I can hear him choking out his words over the phone, and I think of St. Peter, an apostle of Jesus, who, legends say, cried until the end of his life because he had denied Jesus. Peter cried so much, the legend goes, that tears cut permanent furrows in his cheeks.

"From day one I was doing political things that were morally wrong," Marsellus says. "The whole administration was corrupt from the top down, but I chose loyalty above integrity."

He remembers Earnest Knighton. "He was another one I thought shouldn't have died," he says. "During a robbery he shot the storekeeper in the arm — in the *arm* — and the bullet entered the man's heart and killed him. That's not intent to kill, not when someone shoots a man in the *arm*."

"But Knighton was a black man who killed a white person and was tried by an all-white jury,"[8] I remind him.

Marsellus and the Board had upheld the death sentence for Knighton as they did all of the sentences of the six men who appeared before them, and my guess is that the faces of these condemned men will appear and fade and appear again before Marsellus for the rest of his life.

"I did these things," he says, "I sat in judgment on these men like that — the guilty and the innocent. But who was I to sit in judgment? It still bothers me. I'm sorry. I'm really sorry."

CHAPTER
9

I dread hearing what Liz Scott is saying to me. She is telling me about her interview with the Harveys for the *New Orleans Magazine* article. "They're pretty upset with you," she says. "They thought that your visit with them before the Pardon Board hearing had brought you around to their way of seeing things. They feel that you used them, that you only visited with them so you could get 'ammunition' for the Pardon Board hearing. They call you and the other nuns who protest executions the 'sob sisters.' "

It was too much to expect, I tell myself, that I could be friend and comforter to the Harveys while opposing the execution of their daughter's murderer. Intellectually I am not wavering. I am as convinced as I ever was that the execution of Robert Willie is a betrayal of human rights, but I feel guilty that I have added to the Harveys' pain. Liz, good friend that she is, says, "You can't win 'em all."

And I am going back in my mind and clearly remembering sitting there in the car as I was ready to leave the Harveys after my visit, when Vernon had said that we were like two baseball teams that opposed but respected each other. Didn't that mean he understood that we had opposing views? How could they think they had changed my position on the death penalty? Should I have been more explicit? Had I left them with a false impression? Did I betray them?

I decide the best thing I can do for the Harveys is avoid them.

Shortly after the Pardon Board hearing, Robert Willie's trial judge sets the date of execution for December 28. When I hear the date, I know it's real. With Pat, I hoped a stay of execution would come. I did not expect him to die. But I know Robert is finished with the courts, with the Pardon Board, and certainly with the governor. This doesn't make the experience easier but it does make it simpler. Robert will not be torn between life and death, wondering if the ring of the telephone in the death house brings news of a stay of execution. There is only death for Robert now, and waiting for death.

I am now visiting him every week. I have also visited his mother, Elizabeth, and his aunt, Hazel. Robert has three stepbrothers, and Elizabeth says they will come with her on her next visit to see Robert. His aunt Hazel shakes her head sadly at the fate of her nephew. He had lived with her for a while but the boy just wasn't stable, she says, and he and her son had often gotten into trouble together (amply substantiated, I remember, by the juvenile reports). Elizabeth seems to be holding up remarkably well, though she often cries when she talks about Robert. Mandeville, where she lives with her husband, "Junior," and her sons, is a small rural town just across Lake Pontchartrain.

"You know how people talk," she says. "I feel like everybody's watching me when I go into a store. Everybody knows who I am." And she tells of standing near two women in the grocery store and overhearing one say that she "just can't wait to hear that they have finally executed that monster, Robert Willie." She had fled the store in tears. Her husband and children and close relatives seem supportive, and I am glad about that.

Now, seeing Robert for the first time since the Pardon Board hearing, I notice that his demeanor is unchanged — the same jaunty walk and the little black hat.

"Maybe I had a *little* hope goin' in to the Board," he says, "but I knew they were 0 for 3, and I didn't really expect to do better than Sonnier, Baldwin, or Knighton."

He seems matter-of-fact. He seems to accept his fate.

"Speakin' of Tim Baldwin," he says, "Warden Blackburn really liked that guy. I think it was hard on him to see him executed. Every single, solitary time Blackburn'd make a visit to the Row, he'd go on over to Baldwin's cell and have a little chat. Baldwin was an easygoing dude. He never pushed nobody. But Blackburn always goes right past my cell, and when he does talk to me, he never does look me in the eye." He shakes his head. "He doesn't like me. He's afraid of what I might do," and he looks down at his wrists and I notice that his hands are cuffed tight in the black box, a solid, square device that holds the wrists rigidly in place. I have only seen it used when prisoners are transported from Angola — never, like this, in the visiting booth. "Some snitch," he says, "must have told Blackburn I was plannin' to hit the fence. I bet I know who it was, too, a dude who ain't wrapped too tight, who's always kissin' ass with the authorities. Now, I admit I've been talking about gettin' out of this place if I get half a chance — who wouldn't — but" — and he brandishes the black box — "Blackburn sure ain't takin' no chances, is he?"

I'm noticing how he is talking about Blackburn with a tinge of regret in his voice when he describes how the warden had a soft spot for Baldwin but not for him. Blackburn has a kind face and is, in my estimation, a gentle, fatherly figure as prison wardens go, and I sense that Robert would like to have won his confidence. It makes sense. He's never really had a father. His own father spent twenty-seven of his fifty-three years in Angola. Later, I am not surprised when Robert tells me that he has sent Warden Blackburn a Christmas card with the message, "I hope you and your family have a very merry Christmas and a happy New Year."

It makes me think of my own daddy. It has to be one of life's most special feelings to know that your father is proud of you. I was my daddy's scholar, his public speaker, his "pretty little girl," his scribe who kept the travel diary on family vacations. He always had a special tone in his voice when he introduced me to friends and colleagues. *And this is my little daughter, Helen.* In the presence of strangers I would fall silent, standing close against him, my hand holding on tightly to his, my eyes not venturing past the huge, brightly shined black shoes (he never liked brown); and afterward, having emerged unscathed from the Encounter with the Towering Strangers, I would squeeze his hand tighter than ever and teem once more with chatter and questions.

A kid can sail to the moon with that feeling of security from a father.

But Robert Willie . . . Did Vernon Harvey have the facts right? Hadn't he said that Robert's father said his son deserved the chair and he'd be willing to pull the switch himself?

I look across at Robert through the heavy mesh screen. I remember from his juvenile record that he once asked to be kept in jail because he had nowhere else to go.

Robert says, indicating the black box on his wrists, "At first I had real bitter feelin's about this, somebody snitchin' on me, but I'm not really sure which one of 'em snitched, so I was mad at all of 'em and didn't talk to none of 'em for awhile. But life's too short to bear grudges, so, hey, I'm talkin' to everybody now, all of 'em."

Then he says he hopes he gets to see the football play-offs before he goes to the death house because he has two ice creams bet on Miami and he hopes he gets to bring his radio because he can't make it through a day without music and he says how his life-style has changed since he came to the Row because now he's in bed by 10:30 P.M., right after the 10:00 news.

"The dude in the cell next to me will want me to watch some TV program and I say, 'No, man, I'm goin' to sleep.' " He laughs low. "They call me the 'old man,' " he says, and then he describes how neat and fastidious he is and how he's always asking for extra bleach and soap to clean his cell and how he's spent about twenty dollars on toothpaste, shampoo, soap, deodorant — and how in summer when it gets so hot, he strips naked and pours cups of water over him and then uses the mop in his cell ("it's just the mop part, the handle is sawed off") to sop up the water from the floor.

"Some dudes here don't bathe and I tell 'em, 'Hey, man, there's no sign sayin' the shower don't work. It's not like you got to pay a quarter or nothin'.' See, I got a sensitive nose, and I tell 'em, 'Man, you're invading my privacy.' "

I ask him if anything has come of the lawsuit on death-row conditions, and he says that the Department of Corrections has instituted a few changes: an extra TV on each tier, a few new food items from the canteen — peanut butter, jelly, and peppers — and approval for inmates to have two plastic containers to store food items, a radio/tape player, a small mirror, and drawing materials.

"Probably just the threat of the suit was enough to win changes on this piddly stuff," he says, "but eventually, for real, substantial changes, the suit will need to be reworked and pressed and it will have to be someone other than me 'cause I'm not goin to be around."

He has a cigarette going, but with considerable difficulty because of the black box clamping his hands tight to the belt around his waist. He has to bend over almost double to reach the cigarette.

"Whichever inmate takes on the task is gonna have his work cut out for him," he says.

I tell Robert I've been talking to his mother on the telephone and he says that now she's his biggest worry. He can do it, he's "ready to go," but he doesn't know what he'll do if she starts "crying and breaking down" in the death house.

That was what Pat Sonnier had feared most, his mother breaking down and causing him to lose emotional control.

"You don't always have to be this tough Marlboro Man," I say to him. "Real men cry, you know."

He gives a little laugh, a nervous laugh, and I know he's listening.

"There's another mother who's suffering, Robert," I say. "Elizabeth Harvey. She and Faith were very close. They used to talk to each other almost every night on the phone. They used to go shopping together. She had her brother come to dig her daughter's jaw out of a body bag to do a dental check before she could accept that this daughter, whom she loved so much, was really dead. And she will live every day of her life knowing that her daughter died a terrible death — and alone. And, Faith — have you ever really faced her pain, felt it, taken it inside yourself? I'm saying all this to you because I'm your friend and I care about you and I just can't see you going to your death and not owning up to the part you played in Faith's death."

"I am sorry, I really am sorry about Faith," he says, "I hope my death gives the Harveys some peace. I really do. Maybe my death will help them get some relief, some peace."

His head is down and his voice is soft, and when he says this I say to him, just as I said to Pat Sonnier, that his last words can be words either of hate or of love and maybe that's the best thing he can offer the Harveys, a wish for their peace.

The guard comes to tell us time's up. As I am about to leave, I get a message that Major Kendall Coody wants to see me.

The major. That's top brass. This is the man in charge of death row who supervises inmates and guards. I brace myself. He probably wants to assess Robert's seriousness about escaping. Maybe he wants to know if Robert has a "cyanide finale" or something like that planned.

He asks me to pull the door behind me as I step inside his office.

"How's Willie doing?" he asks.

"Okay," I say, "I think he's okay."

He's seated behind his desk and I can't tell how tall he is. I'd guess he's in his late forties. He has a broad, square face, fair skin, and a thick brown mustache. His dark brown hair is neatly combed except for a thick shock that falls in the middle of his forehead. He has light brown eyes and wears glasses. He is a troubled man.

"I'm not sure how long I'm going to be able to keep doing this," he says. "I've been through five of these executions and I can't eat, I can't sleep. I'm dreaming about executions. I don't condone these guys' crimes. I know they've done terrible things. I don't excuse what they've done, but I talk to them when I make my rounds. I talk to them and many of them are just little boys inside big men's bodies, little boys who never had much chance to grow up."

He tells me that he talks to each inmate on the Row almost every day. In his job, that could be a serious occupational hazard — getting to know inmates personally, finding the little boy inside the man — dangerous territory indeed, for a man whose duty is to oversee their execution. One of the personnel at the prison had once told me about the orientation of guards at Angola, and that's the first rule they are taught: never relate on a *personal* level with inmates.

Coody tells me that he also serves on the "Strap-down Team," the guards who accompany the prisoner to the electric chair. That means he's not insulated from the "final process." He's not like the other guards who work day in and day out on death row, feeding men, talking to them, supervising their showers, delivering their mail — but never seeing the green room with the brown wooden chair. But five times now this man has been in the execution chamber at night and then back here on the Row for business as usual the next morning. He's never had to strap them in the chair, he says, but he's walked them to the chair and sometimes been the one to gather up their personal belongings — clothes, toilet articles, books — from the holding cell after they're dead.

"I get home from an execution about two-something in the morning and I just sit up in a chair for the rest of the night. I can't shake it. I can't square it with my conscience, putting them to death like that."

What a spot to be in. Major Coody is not like the governor, the head of the Department of Corrections, the warden, and most of the other guards around here. He can't persuade himself that he's just *doing his job*. My heart goes out to him, and I tell him how I felt watching Pat Sonnier die, and I say that it seems to me that he is someone who is unable to shield himself by rationalization and it may mean that he will need to find another job.

180

DEAD MAN WALKING

It is not a very long conversation.

"I respect you, Major Coody. I'll pray that you follow where your heart and conscience lead," I say to him as I am leaving, and his eyes look into mine as he reaches out for my hand.

It is the last time I see him alive.

I do not run into him again over the next weeks prior to Robert's execution, nor do I notice if he is one of the guards surrounding Robert as he walks to the chair. A couple of months after Robert's execution I hear that he has been transferred to another part of the prison, and then I hear that he has asked for early retirement, and then I hear that he has died of a heart attack.

I wish that before he died he had had a chance to participate in the public debate on capital punishment. I would like to have seen him square off with one of the D.A.'s or the academics who lay out such clean, logical arguments for the necessity of executions. My hunch is that he would say something like: *Look, no matter what reasons you give to justify killing criminals, when you're there and you see it, when you watch it happen with your own eyes and are part of it, you feel dirty. You're killing a man who can't defend himself and that is just as wrong as what he did.*

November has turned into December and the rusty, furry needles on the cypress trees are dropping in clumps now, and everything is getting that sparse, stripped winter look. Robert asks me for a big box of Christmas cards. He says he wants to send a card to everyone he knows.

I tell him that I respect his need for privacy and when he goes to the death house, if he prefers to be alone or just with his family, I won't be offended. I don't want to impose my presence on him. I've only known him a couple of months.

"Yeah, yeah, you be there, ma'am, if it won't put you out too much," Robert says. "I'm gonna want someone to talk to and be with right up to the end. I don't believe in being chummy with the guards who'll be helping to kill me. I've read stories of inmates having these little intimate conversations with the guards in the death house like they're big buddies or something. Not me. I'm only talking to those people when I have to. I don't need no favors from them people. No way."

And he tells me of his recent encounter with one of the prison chaplains and that I had come up in the conversation. "Chaplain

Penton was telling me that this Sister Prejean stirs up emotions in the inmates, that's how he put it — 'stirs up emotions' — and that maybe I'd prefer him instead to be there with me in the death house, and I said to him, 'Look, man, you get your paycheck from these people, you work for these people, and you go along with the death penalty. I don't particularly need your kind of help, man.' "

I remember Penton and our conversation there in the death house while Pat was getting his head shaved, when he had told me to prepare myself for the "visual shock."

"It's hard to resist policies of an organization when you're on its payroll," I say.

"Like biting the hand that feeds you," he says.

And it makes me glad that I do work I really want to do and that I'm free to take moral positions I believe in.

Robert whispers that at first he was afraid to die but he's not afraid now. He's been preparing himself to look death in the eye. "I've had a pretty fulfilled life — women, drugs, travel, rock and roll, school, football — about everything there is." He is scheduled to die five days before his twenty-seventh birthday.

Some inmates, he says, have confided to him that they hope they can go out like him.

He is beginning to give media interviews, lots of them. He seems to enjoy talking to reporters.

To a reporter for NBC news he says he'd like to talk with the executioner face to face and say, "Hey, man, you shouldn't be killing people for no four hundred dollars. You shouldn't be killing people for the government," and wonders out loud if he'd shake hands with the executioner to show he wasn't afraid of him, but decides, "Nah, I wouldn't want to touch his hand."

To local newspaper reporters he bristles when someone suggests that his family life was not all it should have been. He insists that he had a "good family" and that his family is "not to blame for nothin'." He says he admires Adolf Hitler and Fidel Castro because they were "leaders" and "got things done," although he admits that Hitler "maybe went a little overboard with some of his policies." But he thinks "Hitler was on the right track about Aryans being the master race" and says he joined the white supremicist group, the Aryan Brotherhood, when he was in the federal penitentiary in Marion.

He also says the U.S. government does "evil things" through the CIA — "trying to assassinate political enemies like Castro in Cuba,

Allende in Chile, and Sandinistas in Nicaragua through the Contras. I don't trust the U.S. government any further than I can throw 'em, man. They shouldn't be given power to execute nobody. They're too corrupt, man."

When a reporter asks about changes he might make in his life if he had it to live over again, he says he'd join a terrorist organization and bomb government buildings — "not the people, just the buildings" — and he'd rob banks because the government insures banks and it would cost them money and "money is the only language they understand."

When asked if he's scared to die he says, "The electric chair don't worry me, man. I haven't read much about it but I know electricity will fry your ass. I'm going willingly. I'll hold my head up. I've got pride. I don't run from nothin'." He brags about coming out of Marion, "the maximum securiti-est penitentiary in the country" where he "established" himself as a "man and as a convict," and he "doubts that 99 percent of the dudes here at Angola could make it in Marion." He summarizes his life in a few deft strokes: "I'm an outlaw. I've been an outlaw most of my life. If I had it to do all over again, I'd be an outlaw."

On Christmas Eve Robert is moved to the death house. He had told me he wanted to make the move "sooner rather than later" because he wanted to "get his thoughts together," and "meditate."

I go into Baton Rouge to be with my family as I usually do on Christmas Day. I telephone Warden Blackburn, and ask if I might wish Robert a merry Christmas by telephone, but he refuses. I had given Robert Mama's telephone number and told him to call on Christmas, but throughout the day I am moving between her house and my sister Mary Ann's, and I miss his call.

The next day I drive to Angola to see Robert. I haven't been back in the death house since Pat's execution, and here I am, counting on my fingers again: Wednesday, December 26; Thursday, December 27; Friday, December 28. Thursday night, that's it. Robert won't see much of the twenty-eighth — just about ten minutes, because they come for him at midnight. Two more days to live. The twenty-eighth is the feast in the Catholic Church of the Holy Innocents, commemorating the infants slaughtered by King Herod.[1] Vernon Harvey's been telling the press about how he's going to sit in the front row at this execution and that he had put in his request to the trial judge to set the date of execution for the twenty-eighth because Faith was murdered on the twenty-eighth of May. I am sure he would consider the commemoration of Innocents a highly appropriate day on which to exact retribution for the death of his stepdaughter.

Along this road now as I get closer to the prison I can feel the fear mounting, and it feels just the way it does before a hurricane — swooping blasts, then eerie calm and the sense of waters rising. *Jesus, help him, help me*, and I'm back to saying essential prayers.

I wonder how Robert the Outlaw is holding up now in the quiet green holding cell just a few short steps away from "Gruesome Gerty," which is what the inmates call the electric chair. He's got a tougher hide than anyone else I know if he's been speaking the truth in these media interviews, and he had sent me a copy of a poem from "Crazy Dave," a fellow inmate from the federal penitentiary in Marion:

> Gruesome Gertie she waits for a Rebel
> Robert Lee Willie is his name.
> She visits him in his dreams at night.
> She tries to drive him insane.
> But Robert Lee Willie is a Rebel
> and I know his mind is strong.
> And even if you do end up with him
> in our hearts he will always live on!

I arrive at the front gate of Angola. It's Wednesday, a regular visiting day, and a cluster of people are here in the visitor center and the prison bus is waiting to take them back to the camps. A white van is sent to pick me up to bring me back to the green building with the generator outside and the little red geraniums growing in the front. I know the route.

I will be the only one to visit Robert today. He has told his mother not to come until tomorrow. He says he knows his mother couldn't take two days in the death house. Tomorrow will be hard enough. She'll have the boys, Robert's stepbrothers, with her and maybe that will help. Mickey is eighteen, Tim, sixteen, and Todd, eleven.

I notice some differences when we arrive at the death house. No geraniums, no guard with a rifle at the front door, and no armed guard inside the door. They've executed five people now and realize they were overprepared, that a man with hands and legs chained and surrounded by eight to ten guards isn't going very far.

I should feel more prepared for what is coming than I was six months ago with Pat Sonnier, and the title of a film — *After the First* — flashes across my mind. The film tells the story of a young boy who goes on his first deer hunt with his father. When the boy looked at the beauty of the deer poised in the early morning, its antlered head raised above the bushes, he had hesitated, then shot; and as father and son looked down together at the dead deer, the father had said, "After the first it won't be so hard."

But it is hard. It freezes my heart just to step into this place with the cold polished tiles.

I've brought my Bible with me and a guard takes it and thumbs through the pages and then passes the metal detector over me. I empty the pockets of my blue suit for the guard to inspect.

"I'm ready for you this time, young lady. I'll have dinner for you," Captain Rabelais says. I haven't seen him since Pat's execution.

It's hard to believe where I am and what is going to happen here. The sun is shining in through the front glass door and it's Wednesday, the day after Christmas. I feel glad to see Captain Rabelais. I like the man. But I avoid friendly banter. This is the death house and Captain Rabelais is part of the group of people who are going to kill Robert Willie. I walk up to the familiar white metal door with the mesh window where I had waited out the last hours with Pat Sonnier. Robert is out of his cell and seated on the other side of the door, his hands and feet shackled. And there's the guard standing at the end of the short four-cell tier, part of the "death-watch" team which will keep Robert under twenty-four-hour surveillance until he is executed.

"Merry Christmas," I say to Robert.

"I tried to call you yesterday at your mother's," he says.

"I asked the warden to put in a call to you here but he wouldn't," I say.

"They don't put calls through. This ain't exactly the Holiday Inn," he says, and he smiles. I see he has on his jeans and a long-sleeved blue denim shirt with a white T-shirt underneath and the black knitted hat, and I am glad he has the little hat because when they shave his head maybe he can wear it and his head won't be cold. Would they let him wear it to the chair? No, probably not. The guards will not want to deal with any extra clothing to be removed when they get their prisoner in the chair.

All my energies move now to this man behind the screened window of the white metal door. I'll be here with him all day and I take a deep breath and ease in. He's glad to see me, I can tell.

"Were you able to sleep much?" I ask.

"I did," he says. "It's weird, it's a lot quieter here than on the Row. Yeah, I slept. Funny, but I've told the truth about what happened and, like the Book said, the truth sets you free. I used to always think that the truth could hurt you, but I feel free now, kind of innocent even, knowing it, knowing the truth."

This leads to a special request.

"Look," he says, "maybe you can't do this and maybe it's too expensive or whatever, but if you can do this for me, I would really appreciate it. I want to take a polygraph test because I want my mother to know that I didn't kill Faith Hathaway. I don't care if nobody else in the whole world believes me, I just want my mother to know."

A polygraph test. The quickest I could get it for him would be tomorrow. No chance of getting it lined up for today. I weigh it in my mind. There is a question of money. I estimate it'll cost a hundred and fifty, maybe two hundred dollars, and I tell him yes, I'll make a phone call from here, from Captain Rabelais's office, because as a matter of fact I happen to know someone in Baton Rouge who administers these tests and maybe we can pull it off.

This leads me to ask him about a discrepancy in the physical evidence of his case that's been bothering me. I had read it in the transcripts of the trial and Farmer had brought it up during the Pardon Board hearing. Robert claims that Vaccaro, positioned behind Faith Hathaway, her head in his lap, suddenly began stabbing her, and he, Robert, kneeling in front facing her, had held her hands. But the victim's body was found with her arms above her head and her legs up, knees bent, feet on the ground. To hold her hands, then, Robert would have had to reach across her body, blocking Vaccaro from stabbing her.

The pathologist had testified that the victim's hands and feet had to have been held in spread-eagled fashion before she died.

"When we left her, her hands were laying on her stomach and her legs were down flat and her knees together," Robert says.

He states it simply and without remonstrance and exhaustive explanation. That's all he says.

There are three possible explanations that occur to me:

Faith was not dead when Robert and Vaccaro left her, and she moved her limbs into the position in which she was found.

Someone else moved her arms and legs into the position before pictures were taken at the scene of the murder.

Robert is lying.

But if Robert is lying, why this last-minute, privately administered polygraph test for his mother? And why, after arrest, the offer to take a polygraph test for the authorities?

"So, what's all this I hear about you admiring Hitler and wishing you could come back as a terrorist and bomb people?" I say to him, referring to the stories appearing over the last couple of weeks.

"Not the people, just the buildings," he protests. "I didn't say I'd bomb the people. I don't have any love for the U.S. government. The CIA goes around thinking they can assassinate anybody they damn well please, anybody that doesn't agree with their ideology, and look at the death penalty. You never see rich people on death row. They can buy government officials off because the almighty dollar determines what kind of justice you get here in the good ole USA."

I tell him I can agree with some of his criticisms of the U.S. government, but that his violent response is no solution. Our Sisters serving as Latin American missionaries have urged us to write letters to congresspersons protesting U.S.-backed militarist policies in Central America, and I had visited Nicaragua in 1983 and talked to too many people who had had innocent loved ones killed by the Contras — children, women, teachers, health-care workers — to trust U.S. government officials who called such terrorists "freedom fighters."

"So how is bombing buildings going to change anything?" I ask. "That's a pure testosterone solution if ever I heard one."

And he argues that the destruction of government buildings will "at least get the government's attention and they'll have to put a lot of money out to rebuild and *money* is all they understand."

And I say that if our government is doing things we disagree with that it's only us, the people, that can hold them accountable and demand that they change because we're a democracy, and democracy is hard work, a lot harder than the one-act shoot-'em-up solution he's suggesting.

"Violence is such a simplistic solution," I say. "Like these people trying to kill you now. What is your execution going to accomplish other than show that the state of Louisiana can be as violent as you were? And what's this you said about admiring Hitler? People are reading these interviews and thinking you're some kind of nut. It's going to make it easier for people to say 'good riddance' when you're executed. You're not helping yourself or anybody else on death row by saying things like that."

"Hitler was a leader. He advanced things," he says. "He was a supreme being in one way and maybe a nut in another because he went a little overboard. But I admire people who do something, who act, and you gotta say that for Hitler — he acted."

He asked for it, saying something dumb like that, and I tell him what I think — we've got all day to talk — and then what really comes out as we talk is that the Aryan Brotherhood in the federal penitentiary in Marion was a family to him.

"I've got two tattoos here underneath my sleeve," he says, pointing to his arm, "the swastika and the skull, membership badges for the brotherhood. A dude I had met in Terre Haute had sent a letter of recommendation for me to the brotherhood before I got to Marion, and when I got there, as soon as I arrived, they took me in, gave me cigarettes, drugs, the shirt off their backs. Everything they had they was willing to share. That was the best part of it, the sharing. You belonged, man. Once I got hold of a hundred Valiums and I shared them with the brothers. And when the other brothers got stuff, they shared with me. It was one for all and all for one. Once you're in the brotherhood, it's for life — you can't get out until death. That's what the skull represents."

"What would have happened if you decided not to share the Valiums?" I ask.

"They would've killed me," he says.

"Cozy family," I say.

"It was. It really was," he says. "And there's mostly just whites in Marion, not many blacks, and, truthfully, the Aryans run the place. There's not many fights or killings or much homosexuality." He explains that Marion is the highest-security prison in the country, built in 1963 to replace Alcatraz, a "tough pen," he says, where inmates get their heads shaved and wear Army uniforms and boots. "Being there taught me a lot about handling things, prepared me to handle things better here. They have better programs there and it's easier to do your time. Here, it's hard to do time. And in Terre Haute, where I was before I went to Marion, you get a dollar an hour for your work. Here you get two cents. At Marion you could join educational programs and play group sports. I liked football. You got to choose the group you wanted to play with. Here, those on the Row can't play group sports. It's one of our demands in the lawsuit."

He talks about Marion as if it were an alma mater. He talks about the Aryan Brotherhood as if it were a fraternity.

He tells me about the time in Marion when he and a bunch from his tier went to the "hole" because of his "cold baked potato." One day when he was served his lunch tray in his cell, he felt the baked

188

potato and it was cold and he asked the guard to heat it in the microwave but the guard refused, and he threw the potato onto the tier, followed by his tray. Then other inmates threw their trays, followed by soap, toilet paper, books — and some set fires in their cells and everybody was yelling about "messing over Robert." He chuckles. The memory of it pleases him — all the guys getting into the act like that, all protesting together over the cold baked potato.

"I must have been in the hole thirty-eight days or so for that baked potato. The hole there ain't nice like the one here. You're kept naked and you have terrible food, I mean *terrible*, and they come and hose you off every three days and you have to lather right away because they only give you a few seconds and they only give you one book to read, like one of those 'See Dick run' books."

Obviously he had made it through all these experiences and lived to tell the tale. Obviously he is one tough dude. He takes a long draw from his cigarette, and for a good long time he talks about Marion. Captain Rabelais brings us cups of coffee, and I drink one cup to Robert's three. It reminds me of Pat, being here, the coffee, the cigarettes, the talking and talking to keep the terror at bay. *He's going to die, he's definitely going to die. Just follow the stream, let him take the lead, accompany him. But be honest, don't condescend because he's going to die.*

And I have to keep positioning myself inwardly to grasp the reality of imminent death, because Robert Willie, through mysterious resources of his own, seems to have a firm foothold in the present moment and is calm and obviously enjoying this conversation very much.

Captain Rabelais brings lunch in heaping amounts, a tray for each of us, and I tell Robert about the fainting episode and the one rule in the prison I succeeded in changing, and Captain Rabelais keeps saying, "Eat, young lady, eat" and tells us there's more where this came from and there's this "Eat hearty, mates" spirit in his voice. Robert is eating with gusto and saying that this food is so much better than what they get on the Row, and I find myself eating all the meat loaf and mustard greens and half of the huge slab of corn bread.

Robert tells me of the "blowout" that happened in Marion last October when two guards and an inmate were killed. "They get real upset when guards are killed," he says, and I recall having seen a newspaper article among his papers, a letter to the editor by an inmate at Marion, giving his version of the incident.

Robert says that after the guards at Marion were killed, a large contingent of guards, the "A-Team," "systematically dragged out every member of the brotherhood and beat the shit out of them." I remember the inmate's article had talked about the beatings and that afterward even lawyers were barred from the prison and the whole prison was put on lock-down, with educational and recreational programs curtailed.

He pauses and is quiet awhile and says to please excuse him but he has to use the "can," and I figure this is a good time to telephone and check out the possibility of the polygraph test. Amazingly, by the second phone call I reach Don Alan Zulke, a family friend, who says he's available and can come to the prison early tomorrow morning to administer the test. As we are lining it up, he says he must honestly say that if this test is to be administered in the death house on the very day of the client's execution, there is a high probability that the sheer stress of the situation will skew the results because the test measures emotional stress. I weigh what he is saying. The cost of the test, about two hundred dollars, is a lot of money in this work where we scrabble even to pay telephone bills. Two hundred dollars for a test which is probably not going to be accurate anyway? Against that, I weigh a man about to die who wants to assure his mother that he's telling the truth. "Let's do it," I say, and we make tentative plans, which I explain must meet with the warden's approval. I tell him to make the test as early in the morning as possible and I give him directions to the prison.

I'm in Captain Rabelais's office, and just as I finish the phone call I smell a cigar and in walks Warden Blackburn. Robert's execution will be his third. I wonder if the deaths are starting to "get next to him." I wonder how long it will be before he talks to Major Coody.

"How's he holding up, Sister Prejean?" (He says "pree-jeen," as most people do who don't know French.)

"Amazingly well," I say, and immediately, wish I hadn't said that. I don't want to grease the wheels. I want to jag, jar, and jimmy this death process any way I can. I know that's what this warden wants more than anything else — for the execution to go as "smoothly" as the others have gone. Above all, he doesn't want a Leandress Riley scene — any warden's execution nightmare.

Riley was a black man executed in San Quentin's gas chamber on February 20, 1953. He was small, only eighty pounds or so, and he was terrified. The guards had to carry him screaming and struggling into the gas chamber where, with difficulty, they strapped him into the metal chair and bolted the door. But just before they dropped the cyanide pellets into the vat of acid, Riley managed to pull his slim wrists out of the restraints and jumped up, racing around inside the chamber, beating frantically on the glass windows where witnesses and media watched horrified. Prison officials had to stop the process, open the chamber, and strap him in again. This happened three times. And then he screamed in terror right up to the end, right up until he inhaled the gas.[2]

Word has it that most of the guards who worked on Riley's "tactical unit" could never work another execution. I think Blackburn knows that if any inmate is a "fighter," it's Robert Lee Willie. I know he wants to get any kind of reassuring signal he can that this man is going to go "peacefully." It is a reassurance I cannot give him.

I tell him of Robert's request for the polygraph test and the plans I have just set in motion, and he approves the test provided it's administered early enough in the day.

Now, once again, here's the familiar feeling of the tight, cold grip of fear in the hollow of my stomach. Talking through the morning with Robert, I had forgotten where I was. But now, talking to Warden Blackburn, I know all too well where I am, and I say, "I have to get back to Robert."

"Robert sent me a Christmas card, which was real nice and I thanked him," Blackburn continues. "You know, it wasn't my decision to send him here on Christmas Eve. I was willing to let him stay with his buddies on the Row until after Christmas. It was his choice," he says.

I go back to the white metal door. It seems that this day is lasting a hundred years. It also seems that the day is flying. Death-house time is like no other.

Robert stands by the chair to stretch his legs a bit, and I stand up too.

"I shouldn't have said all those things about Hitler and being a terrorist, all that stuff," he says. "It was stupid." He says that Blackburn told him this morning that there would be no more media interviews. "Actually," he says, "I have a legal right to do more if I want to, but I don't feel like doing any more. Still, the warden shouldn't just exert his authority like that."

I tell him that the polygraph test is set up for early tomorrow morning.

"Wow. Quick work. You did that already?" he says, and I can tell he's happy it's going to happen. It seems to mean a lot to him.

I tell him what Zulke had said about the accuracy of the test being jeopardized by the stress of the situation. I want to prepare him because I sense he will probably be disappointed in the results. How can he *not* feel stress in a situation like this? I ask him, and I tell him that stress is not always a conscious thing.

"I wonder what would have happened if they had let me take this test after I was arrested like I asked them to," he says. "I know they couldn't have used the results in court or nothin', but doubt, that's what I was after. If the D.A. had doubts, maybe he would've offered me a plea."

Warden Blackburn approaches us and says that time's up for today and I'll have to leave now. Robert takes a quick look at his watch and then at the warden. He's been enjoying the company, and I know he'd like me to stay longer. There are no set rules regarding "special" visits in these "last days." Robert shrugs his shoulders.

"Just a moment longer, Warden," I say, "I'd like a chance to pray with Robert." Blackburn nods his head and leaves. Robert winks. "*That* was an offer he just couldn't refuse, 'cuz ain't he a minister or somethin' in his church?" Robert says and smiles. One of the things he had told a reporter was that yes, he had religious faith and believed in Jesus Christ and had a spiritual adviser, but he was no "religious fanatic or nothin'," not "one of those jailhouse religious hypocrites who only use religion for their own purposes." He was an "ordinary person," he had assured the reporter, and continued to "curse a lot."

That had made me smile. I have never before met a man quite like Robert Willie.

I put my hands upon the screen as close as I can get to him and say a prayer. He bows his head and I find myself looking at the top of the black knitted hat, which he will give to me as a gift there at the end right before he walks to the chair, the black hat that covers the head of the Outlaw, the Aryan brother, the "Marlboro Man," the "Rebel" — the kidnapper/rapist/murderer. I ask God to give him what he needs — mercy, courage, remorse for the pain he has caused — and freedom of heart to accept death when he meets it. I also pray for the Harveys, who will be there to watch him die.

At the end of the prayer he says, "Amen. Thank you, ma'am, for the nice prayer. I don't know if I can be everything the prayer says, but I'm sure gonna try."

I leave him with a parting word about the God I believe in not being a God of blood who demands torture and death but a God of love, of compassion. I refer him to the Gospel of John, to a passage he might want to read before he goes to sleep tonight (his last full night on earth), where Jesus talks about living freely and dying freely:

> I lay down my life
> in order to take it up again
> No one takes it from me;
> I lay it down of my own free will . . .
> (John 10:17–18)

"Not that they're right to take your life," I say to him. "It's wrong and it ought to be resisted and denounced, but you have within yourself the freedom to choose the way you die — with love or hate." And I tell him that I care about him, I value his life, and I will stand by him until the end.

And I'm out of the death house and into the pale yellow December sun. Robert has asked me to come tomorrow at two in the afternoon when his mother and brothers will visit. I dread that, watching the pain of his family in such a place. Todd is only eleven years old.

But that's tomorrow and I don't want to think about it. Today — now — that is what I'll think about. I'm driving through the curvy Tunica hills out to Highway 61 and Baton Rouge and Mary Ann's house for supper tonight, where her five children are all home from college for Christmas.

Christmas?

Robert had sent out Christmas cards from the death house.

A snatch of a Christmas carol comes to me and I fiddle with the words.

> *God rest ye merry gentlemen*
> *let nothing you dismay.*
> *We'll pick our day to execute*
> *In June or Christmas day . . .*

I think of the running debate I engage in with "church" people about the death penalty. "Proof texts" from the Bible usually punctuate these discussions without regard for the cultural context or literary genre of the passages invoked. (Will D. Campbell, a Southern Baptist minister and writer, calls this use of scriptural quotations "biblical quarterbacking.")

It is abundantly clear that the Bible depicts murder as a crime for which death is considered the appropriate punishment, and one is hard-pressed to find a biblical "proof text" in either the Hebrew Testament or the New Testament which unequivocally refutes this. Even Jesus' admonition "Let him without sin cast the first stone," when he was asked the appropriate punishment for an adulteress (John 8:7) — the Mosaic law prescribed death — should be read in its proper context. This passage is an "entrapment" story, which sought to show Jesus' wisdom in besting his adversaries. It is not an ethical pronouncement about capital punishment.

Similarly, the "eye for eye" passage from Exodus, which pro-death penalty advocates are fond of quoting, is rarely cited in its original context, in which it is clearly meant to limit revenge.

The passage, including verse 22, which sets the context reads:

> *If, when men come to blows, they hurt a woman who is pregnant and she suffers a miscarriage, though she does not die of it, the man responsible must pay the compensation demanded of him by the woman's master; he shall hand it over after arbitration. But should she die, you shall give life for life, eye for eye, tooth for tooth, hand for hand, foot for foot, burn for burn, wound for wound, stroke for stroke. (Exodus 21: 22–25)*

In the example given (patently patriarchal: the woman is considered the negotiable property of her male master), it is clear that punishment is to be measured out according to the seriousness of the offense. If the child is lost but not the mother, the punishment is less grave than if both mother and child are lost. *Only* an eye for an eye, *only* a life for a life is the intent of the passage. Restraint was badly needed. It was not uncommon for an offended family or clan to slaughter entire communities in retaliation for an offense against one of their members.

Even granting the call for restraint in this passage, it is nonetheless clear — here and in numerous other instances throughout the Hebrew Bible — that the punishment for murder was death.

But we must remember that such prescriptions of the Mosaic Law were promulgated in a seminomadic culture in which the preservation of a fragile society — without benefit of prisons and other institutions — demanded quick, effective, harsh punishment of offenders. And we should note the numerous other crimes for which the Bible prescribes death as punishment:

contempt of parents *(Exodus 21:15, 17; Leviticus 24:17);*
trespass upon sacred ground *(Exodus 19:12–13; Numbers 1:51; 18:7);*
sorcery *(Exodus 22:18; Leviticus 20:27)*
bestiality *(Exodus 22:19; Leviticus 20: 15–16);*
sacrifice to foreign gods *(Exodus 22:20; Deuteronomy 13:1–9);*
profaning the sabbath *(Exodus 31:14);*
adultery *(Leviticus 20:10; Deuteronomy 22: 22–24);*
incest *(Leviticus 20:11–13);*
homosexuality *(Leviticus 20:13);*
and prostitution *(Leviticus 21:19; Deuteronomy 22: 13–21).*

And this is by no means a complete list.

But no person with common sense would dream of appropriating such a moral code today, and it is curious that those who so readily invoke the "eye for an eye, life for life" passage are quick to shun other biblical prescriptions which also call for death, arguing that modern societies have evolved over the three thousand or so years since biblical times and no longer consider such exaggerated and archaic punishments appropriate.

Such nuances are lost, of course, in "biblical quarterbacking," and more and more I find myself steering away from such futile discussions. Instead, I try to articulate what I personally believe about Jesus and the ethical thrust he gave to humankind: an impetus toward compassion, a preference for disarming enemies without humiliating and destroying them, and a solidarity with poor and suffering people.[3]

So, what happened to the impetus of love and compassion Jesus set blazing into history?

The first Christians adhered closely to the way of life Jesus had taught. They died in amphitheaters rather than offer homage to worldly emperors. They refused to fight in emperors' wars. But then a tragic diversion happened, which Elaine Pagels has deftly explored in her book, *Adam, Eve, and the Serpent*: in 313 C.E. (Common Era) the Emperor Constantine entered the Christian church.

Pagels says, "Christian bishops, once targets for arrest, torture, and execution, now received tax exemptions, gifts from the imperial treasury, prestige, and even influence at court; the churches gained new wealth, power and prominence."[4]

Unfortunately, the exercise of power practiced by Christians in alliance with the Roman Empire — with its unabashed allegiance to the sword — soon bore no resemblance to the purely moral persuasion that Jesus had taught.

In the fifth century, Pagels points out, Augustine provided the theological rationale the church needed to justify the use of violence by church and state governments. Augustine persuaded church authorities that "original sin" so damaged every person's ability to make moral choices that external control by church and state authorities over people's lives was necessary and justified. The "wicked" might be "coerced by the sword" to "protect the innocent," Augustine taught. And thus was legitimated for Christians the authority of secular government to "control" its subjects by coercive and violent means — even punishment by death.

In the latter part of this century, however, two flares of hope — Mohandas K. Gandhi and Martin Luther King — have demonstrated that Jesus' counsel to practice compassion and tolerance even toward one's enemies can effect social change. Susan Jacoby, analyzing the moral power that Gandhi and King unleashed in their campaigns for social justice, finds a unique form of aggression:

" 'If everyone took an eye for an eye,' Gandhi said, 'the whole world would be blind.' But Gandhi did not want to take anyone's eye; he wanted to force the British out of India . . ."

> *Nonviolence and nonaggression are generally regarded as interchangeable concepts — King and Gandhi frequently used them that way — but nonviolence, as employed by Gandhi in India and by King in the American South, might reasonably be viewed as a highly disciplined form of aggression. If one defines aggression in the primary dictionary sense of "attack," nonviolent resistance proved to be the most powerful attack imaginable on the powers King and Gandhi were trying to overturn. The writings of both men are filled with references to love as a powerful force against oppression, and while the two leaders were not using the term "force" in the military sense, they certainly regarded nonviolence as a tactical weapon as well as an expression of high moral principle. The root meaning of Gandhi's concept of* satyagraha . . . *is "holding on to truth" . . . Gandhi also called* satyagraha *the "love force" or "soul force" and explained that he had discovered "in the earliest stages that pursuit of*

truth did not permit violence being inflicted on one's opponent, but that he must be weaned from error by patience and sympathy . . . And patience means self-suffering. So the doctrine came to mean vindication of truth, not by the infliction of suffering on the opponent, but on one's self.

King was even more explicit on this point: the purpose of civil disobedience, he explained many times, was to force the defenders of segregation to commit brutal acts in public and thus arouse the conscience of the world on behalf of those wronged by racism. King and Gandhi did not succeed because they changed the hearts and minds of southern sheriffs and British colonial administrators (although they did, in fact, change some minds) but because they made the price of maintaining control too high for their opponents[5] [emphasis mine].

That, I believe, is what it's going to take to abolish the death penalty in this country: we must persuade the American people that government killings are too costly for us, not only financially, but — more important — morally.

The death penalty *costs* too much. Allowing our government to kill citizens compromises the deepest moral values upon which this country was conceived: the inviolable dignity of human persons.

I have no doubt that we will one day abolish the death penalty in America. It will come sooner if people like me who know the truth about executions do our work well and educate the public. It will come slowly if we do not. Because, finally, I know that it is not a question of malice or ill will or meanness of spirit that prompts our citizens to support executions. It is, quite simply, that people don't know the truth of what is going on. That is not by accident. The secrecy surrounding executions makes it possible for executions to continue. I am convinced that if executions were made public, the torture and violence would be unmasked, and we would be shamed into abolishing executions. We would be embarrassed at the brutalization of the crowds that would gather to watch a man or woman be killed. And we would be humiliated to know that visitors from other countries — Japan, Russia, Latin America, Europe — were watching us kill our own citizens — we, who take pride in being the flagship of democracy in the world.

And here I am driving to Baton Rouge from the death house, where tomorrow a man is going to be executed, and it's going to happen all over again and I'm going to be there and there's nothing I can do to stop this senseless, futile killing.

It all seems so overwhelming.

A good night's sleep, that's what I need.

I take several long, deep breaths. I'm coming into Baton Rouge.

No need for phone calls this time to line up the funeral and burial. Robert's family is taking care of that. Sisters Kathleen and Lory say they'll be at the gates of the prison tomorrow night during the execution, and other Sisters will be there, too. The "Sob Sisters," as Vernon Harvey calls us. The plan is for me to get to the prison by two o'clock in the afternoon and, after the execution, if I'm up to it, to drive the car back. If I'm too upset to drive, one of the Sisters will drive my car.

A phone call comes from Jason DeParle, a close friend and reporter at the *Times-Picayune*; he wants to offer me his support. There are calls from Bill and Debbie Quigley and Millard, Tom Dybdahl, and other friends and coworkers. Pilgrimage for Life, our statewide anti-death-penalty group, will conduct prayer vigils in New Orleans and at the Governor's Mansion in Baton Rouge.

Jason DeParle has interviewed Robert and written a long article about him which carried the headline: "Murderer Willie Going to Chair a Proud Man." Jason told me he had struggled with the story because throughout the interview Robert had presented such a "macho" and unrepentant image, and as a reporter, of course, he had no choice but to render the image Robert projected. He tells me this somewhat apologetically because he knows I am Robert's spiritual adviser and trying hard to "work" with him. Jason will be doing follow-up stories of the execution and the funeral. He's young, an excellent writer, and sensitive to issues of social justice. When his schedule allows, he comes to the potluck suppers at the Quigleys'.

I get a good night's sleep, thanks to the now familiar getting-through-an-execution formula of a sleeping pill and a cup of hot milk. I awake rested and ready. The feelings of futility and despair of yesterday have washed away. It's December 27, the feast of St. John the Evangelist. He was the one to record in his Gospel the words of Jesus, "You shall know the truth and the truth shall make you free."

At two o'clock I arrive at the prison. I look at the visitors' building there in the bright sunlight and I find myself playing a childhood game: when I look at this building again, the execution will be over, and what will the building look like then? When I was a child setting out on a family vacation I'd look at a particular bush in the front yard or the doorknob on the kitchen door. Then, when we returned home, I'd look at the object again and remember that I had looked at it before. I guess it was a child's way of plumbing time, of sensing its passage.

Now I look at the building and know that when I see it again, Robert Lee Willie will be dead.

The prison vehicle is waiting for me.

As I enter the death house, I see that Elizabeth, Robert's mother, and her three sons, Robert's stepbrothers, are already there.

Mickey and Todd are sitting closest to the white metal door. In chairs behind them are Elizabeth and Tim. I met them when I visited Elizabeth. They are handsome, healthy-looking kids. I can tell it's eighteen-year-old Mickey, the oldest, who's keeping the conversation going. He's teasing Robert, accusing him of trying to steal his girlfriend during one of Robert's last calls home. "She was only on the phone a few minutes," says Mickey, "and there she was falling for the ole Robert charm. I had to take back that phone."

I pull up a chair and look at my watch. It's 2:10. Rules say the family can visit until 5:45.

The talk goes on for a while about Mickey's girlfriend and then all the girlfriends Robert has had, and Robert asks Todd if he has a girl. Todd still has a little boy's round face, and when Robert asks him about a girl, his ears and the sides of his cheeks and neck turn pink, and he says he doesn't have time for girls, that he has too much fishing and camping to do, and talk turns to the tent and camping equipment he got for Christmas. Tim tells him to tell Robert about his recent experience of sleeping in the back yard. There are smiles at this and Elizabeth tries to divert the teasing, saying, "I made him come in. I was worried. I went out there and made him come into the house."

Robert asks Todd what happened and Todd is suddenly tired of sitting in the chair and he stands up near the door and moves his fingers up and down the mesh screen and says how he and his buddy put up the tent by themselves and cooked their own meal outside and stayed in the tent until about midnight, when they heard some kind of animal prowling around and making noises — not a cat or dog or anything like that, they could tell, but some kind of "wild animal."

I can tell Robert is highly amused. Probably he hasn't had many conversations like this with his stepbrothers, especially Todd, who would have been only seven years old when Robert was arrested in 1980.

He asks Todd which it really was — that he came inside because he was scared or because his mother came out and got him — and Mickey gives Todd a tap on the back and says, "Tell the truth now, tell the truth," and Todd is shifting from foot to foot.

He's just a kid, and I have to smile, remembering when I was a kid and all the times we set out to spend the night in the back yard. We'd throw sheets over the clothesline for our tent and talk and sing songs from Girl Scout camp and, inevitably, around midnight or so, sounds of "wild animals" would drive us inside.

Sometimes there are silences between the stories, and now and again a guard passes by as he goes through the back glass door to Camp F, and you can hear the swish of the air and feel the gush of cold as he opens the door. Elizabeth tells Robert that some people have been asking her about the funeral and she says she wouldn't talk about that and told them, "He's not dead." She is standing up by her chair and smoking and Robert must be relieved because she seems to be holding up and isn't crying. Maybe it's the unreality of the place, the sun shining so bright and all of her boys sitting around, teasing each other, *appreciating* each other — except that Robert will soon be dead, this could be a pleasant family visit.

As Blackburn approaches, I glance at my watch and see that it's three o'clock and already an hour has gone by, and Blackburn tells the family that they will have to be leaving now.

I look at Robert and he says to the warden, "Already? Isn't it kind of early?"

I know Robert knows what the rules say, about families being permitted to stay until 5:45. We had talked about it before.

Warden Blackburn repeats, "It's time for you folks to be leaving now."

Robert could protest this and I would join him in it. He's being cut out of three hours with his family on the last day of his life and for some reason he isn't upset. Maybe he doesn't want to get into a confrontation with the warden which will upset his mother.

Robert stands up and says he's collected his stuff in two pillow-cases and he'd feel better if they just took his stuff home with them now rather than having the prison send it later. He wants to make sure they get it. The guard on watch at the end of the tier moves to get the white bags and asks Robert to step back to the opposite end of the tier while he opens the door. He hands the two bags to Captain Rabelais.

"This is all my stuff here. Mick, ya'll can see about dividin' it up. Except my boots from Marion. I'm gonna walk to the chair in them boots. No cryin' now," he says, "I don't want no cryin'. I'm not tellin' ya'll good-bye yet. I'll call you tonight."

I ask the warden if the family can hug Robert and he shakes his head no. "Security," he says.

"See ya, man. Stay strong," Mickey says, and he almost gets it out, but there is a crack in his voice when he says "strong." Tim and Todd are beginning to walk out. Todd's face is crumbling into tears. Mickey and Elizabeth are moving toward the foyer. Elizabeth keeps jabbing a Kleenex to her eyes. "We love you, Robert," she says.

"No cryin'. I'll call you tonight. I'll call you."

There's some sort of mix-up over the two pillowcases, some inventory slip that needs to be signed before the bundles can be released. Tim has taken Todd outside and Elizabeth, Mickey, and I are standing in the foyer with the two pillowcases on the floor at our feet. Mickey, his voice barely containing his anger, says, "These people ought to get *organized*."

Robert, behind the door, can hear voices though he can't see us. "What's the holdup?"

"Somebody's got to sign some paper," Mickey says.

Robert gives a scornful laugh. "These people," he says. "This place sure ain't Marion, I'll tell you that."

It takes fifteen minutes or so for the inventory paper to be produced and signed. Tim and Todd are walking together in the parking lot in the front of the building. I put my arm around Elizabeth and walk with her to the front door. "Don't worry, I'll be with him. He has a lot of spunk, a lot of inner strength," I tell her.

"I know. I know. He's stronger than any of us," she says.

I watch through the front glass door as the boys and Elizabeth get into the van. The doors slam, the motor starts, and the vehicle drives away. One of the boys gives a little wave to me as they are driving off, and I see that Mickey has an arm around his mother's shoulders. She has her head in her hands.

I look down at my watch: 4:15, and here it is, the coldness in my stomach, the aloneness, and this time the *exact knowledge* of what each hour of this night will bring.

I recall a snatch of the Miserere, Psalm 51, that we used to recite each day as we moved to the dining room after the noontime examination of conscience. We also recited the psalm when a Sister was dying. *Have mercy on me, God, in your goodness; in the greatness of your compassion wipe out my offense ... Do not cast me from your presence and your holy spirit take not from me ...*

No, I realize, I don't have *exact knowledge* of what the night will bring. The protocol, yes, I know the protocol, but Robert Lee Willie? What if he rages and fights all the way to the chair? What if the tough veneer cracks and he sobs or faints?

I turn back to the white metal door.

Robert is standing near the door and taking slow drags from his cigarette. I wonder if the spell of control is broken. I wonder now what he'll do, what he'll say, but I can see that his hand is firmly on the helm of his feelings, that he's in charge of his own agenda. Maybe he's even relieved now that the family visit is over. His mother had barely cried, and it had not been a tearful, wrenching parting. Maybe that's why he didn't protest when the warden asked the family to leave early. Maybe now in these last hours it's easier just to take care of himself. It is, after all, what he's been doing since childhood.

"I'm goin' out with my boots on," he says, "and if it ain't too much trouble for you, ma'am, I'd sure appreciate bein' buried in these boots."

The air is still heavy with the finality of his family's leaving, and I start moving away the four empty chairs facing the white metal door. There will be only one chair now. It is darkening outside. The fluorescent lights have been turned on. *Create a clean heart in me, O God, and a steadfast spirit renew within me.*

Robert asks me about the results of the polygraph test.

Zulke, who had conducted the test this morning, had processed the results at his office in Baton Rouge. Since prison rules prohibited his telephoning the results directly to Robert, he called me.

"Zulke said your answers showed stress, just as he had predicted," I tell him. "He said the results were inconclusive."

The news surprises him. "Man!" he says. "Is the dude sure? Is he absolutely, positively sure? I felt at ease answering all the questions. I didn't feel no stress at all. Man! I can't believe I failed that test."

"Zulke didn't say you failed the test," I say. "He said that your responses registered stress, which may in normal circumstances be associated with lying, but here, facing death like this, who wouldn't show stress? All Zulke said was that the test showed stress, which he fully expected it would."

It amazes me that Robert actually thought he could transcend feelings of stress here in this death house on the day he's scheduled to die.

"Robert, you'd have to be a robot or insane not to feel stress," I say, and I tell him that mothers have a way of knowing the truth about their children, and that surely his mother is not going to rely on a semiscientific test to determine whether she believes him or not.

"Man!" he says. "I just can't believe that test didn't come out right." (I realize he must be struggling to clean up his language for me. In his disciplinary reports, which include verbatim accounts, "man" was certainly never included in his personal arsenal of expletives.)

I can see that he needs time to work through his disappointment and nothing I can say will help. I decide that maybe now's a good time to bring up the "niggers, spics, and chinks" discussion and I say he's *got* to be kidding, that he can't really buy all this Aryan white supremacy garbage, and doesn't he think it just a bit ironic that he, of all people, with his track record of crimes, should be claiming supremacy over anybody? Him?

"Forget the 'spics' and 'chinks,' " he says. "I just sorta threw 'em in. It's the niggers, really. I never have gotten on too good with 'em. Me and my cousin used to ride our bikes down the road and throw rocks at 'em and Junior kept warnin' us that they were going to beat us up, and, sure enough, one time they waited their chance and got ahold of our bikes and tore 'em up."

What he says about black people is classic racist stereotype. It's all about blacks being lazy, content to be on welfare, having babies out of wedlock, committing most of the crimes, and using up tax dollars in the process. "Slavery's long over," Robert says. "They keep harpin' on what a bad deal they've had. I can't stand people that make themselves out to be victims."

And I talk about the pervasiveness of racism in our society and how it's been with us from the beginning of this nation, which has built itself economically, at least in some measure, from the slave labor of blacks, and how, even when the slaves were freed through the Emancipation Proclamation, they were only partly freed because most of them were not allowed a chance to compete. In an agricultural society, most of them had no way of getting land. I tell him stories of black people I know in St. Thomas — good, hardworking people — and I argue that he ought to take a closer look at Reagan's economic policies — taxing working people while exempting the

rich, bankrolling defense contractors while abandoning the cities —
to see if poor blacks are the real culprits "gobbling up" our tax
dollars.

I ask him if he's ever been the object of prejudice.

He says, no, not until he got to prison, and he says how people
in society "talk bad" about prisoners, saying they're monsters or
animals or without human qualities of any kind. "What do they say
about us?" he says with a laugh. "That we are without socially
redeeming qualities, isn't that the way they put it?"

But mostly, he says, he doesn't like people who act like victims.
He likes people who put up a fight. "And that includes inmates,
too," he says. "Some of these sad-asses around here won't lift a
finger to stand up for their rights or better their condition, so they
get what they deserve, in my opinion. I think it was a great moment
when Martin Luther King led his people and they marched in the
streets all the way to the nation's capital and kicked the white man's
butt. I liked seein' that. They just didn't lie down and moan 'racism,
racism.' I wish they'd do more of *that*."

I am surprised when Captain Rabelais and the warden appear
with Robert's last meal. It's six o'clock.

His last meal.

When Robert sees the trays of food, he smiles and rubs his hands
together and says this is one meal he's going to enjoy.

I say, teasing him, "Hey, what about your saying you wouldn't
accept any favors from these people?"

He says that principle applies to everything but fried seafood. He
loves fried seafood.

A guard places three trays of fried shrimp, oysters, and fish, fried
potatoes, and salad on three chairs in front of him. Pat had sat inside
his cell to eat his meal so the handcuffs could be removed, but
Robert remains here by the door with the handcuffs on but detached
from the leather belt, so he can move his hands to eat.

Captain Rabelais serves me a tray of beef stew and corn, but at
the sight of it my throat closes and I fight back a wave of nausea. It
is 6:00 P.M. and it's been dark outside for some time, and all the
lights in the building are on and will not be turned off until tonight's
"task" is completed, and as some of my black friends say, "I know
what time it is."

I take a sip — a tiny one — of the iced tea. Robert, occupying a
universe of his own, picks up a fried shrimp with his fingers, smells
it with obvious delight, and eats. And eats and eats and talks and
eats, and it is hard for me to realize that this is his last meal. He

seems to have found some space, some grace, some kind of lagoon in the present moment, even though close by are white, crashing rapids.

Maybe his experience in life has taught him early on that life is waves, not particles, that nothing is really solid, that everything is flow. Or maybe his fierce "macho" stance has inured him from appropriate feelings. *"Electric chair don't scare me, man."* I quietly ask God to help me let go of life freely when it's time for me to die. Ignatius of Loyola, Theresa of Avila, John of the Cross, Francis of Assisi — every saint has taught the paradox that lies at the heart of the spiritual life: to love passionately but with freedom of spirit that does not cling even to life itself.

Robert says, "I feel kind of high but not like it was with the drugs. I know I'm going to a better place." And I move into the space with him and relax and my throat is not so tight and I sip the iced tea and take a taste of the stew.

Talk turns to family.

He talks about how "Junior," his stepfather, tried his best to be a father to him, but he was a rebellious teenage kid. He was using drugs and not taking orders from anybody.

"When we got the house my family has now," he says, "I had my own room and Junior said I could decorate it any way I wanted to, so I was hammering away, putting up my rebel flag on the wall, when Junior opened the door and said, 'but *no* putting nails in the wall.'" And he smiles at this and says how Junior had "a big thing about working for what you wanted and not expecting it just to be handed to you," and when he was thirteen, Junior bought him a lawn mower so he could get jobs cutting lawns. "He'd pay me a dollar to cut our lawn," he says. "That would give me twenty-five cents to get in the football game and seventy-five cents to spend."

But he could never hold a job for long, he says. He'd get a job, make some money, then stop working so he could enjoy the money he had earned. He drove trucks, worked on barges, grew marijuana and sold it.

I ask how he could grow marijuana without being caught, and he explains that he set his "patch" deep in a wooded area near Covington. "You have to be sure you have enough landmarks to find it yourself but without others being able to find it — either the law or other dealers, because the other dealers will get in there and steal your crop from you."

There's big money in drugs, he says, but it's dangerous, and after he and his cousin had drowned the drug dealer, he had made a resolution to get "regular" jobs. That included working on a push boat moving forty-eight barges from Grand Isle, Louisiana, to Cairo, Illinois, and he says how scary it was to walk on the barges at night, stepping across the open spaces with the barges rocking and swaying even though cables through iron loops were there to steady them and keep them all hooked together.

"One night," he says, "me and another dude had to go up to the first barge to set up a light, and afterwards, we sat on the front awhile and smoked a joint and calmed our nerves before making the trek back. The river is real, real mysterious at night with the lights makin' little flicks in the water and the swish of the current under you and you have this feeling and it's like an adventure, being away from home and on a long river like that, which you know goes by cities and towns and different parts of the country and finally to the sea."

The job, he says, included opening the hatches of the barges to check on the grain inside, and there would be rats "as big as dogs or cats" in the grain and so they would always bang on the lids before opening them to scare off the rats.

He holds an oyster up. "The last of the oysters," he says, and he recalls how they fed them well on the barges. "You shoulda seen the food we ate — big juicy steaks fixed any way you liked every single day if you wanted it and when you got off duty at night, cakes and pies and quarts of milk, which if you didn't finish, you were supposed to throw over the side, but I hated to waste food like that, knowin' there are people starvin' in the world. I've always been like that about not wastin' food."

He tells how it was dangerous work because you could fall between the barges and be crushed, or if the barges strained too hard the cable connecting them could snap, and once he had witnessed with his own eyes a cable snap and whip around and cut a man in half.

"Right at the waist, it cut him in two like a knife and his waist and legs dropped into the water, and he just looked down and died. I think the shock killed him, watching half his body drop into the water like that."

Robert reminds me of my cousins Jimmy and Wayne who worked on the oil rigs out in the Gulf and told stories like this. We'd be at our camp at Grand Isle, playing cards and talking, and they would tell us about the food and the accidents and about how they would go swimming in the clear green water and sometimes put on scuba gear and go down the steps of the rig way down deep where huge fish — two hundred pounds or so — would come right up to them. I envied boys who could get such adventurous jobs which were off-limits to girls.

"Man!" Robert says, "I can't believe I didn't pass that lie-detector test." He shakes his head, a fried potato between his fingers. "I wish I had been able to take the test sooner before I came in here."

He asks me to tell him exactly what the procedures are going to be — when they shave his head, everything, because he doesn't want to be surprised. He wants to be prepared.

His question jolts me. He had caught me up in the stories of the barges and the river, but now here we are. He has finished the last meal he will ever eat in his life and it is seven o'clock in the evening and he has five more hours to live.

I tell him everything I know: how they will shave his head, cut his left pants leg at the knee, give him a new white T-shirt, and put a diaper over his undershorts. I tell him about the walk to the chair, the opportunity to say his last words, and the straps they will use to fasten him to the chair, including his jaw, and the mask they will put over his face — everything.

I feel scared and cold telling him this, knowing that in a few short hours this reality will be his. A couple of weeks ago he had decided that he would like his execution to be televised. "It would be a good thing for the people to see what they are really doing, executing people. I'll bet if they saw it, it would change some minds," he had said. But state rules prohibit televising executions, and there was no way to challenge the rules, so he had let it go.

Now he wonders if he ought to shake Warden Blackburn's hand, but he decides he won't do that. "I don't wanna say nothin' to him like 'it's okay, I know you're only doin' your job.'"

It's on his mind, what he wants to say at the end. He knows for certain he wants to say something about the death penalty being wrong, and he's considering other things too. I wonder what I would say with the microphone before me, knowing that the words I say would be my last. I wonder if I would even know what I was saying. With Pat, the words had been so ordinary, in a way. What made them extraordinary was knowing they were the last.

Robert tells me he had called his lady friend in Texas, the one he loved, to tell her about the execution. He says he invited her to come see him in the death house, but she was shy about the publicity that might come her way. He had said that he didn't want to put pressure of any kind on her and that if she didn't want to come, it was okay, that he understood. Before he hung up he had thanked her for all the good times they had had.

We get to talking about the earring in his left ear. "It means I'm heterosexual and not no homo," he explains to me.

"The Marlboro Man," I tease him.

"Well, actually, I don't have a big thing about wearing an earring to assert my manhood," he tells me, "but the wife of a friend of mine offered to pierce my ear for me, and she told me to put my head in her lap and she'd do it, and" — he smiles — "I just couldn't pass that up."

Time is washing away now. It's close to 9:30. Robert is getting ready to telephone his family. I tell him that tears are a sign of humanity and strength, not weakness, and that Jesus had cried when a good friend of his died and during the agony before his own death. "Marlboro men are only on cardboard," I say.

"When I talk to Mom I'm gonna let it flow," he says.

I walk back and forth in the foyer as Robert makes his phone calls.

The last-minute preparations for the execution have begun. Chaplain Penton is here and approaches the door to let Robert know he's available if he needs him. The secretary is setting up her typewriter in the room with the coffee pot. A number of the associate wardens with their walkie-talkies have arrived. No press yet, no witnesses. They'll be brought over around eleven o'clock. After five executions they've got the protocol down pat.

I go back to the white metal door. The phone receiver is back on its hook and Robert is in his cell. I can hear him blowing his nose. When he comes to the door I can see he has been crying.

"I just let it flow," he says. "I told my mother and Junior that I loved them. I talked to each of the boys."

"You're a real man now, Robert," I say.

"I hated to say good-bye," he says. "I told them if I get a chance I'll call 'em back right before I go."

I ask him if he would like to pray with me and he nods his head and I am reading the words of Jesus, "You will learn the truth and the truth will make you free," when Slick with his shaving kit approaches the door.

"You have a dignity, Robert, that no one can take from you," I say to him.

In the foyer I walk slowly up and down, just as I had done for Pat, and here again is the same circle of light and strength, and I pray to Pat and ask him to help Robert, and I ask God to help Vernon and Elizabeth Harvey.

Back at the visitor door Robert rubs his hand on his shaved head. "Wow, they even took off the eyebrows," he says.

It's the first time I've seen him without his long-sleeved denim shirt. His arms are covered with tattoos. He lowers his eyes and won't look at me and says, "You're gonna think I'm a bad person, seeing all these tattoos," and I can tell he is very embarrassed. There's a swastika and a skull, women's names, and on one arm a naked woman.

"Doesn't it hurt to get tattoos?" I ask.

It's something to talk about.

Robert tells me about the man in Marion that did most of his tattoo work, and that when you get it done you want to get it done by an expert so you don't get infections. He says that on his chest he has the "Grim Reaper" on one side and a woman's body on the other.

It's all stream now, the talk, weaving and flowing and not following any pattern.

"I have to make a confession to you," he says, and he explains that when he first heard I was a nun he thought he was really going to be "in for it." "I thought you'd be doin' nothin' but preachin' repentance at me, but after our first visit, I saw I could just talk to you like a friend, and I told my mother that I met this real nice lady."

I tell him that when Millard Farmer had first told me about his crime I thought he was some kind of sociopath. I thought he must be mentally deranged.

"And now that you've met me, you're sure of it," he says and gives his little soft laugh. "I was deranged all right to let myself go along with Joe Vaccaro."

It's a few minutes past 11:00. We can hear the front door opening and closing, opening and closing. The witnesses and press are arriving. Vernon and Elizabeth Harvey must be inside the building now.

"Think I'll call my family one more time," he says. "Just stay here. Don't go out there with all those people."

The guard at the end of the tier comes down to hand the receiver to him. The operator will say, "A collect call from Robert Willie at a correctional institution. Will you accept charges?"

"Yes," someone from the family will say, "we'll accept the charges." One more phone call. The last time the family will ever hear his voice. I wonder how little Todd is doing, and Mickey and

Tim. Maybe there will be some sort of relief when it's all over and the phone doesn't ring any more. Not that they want him to die, but each time the phone rings, their hearts must race to their throats. The dread must be terrible.

It's 11:30 and the team of guards goes into the cell with Robert to put the diaper on him. I hear the murmur of voices. I hear the toilet flush. *A clean heart create in me, O God, and a steadfast spirit renew within me . . . for you are not pleased with sacrifices . . . a heart contrite and humbled, O God, you will not spurn . . .*

Robert is back at the door and has the guard hand me his parting gift, the black knitted hat. "It's probably pretty dirty," he says. "You'll have to wash it."

I thank him for the hat.

He thanks me for teaching him about God. "I know God knows the truth about what happened," he says. "I know I'm gonna be okay, and look, when I get in the chair, I'm gonna let you know I'm okay."

"Look at me," I tell him, "look at my face."

He seems confident that he is going to a better place. "I'm not worried at all," he says, but he shivers and the guard comes and puts his denim jacket around his shoulders.

And here we go again, we are doing this all over again, with Blackburn, not Maggio, this time coming to the door at midnight with the full squad of the "Strap-down Team," saying, "Time to go, Willie."

He is already standing. He is ready.

I step back as the guards bring him out and surround him. As we walk, I read to him from the Gospel of John, and if he can hear, if he can take in the words at a moment like this, he hears the words of Jesus about laying down his life in order to take it up again, and as I read the words I look up and see that Robert is walking with the same little jaunty walk, up on the balls of his feet, the only way I have ever seen him walk.

As we approach the death chamber the guards direct me to a chair with the other witnesses. I see Vernon and Elizabeth Harvey on the front row. They are serious, silent, looking straight ahead. The lights are very bright, the dark oak chair gleams, the big clock on the wall behind the chair says 12:07.

Robert says his last words:

"I would just like to say, Mr. and Mrs. Harvey, that I hope you get some relief from my death. Killing people is wrong. That's why you've put me to death. It makes no difference whether it's citizens, countries, or governments. Killing is wrong."

He sits in the chair and the guards begin to strap him in. He watches as they strap his arms and legs. They put the metal cap on his head and the electrode on the calf of his left leg, and they are ready to put on the chin strap and the mask over his face when Robert takes one more look around the room at the world he is leaving. He looks at me and winks, and then they strap his chin, lower the mask, and kill him. This time I do not close my eyes. I watch everything.

CHAPTER

10

I walk into a blur of television camera lights outside the prison.

Vernon Harvey pours himself a drink and smiles, and says to the clutch of reporters that he's sorry every victim doesn't have the satisfaction of watching a murderer die. But he says Willie died too quickly, and he wishes Willie could have had the same kind of painful death that Faith had, and he hopes he fries in hell for all eternity. When asked if he's happy, Vernon Harvey says, "Do you want to dance?"

Elizabeth Harvey says Willie's unrepentant attitude made her want to witness his execution and that she's glad he's dead and won't be able to kill any other people.

Fourteen-year-old Lizabeth Harvey, who was not permitted to view the execution because of her age, has been waiting outside the gates with friends and supporters. Inside the family van, she has helped to make posters supporting capital punishment. A picture of her smiling and hugging her mother and a family friend after the execution will make its way into a two-page spread in *Life* magazine. She tells reporters that this has been the "best Christmas" she has had in a long time, knowing the man who had killed her sister was finally executed. "That ought to tell murderers that if they kill somebody, they're going to face the electric chair."

When reporters turn to me, I say, "What have we accomplished by killing Robert Willie? Now two people are dead instead of one, and there will be another funeral and another mother will bury her child."

Reporters ask me if Willie showed any remorse. I tell them of his last words to the Harveys, that he hoped his death would give them peace.

For a second, in the glare of the lights, Vernon Harvey and I look across at each other. It is only for a moment. Then he disappears among his supporters, their signs bobbing under the glare of the lights: "Just Revenge," "Remember the Victims," "Murder in La. and Die." And I, with the Sisters, head to the waiting cars in the parking lot.

When the jolts hit him, the way he was strapped to the chair, his body didn't move much. He lifted somewhat in the chair and his chest pushed against the straps and his hands gripped the edges of the chair, but there wasn't much movement. Three times the current hit, and I couldn't see his face. I had prayed out loud, "God, forgive us, forgive all who collaborate in this execution."

The morning after the execution I awake at Mama's, thinking of Robert's words — he had said not to mourn him but "maybe now and then go and pour a beer on my grave." He had not gone to the chair in his boots. He had gone in white terry-cloth slippers.

The phone is ringing. Mickey, Robert's stepbrother, calls to say the funeral will be held tomorrow at the Brown-McGeehee Funeral Home in Covington, with burial in the family plot in nearby Folsom. The warden's office calls to tell me that they have Robert's boots and I can come pick them up. Friends and supporters call, including some who had participated in the anti-death-penalty prayer vigil last night in front of the Governor's Mansion; and they describe how their prayers kept mingling with the merriment of Yuletide revelers who had come to admire the governor's forty-foot Christmas tree there on the lawn.

By afternoon I feel the fierce desire to do something *normal*, and I'm in jeans and an old sweatshirt washing the car when the call comes from *ABC Evening News* in New York, asking if I will consent to an interview about Robert Willie's execution with Peter Jennings. I wipe the back of my wet hand on my pants and weigh the invitation. I look at my watch. It means changing into my suit and heels and getting to the television station *now*. The shortness of time is a good excuse to say no, and I want to stay in this protected, private space and finish washing the car. Besides, this is *national* television and *live*, and I need my wits about me, and I know that I am tired and wrung-out.

"I'll be there," I tell them.

I know I have to be there because it's an opportunity to talk about the death penalty, and I always make it a rule to say yes to such invitations if I'm able.

I change clothes and drive to WBRZ, the ABC affiliate station in Baton Rouge.

As soon as I arrive, a technician, working quickly, hooks the microphone onto the lapel of my coat, hands me a small hearing device to insert into my ear, and in a few short moments I am hooked up to New York. Before we go on the air, Peter Jennings practices saying "Prejean" — "Pray-zshawn." He recognizes that it's French and wants to make sure he pronounces it correctly. To tell you the truth, he tells me, they want my viewpoint because they are featuring the Harveys and they don't want to present only one side of the issue. It's unusual, he says, for a state to allow the victim's family to witness an execution, and that's what sparked their interest in this story in the first place. The technician advises me not to look at the monitor when I speak because the picture is a second behind the audio and it can be confusing.

The story opens showing the Harveys outside the prison after the execution. Someone is holding a sign that says "Have 'Faith' in the Justice System."

Vernon says he wishes every victim could have the opportunity he had tonight. Lizabeth says that since Robert Willie saw Faith die, her parents should see him die. Warden Blackburn is shown announcing that Robert Willie was pronounced dead at 12:15 A.M. and then Robert's last statement is read. Then they go back to Elizabeth and Vernon Harvey, and Vernon says he feels it was too easy and quick for Willie, "he didn't suffer no pain, and my daughter had to."

Jennings asks me what purpose is served by letting the victim's parents attend the execution.

I say that Louisiana officials feel that if any people have a right to witness, it should be the parents of the victim, but I feel that this merely emphasizes that an execution is an act of personal vengeance.

"Are people there for vengeance?" Jennings asks.

Yes, I say, they are, out of their deep pain, and I sympathize with them in the loss of their daughter.

Jennings asks if I feel it would be a good thing for people to be exposed to executions, and I say yes, because then they would see the violence unmasked and this would lead them to abolish executions. I say that an execution is a brutal and horrible thing, and that I heard Mr. Harvey say Robert experienced no pain, but that the pain came every time he looked at his watch, knowing that in a few days, a few hours he would die.

Jennings thanks me and turns to George Will, the political commentator, and asks whether he thinks people should be able to witness executions.

George Will says the American people favor capital punishment, not primarily because they believe it's an effective deterrent, but because it satisfies a deeply felt moral intuition that there are some crimes for which death is the only proportionate punishment, and this murder certainly seems to be one of those crimes. That is what the American people feel, he says, and he thinks they're right and that vengeance, far from being shameful, can be noble.

Jennings presses the original question of whether people, if allowed to witness executions, would be repelled by capital punishment.

Will says he thinks that's arguable and that some people who see it as a deterrent say we ought to show it on television and make it as grisly as possible, but he believes that would have a "very bad coarsening" effect on the country. Capital punishment, he says, can be done in private and still perform the essential function of expressing the community's vengeance, not just for the loved ones but for the whole community of Louisiana, which, he believes, was expressing itself last night.

That's it. That wraps up the death-penalty segment of the evening news. I look up and see that a small group of WBRZ staff has assembled to watch the encounter. I guess this is a pretty big occasion, for a local affiliate to be featured on national news like this. One of the technicians remarks to me, as he unthreads the microphone wire from the sleeve of my coat, that for national prime-time television, that was a "large hunk" of time I was given. Usually, he says, it's a forty-five-second or one-minute spot, especially when it's live. But all I can think is that George Will said that the expression of vengeance in an execution is not shameful, but noble.

Noble?

Yet, he was quick to add that only a very few people in a private setting should witness an execution because public exposure would have a "coarsening" effect on society.

How, I wonder, does a *noble* act *coarsen* society?

Another death-penalty advocate, Walter Berns, author of *For Capital Punishment: Crime and the Morality of the Death Penalty,* concurs with George Will on the necessity of restricting the number of witnesses at executions. He, too, fears that public viewing of such events would have a "coarsening" effect upon the populace: "No ordinary person can be required to witness [executions], and it would be better if some people not be permitted to witness them — children, for example, and the sort of persons who would, if permitted, happily join a lynch mob. Executions should not be televised, both because of the unrestricted character of the television audience and the tendency of television to make a vulgar spectacle of the most *dignified event*"[1] [italics mine].

But it's not the presence of television cameras or the composition of the crowd or even whether the crowd acts politely or not that makes the execution of a human being ugly. An execution is ugly because the premeditated killing of a human being is ugly. Torture is ugly. Gassing, hanging, shooting, electrocuting, or lethally injecting a person whose hands and feet are tied is ugly. And hiding the ugliness from view and rationalizing it numbs our minds to the horror of what we are doing. This is what truly "coarsens" us.

I think of the moment when Warden Ross Maggio stood at the microphone to announce the time of Pat Sonnier's execution. His eyes happened to meet mine, and he lowered his eyes. It was instinctive. He had helped kill a man. There was nothing noble about it.

Camus held that executions are performed in secret because they are shameful deeds. State governments, he said, who wish executions to continue, know to keep them hidden from view, not only physically but also symbolically in the euphemistic language used to describe them. (p.176).

When the death penalty is talked about, a strange lexicon of euphemisms emerges:

- Mob vengeance, when enacted by government officials, is called *noble*.
- The torture and killing of a convicted prisoner is commensurate with his or her *dignity*.
- Death by lethal injection is *humane*.

Ronald Reagan voiced this last euphemism in 1973, when, as governor of California, he advocated lethal injection as a method of execution: "Being a former farmer and horse raiser, I know what it's like to try to eliminate an injured horse by shooting him. Now you call the veterinarian and the vet gives it a shot and the horse goes to sleep — that's it."[2]

Surely, the reasoning goes, lethal injection is a far more "humane" method of execution than methods practiced in times past (and not-so-past — the last four methods on the following list are current): poisoning, stoning, beheading, crucifying, burning, casting from heights onto rocks, pouring molten lead on the body, starving, sawing into pieces, burying alive, impaling, drowning, drawing and quartering, crushing with heavy weights, boiling, throwing into a pit with reptiles, giving to wild animals to be eaten alive, disemboweling, garroting (strangulation), beating to death, breaking on the wheel, stretching on the rack, flaying, hanging,* electrocuting, shooting, gassing.[4]

Witnesses will be "bored," Deputy Warden Richard Peabody, who supervises executions at Angola, said when Louisiana switched in 1990 from the electric chair to lethal injection. "About the only thing that witnesses may observe is that during the injection of sodium pentathol, the man may gasp or yawn. There doesn't seem to be any other activity that's going to be physically seen."[5]

Louisiana became the nineteenth state to use lethal injection to kill prisoners since the state of Oklahoma inaugurated its use in 1977. The method is preferred because it virtually eliminates visible, bodily pain. There is only the "uncomfortableness" of a needle prick into a vein. There remains, however, one dimension of suffering that can never be eliminated when death is imposed on a conscious human being: the horror of being put to death against your will and the agony of anticipation. As if, when they strap you down on the gurney, your arms outstretched, waiting for the silent deadly fluid to flow — the sodium pentothol, which comes first to make you unconscious so you do not feel the pancuronium bromide when it paralyzes your diaphragm and stops your breathing and the potassium chloride which causes cardiac arrest and stops your heart — as if you feel the terror of death any less because chemicals are being used to kill you instead of electricity or bullets or rope?

There is an elaborate ruse going on here, a pitiful disguise. Killing is camouflaged as a medicinal act. The attendant will even swab the

---

*The states of Washington, Montana, Delaware, and New Hampshire still allow hanging. On Tuesday, January 5, 1993, the state of Washington hanged triple-child killer Westley Allen Dodd. In a twelve-page list of instructions the Department of Corrections specifies a thirty-foot Manila hemp rope ¼-to-1¼ inch in diameter which is boiled to eliminate stiffness and lubricated with wax, soap, or oil to ensure tightness when the noose is placed around the neck. According to the manual the distance a standing person must fall to generate enough force so the knot breaks the spine depends on weight. For Dodd, that was calculated at 7 feet, 1 inch. If the condemned feels faint while waiting for the trapdoor to be sprung, a board with straps is nearby to prop him or her up.[3]

"patient's" arm with alcohol before inserting the needle — *to prevent infection.*

Admittedly, when executions were public, it was not a pretty sight. People sensed blood, drama. They came in droves, in the thousands sometimes — men, women, and teenagers, and some children too. Some came early to get a "good seat" right up under the gallows. Some packed lunches and ate in the shade of trees and waited for the big event — "There's gonna be a hanging." Some cheered. Some taunted. Some were silent. All watched. When a black person was executed, the racism was not disguised. "Whooie, niggah boy, they're gonna hang your ass now." It was awful to see, and fascinating. And visible. It was truthful. They didn't call it "noble" or "dignified" or say they were putting a person to "sleep" like a horse. It was cruel. It was unusual. And it was obviously punishment. It was death. Forcible, violent, premeditated death. And the people knew it, and the people came to watch because it was death, because death, when you can see it happening in front of your eyes, is always something to watch.

These public executions were called "vulgar" spectacles, which meant not that the execution itself was vulgar, but that the people witnessing it did not act in a seemly or dignified manner.

Then, the "coarsening" effect of executions on people was clear. Now, with executions hidden, the "coarsening" effect is more subtle. But there are symptoms:

- We stand by as the Supreme Court dissolves Eighth Amendment protection against cruelty and torture.*
- Some of us openly acknowledge that even though the death penalty is racially biased and unfairly imposed upon the poor we nevertheless approve its practice.[6]
- Some of us say that even if *innocent* people are sometimes executed along with the guilty, we support the death penalty anyway.[7]

If the innocent are executed?

A two-year study of capital punishment in the U.S. by Hugo A. Bedau of Tufts University and Michael L. Radelet of the University

*Is this because we Americans seem to hold our civil liberties lightly? Two out of every three Americans don't know that the Bill of Rights is the first ten amendments of the Consitution. Twenty-three percent of Americans believe the President can suspend the Bill of Rights during wartime.[8] Fifty-five percent support mandatory drug testing for all Americans.[9]

of Florida documents that in this century 417 people were wrongly convicted of capital offenses and 23 were actually executed.[10]

In recent years cases have surfaced of people sent to death row in error and later released.

- Randall Dale Adams (released in March 1989, Texas)
  The subject of the acclaimed documentary *The Thin Blue Line*, Adams was sent to death row in 1977. Prosecutors manufactured evidence to convict Adams and relied on the perjured testimony of the man who actually murdered the police officer. The Texas Court of Criminal Appeals unanimously set aside his conviction in 1989.[11]
- William Jent and Earnest Lee Miller (released in 1988, Florida)
  Convicted and sentenced to death in 1979 by prosecutors who withheld exculpatory evidence. A federal judge in 1988 ordered a new trial within 90 days. Instead, the state offered to free the innocent men in exchange for a plea of guilty to second-degree murder.[12]
- James Richardson (released in 1989, Florida)
  Originally sentenced to death in 1968 for poisoning his children. Numerous examples of misconduct by the prosecutor finally led the Miami State Attorney's office to undertake a complete examination of the facts of the case, an examination which concluded Richardson was innocent.[13]
- Henry Drake (released in 1987, Georgia)
  Sentenced to death in 1976, Drake was granted a new trial by the Eleventh Circuit Court of Appeals in 1985. At his second trial the jury could not reach agreement. At his third trial he was again convicted but sentenced to life. Six months later he was totally exonerated by his alleged accomplice, and the parole board set him free.[14]
- Anthony Silah Brown (released in 1986, Florida)
  Sentenced to die in 1983, despite a jury recommendation of life imprisonment, Brown was given a new trial because of trial errors. At his retrial the state's chief witness against Brown admitted that his original testimony had been perjured and Brown was acquitted.[15]

These are the lucky ones. A good attorney like Millard Farmer comes into their lives and struggles vigorously to keep them alive or, as in the case of Randall Adams, the subject of *The Thin Blue Line*, a film producer aggressively pursues the evidence and exposes prosecutorial misconduct. In the last twenty years at least forty-six people have been released from death row because the errors in their convictions were found in time to save their lives.[16]

Some are not so lucky.

James Adams, for example, executed in Florida in 1984.

> *In 1974 Adams, a black man, was convicted of first-degree murder and sentenced to death. Witnesses located Adams' car at the time of the crime at the home of the victim, a white rancher. Some of the victim's jewelry was found in the car trunk. Adams maintained his innocence, claiming that he had loaned the car to his girlfriend. A witness identified Adams as driving the car away from the victim's home shortly after the crime. This witness, however, was driving a large truck in the direction opposite to that of Adams' car, and probably could not have had a good look at the driver. It was later discovered that this witness was angry with Adams for allegedly dating his wife. A second witness heard a voice inside the victim's home at the time of the crime and saw someone fleeing. He stated this voice was a woman's; the day after the crime he stated that the fleeing person was positively not Adams. More importantly, a hair sample found clutched in the victim's hand, which in all likelihood had come from the assailant, did not match Adams' hair. Much of this exculpatory information was not discovered until the case was examined by a skilled investigator a month before Adams' execution. Governor Bob Graham, however, refused to grant even a short stay so that these questions could be resolved.[17]*

The fact that mistakes are made will not surprise anyone with even cursory knowledge of the criminal justice system. It has been a sobering discovery for me to see just how flawed and at times chaotic the system of justice is. Examining capital cases, Bedau and Radelet found numerous instances of overzealous prosecution, mistaken or perjured testimony, codefendants who testify against the other to receive a more lenient sentence for themselves, faulty police work, coerced confessions, suppressed exculpatory evidence, inept defense counsel, racial bias, community pressure for a conviction, and, at times, blatant politics — such as a D.A.'s decision to press for the death penalty in a particular case because he's campaigning for reelection.

DEAD MAN WALKING

In England the hanging of an innocent man, Timothy Evans, in 1949, mustered public outrage which led to a moratorium on the death penalty for murder in 1965 and permanent abolition in 1969. And Camus in his "Reflections on the Guillotine" mentions the effect that the execution of an innocent man, Lesurques, had on Victor Hugo:

> *When Hugo writes that to him the name of the guillotine is Lesurques, he does not mean that all those who are decapitated are Lesurques, but that one Lesurques is enough for the guillotine to be permanently dishonored. (pp. 212–13)*

In contrast, Ernest van den Haag, a professor of jurisprudence and public policy at Fordham University, when asked to respond to the Bedau-Radelet study showing that innocent people have actually been executed in this country, said: "All human activities — building houses, driving a car, playing golf or football — cause innocent people to suffer wrongful death, but we don't give them up because on the whole we feel there's a net gain. Here [executions], a net gain in justice is being done."[18]

A handful of relatives and friends gather at the Brown-McGeehee Funeral Home in Covington to bury Robert Lee Willie. When I see Elizabeth she holds me tight and cries and I try to comfort her, telling her about the last hours of her son and how bravely he had met his death.

The three boys hover close to their mother, and Junior is here, too. Little Todd keeps taking his mother's hand and holding it.

I walk over to the open casket and look down at what remains of Robert Lee Willie. His body is dressed in blue jeans and a white T-shirt, and I notice a couple of tattoos on his arms that I hadn't noticed before — a peacock and marijuana leaves. It is a shock to see him so quiet and still like this, his eyes closed, his lips not moving.

There is a flutter of commotion and some laughter when word spreads that Robert's aunt Bessie, waving her shoe, just chased away a reporter who tried to enter the funeral home.

When the funeral director announces that the last good-byes are to be said, Elizabeth approaches the casket. "Oh, Robert, Robert, my boy, O God, help me," she says, weeping. "Oh, Robert, how much I loved you," and she leans over to kiss him and faints, collapsing on the floor. "Mama! Mama!" Todd says and he begins to cry. Elizabeth is brought to an adjoining parlor and remains there for the rest of the service.

A local minister, addressing the young people, gives a sermon about the evils of drugs and prays, asking God to spare Robert Lee Willie the pains of everlasting hellfire. I talk about Robert and the last days and hours of his life and how Jesus taught us to love each other no matter what, and I tell them what Robert had said to the Harveys before he died — how he hoped his death would give them some relief.

The minister says a short prayer at the grave site and someone whispers to me that Robert's father is here, and after the ceremony I go up to him standing here in his denim overalls near the freshly dug grave of his son, and I take his hand and do not know what to say to him except "Mr. Willie," and I begin to cry.

Elizabeth and the boys invite me to the house and I go and we sit around the dining-room table and drink coffee and look at a photograph album and Elizabeth gives me a wallet-sized photograph of Robert as a small boy, maybe six years old, with his thin little face and a slight smile and his hair all slicked close to his head. She also gives me another photo, one Robert had sent her from Marion, where he is standing, unsmiling, dressed in khaki pants and a white, tank-top undershirt, a cigarette limp in his hand, and on the back the inscription, "Hello, Mom, here is the picture of me living every day to the fullest."

CHAPTER

11

The best thing I can do for the Harveys is avoid them. Definitely, I decide, this seems the best course of action. Here I am, spiritual adviser to yet another man on death row,[1] giving lectures, conducting workshops, and organizing public demonstrations for the abolition of the death penalty. The Harveys, on the other hand, don't miss an execution. Each time, there they are outside the front gate of Angola, celebrating as another murderer is killed.

On what common ground could we possibly meet?

Good-bye, Harveys. Or so I think.

I have decided to avoid the Harveys, but they have not decided to avoid me.

Two years after Robert's execution, in 1986, our abolition group is sponsoring a weekend seminar on the death penalty at Loyola University. Not a big event by any means, attended by a hundred or so of those most dedicated to the cause. Proponents of the death penalty *never* attend these seminars.

Except the Harveys.

As we are about to begin the first session I look across the room and see them. I avert my eyes. All day I avoid them. Why have a confrontation over irreconcilable differences, a confrontation that can only lead to further estrangement and pain?

223

I make it through the whole day without meeting them. The day is ending. People are beginning to leave. Elizabeth is standing near the exit and I don't see her ahead of time and suddenly here she is and here I am and she says, "You haven't even looked at us all day. We haven't heard from you in such a long time. When are you coming to see us?"

I'm stunned. I tell her I'll be glad to come see them if they want me to come. Vernon, standing near Elizabeth, nods. Yes, they want me to come.

I realize that in their sorrow they must be lonely, but even more, I know it's rough going organizing victims' families in Louisiana. *They want me to visit.* It is an invitation for which I haven't dared to hope. I remember Vernon saying he liked apple pie. I decide to bake an apple pie. When sorrow and loss and conflict are overwhelming, bake a pie.

A few weeks later I drive up to the Harvey home in Mandeville across Lake Pontchartrain. Same tall trees near the house. Same swing on the porch. Vernon is recuperating from hip surgery. He's glad to get the pie. Elizabeth says, "For disagreeing with somebody so strongly, you sure are tearing into her pie." Vernon just smiles and eats. I sit in their kitchen and we talk and drink coffee. I am glad to be in their company again. They talk about helping victims' families — going with them to court, telling them what to expect, educating them on their rights. "Which we have had to learn on our own," Elizabeth says, "because we sure didn't have anyone to teach us," and then she says how they experienced two victimizations — one with Faith's murder and the other at the hands of the criminal justice system. "All the rights of the criminal are protected — they have lawyers appointed to them if they can't afford one and their rights are all spelled out and they are told what those rights are, but nobody told us our rights. We didn't even know we had rights. Like the right to see the autopsy report and Faith's body. They kept me from seeing Faith's body and then once the chance had passed it was too late. I know they were trying to protect me but that was my decision, not theirs, to make."

"What people don't know," Vernon says, "is that if they get stonewalled by local law-enforcement people, they can call up elected officials — politicians — and get some action."

"In dealing with the D.A. and the police," Elizabeth says, "you could probably get more information when you get your car stolen than if your child is killed because then you're the victim, but when someone's killed, they figure the one killed is the victim, not you, and you're pushed to the sidelines. You and what your needs are don't even count and you can call them until you're blue in the face and they won't call you back. Some do. Some are understanding, but not most of them. They're too busy prosecuting the criminal to be concerned about the victim's family."

Elizabeth says that she tells victims' families to be calm and unemotional when they telephone the D.A. or the police for information. "They don't deal well with emotionally upset people, they just hang up on you, and it's real important to keep lines of communication open with them. There's one case I'm thinking of where the woman's daughter could talk to the police calmer and easier than her mother, and so the daughter was the one who always made the phone calls for information. I tell them that after they hang up the phone, then they can cry and scream all they want, but not when they're talking to law enforcement people."

Vernon says prosecutors may not even want victims' families in the courtroom. "After all their hard work they're scared some relative of a victim might lose control and blurt something out and the jury will hear it and they'll lose the case."

"Some people don't know that they can give a victim impact statement," Elizabeth says, "and most don't know about the victim assistance programs that are available. Again, it's the sheriffs and D.A.'s who are supposed to let folks know about these programs, but plenty of them don't get the word out. There's no votes in it for them. They don't get elected or reelected for helping victims. We're making progress and now more people do know about the programs, but not nearly enough."

Dealing with the law enforcement officials is one thing, Vernon and Elizabeth say, and the way they were treated had surprised them, but what had surprised them even more was the way all their friends and even Faith's friends stayed away from them after the murder. Few, they say, came to visit them and very few came to the funeral.

"I think everyone was denying that this sort of violent death could hit so close to home," Elizabeth says. "They didn't want to admit it had happened to Faith because then they'd have to admit that it could happen to them, and people don't want to face that."

Vernon talks about the abolitionist seminar they had attended at Loyola University. He says he had told Elizabeth, " 'We better watch that nun, we better watch her. She's gonna abolish executions if we don't watch out.' "

He says it half joking, half serious. It's easy. The conversation is easy — even with Vernon shingling in his favorite death-penalty arguments and my countering with my own. I tell them about Robert's last hours and his struggle to formulate his last words. I tell them that I believe he was sincere when he said that he hoped his death would relieve their suffering.

Vernon begins to cry. He just can't get over Faith's death, he says. It happened six years ago but for him it's like yesterday, and I realize that now, with Robert Willie dead, he doesn't have an object for his rage. He's been deprived of that, too. I know that he could watch Robert killed a thousand times and it could never assuage his grief. He had walked away from the execution chamber with his rage satisfied but his heart empty. No, not even his rage satisfied, because he still wants to see Robert Willie suffer and he can't reach him anymore. He tries to make a fist and strike out but the air flows through his fingers.

I reach over and put my hand on his arm. My heart aches for him. I sympathize with his rage. Reason and logic are useless here. In time, I hope Robert's final wish comes true: that Vernon and Elizabeth find peace. But I know that it will not be Robert's death which brings this peace. Only reconciliation: accepting Faith's death — can finally release them to leave the past and join the present, to venture love, to rejoin the ranks of the living.

Some months later I meet the Harveys again — on the steps of the Louisiana Supreme Court building in New Orleans. They are there with a small group of supporters holding signs — "What about the victims?" — waiting for us as we conclude a weeklong abolition campaign across the state. It has been the longest trek yet for Pilgrimage for Life, about two hundred and fifty miles. All along the way we have gotten excellent media coverage and used the opportunity to educate the public on the death penalty.

This is getting to be familiar — the Harveys and their friends waiting for us here at the end.

During the rally Elizabeth asks me if she can have the microphone to speak to the group. As an organizer I know that one thing you *never* do at a public demonstration is hand over the microphone to the opposition. The media just might choose to feature them on the evening news, and you lose a hard-earned opportunity to get your message across.

But this is Elizabeth Harvey.

I hand her the microphone.

The television cameras zoom in.

She says that Congress is about to cut funds for victims' assistance and asks us to join them in writing letters to protest the cuts. Her request is met with hearty applause.

Two weeks after Elizabeth's appeal, a group of us from Pilgrimage send a signed petition to our congresspersons protesting the proposed cuts. I send the Harveys a photocopy of the petition and a personal note of support.

Our next encounter outside the prison gates, in August 1987, is more painful.

I've come with several fellow nuns to support Sister Ruth Rault, D.C., when she returns to the front gate after the execution. It's her nephew, Sterling, who will die tonight[2] and she will be there with him at the end. I had promised her that I would be waiting for her at the gate when she came out.

All the way there I am praying, *Please, God, please don't let the Harveys be there.* But here they are in the amber prison floodlights, with their daughter, Lizabeth, seated in folding chairs near the gates. A few friends are with them, and so are their posterboard signs, propped up on chairs.

"How are ya'll doing?" I say as I walk across to meet them. I nod respectfully toward the couple with them. Things are stiff.

"Hey, take a look at my new poster," Vernon says.

It's done in two frames, the first with the words, "Murderer's Rights: You have the right to an attorney" in bold black letters, and the second showing a tombstone with "R.I.P." on it and the words "You have a right to remain silent."

"He'll be silent all right—forever," Vernon chuckles. He is pleased with the poster. I admit that it makes its point very well. Propped up next to the Harveys are signs that are now familiar to me. One of them says, "Tell them about Jesus, then put them in the electric chair."

"How's the hip?" I ask Vernon. He has recently had a hip replacement.

"Coming along," he says.

My fellow nuns have formed a small circle about thirty feet away. They hold lighted candles and pray. Some of their words to God float over, words that the victims' families couldn't disagree with more.

The daughter of a couple seated near the Harveys was murdered several years ago. They are bitter that her murderer was given a life sentence, not death. They drive more than 100 miles to the penitentiary to join the Harveys for executions.

The woman says to me, "Have you read the Bible, the part where

God says, 'An eye for an eye,' and 'Whosoever doth shed blood shall have his blood shed?' Have you read that?" I say, yes, I'm familiar with the quote.

"Do you know what Romans 13 says?" she asks.

"About obeying civil authority, obeying the law, is that the one you mean?" I ask.

"Yes," she says, her voice clipped. But she doesn't want to talk to me anymore, about the Bible or about anything.

"You haven't lost a child. You don't understand anything," she snaps. "You're upsetting me. Just go away and leave us alone."

"I'm sorry about your daughter," I say as I move away. I hear Elizabeth saying something to her, something about my being "all right" and that I don't try to "change" them. And I hear Vernon saying something, too, and then I'm with the Sisters, praying and looking at my watch and knowing what's going on inside the prison and I can't hear them anymore.

The killing is done.

The guards at the gate announce the time of death. The news media interview us. And everyone leaves to go home. Everyone but the Harveys and me.

I'm waiting for a British reporter to come out of the prison. She wants to interview me and I agreed to ride back to New Orleans with her. The Harveys drive up to where I'm standing. Vernon says, "Look, I'm sorry our friend said those things to you. I guess she's just upset."

I say it's okay, I know she's in a lot of pain, and I thank him and Elizabeth for coming to my defense. I lean over toward them seated in the front seat, my arm resting on the ledge of the open window, and we talk for a while. Vernon says that it looks as if I've lost another one in the chair tonight and that we'll be having executions in this state for a long time to come, if he has anything to do with it. And I say, the day will come, someday, when the electric chair will be in a museum. He says, "Don't hold your breath," and he says something teasing and everybody laughs, including Lizabeth in the back seat, who listens and chimes in and pokes Vernon affectionately on the back of the head.

"Look," Vernon says, "it's time you came with us to a Parents of Murdered Children meeting. You've been helping all these scumballs. You ought to come find out what victims go through."

I know that he and Elizabeth have helped organize a victims' group, and I had considered going to one of the meetings but backed off. I am discovering that many victims' families, like the woman tonight, are angry at me because I oppose capital punishment. They think that compassion toward the murderer means betrayal of the victim. Why go to a meeting where I will upset people further? Already their pain is immeasurable. Why add to it? Especially since I know that there is something I cannot give them, something they may demand as a sign of loyalty and care: that I too desire the death of the one who killed their child. I know I cannot give them that. And that may only serve to upset them further.

But I also realize I'm protecting myself. I've been avoiding the victims because I'm afraid they'll turn on me and attack me. I fear their anger and rejection. Plus, I feel so helpless in face of their suffering. I don't begin to know how to help them. In all my life I have never felt such feelings and counterfeelings, such ambivalence. On one side, I oppose the death penalty; on the other, I feel sympathy for the victims. But what to do? What to do?

The Harveys break through my paralysis by inviting me to this meeting. If Vernon Harvey is inviting me, I must go. If I listen to people at the meeting and learn from them, I might discover a way to show I care.

The Harveys drive off and I am standing here alone waiting for the reporter. I notice one of the guards at the gate looking intently in my direction. He knows the Harveys and what they stand for and me and what I stand for. Seeing us together like this, laughing and talking, must be puzzling to him, the way we're acting — like friends.

I am standing outside the door and looking down at the doorknob. I take a deep breath and ask God's special help before I turn the knob and enter the room where the Parents of Murdered Children's group is meeting. I immediately search out the Harveys across the room and make my way over to them. "She's coming around, she's beginning to see the light," Vernon says as he introduces me to friends. I look around. It's an all-white group — middle-income, working folks. This doesn't surprise me. All of the counterdemonstrators we've encountered in our public campaigns have been white.

I'm nervous. When the meeting begins I sit between Vernon and Elizabeth and feel safer. I feel guilty. It has taken me four years to attend one of these meetings.

The motto of the group is "Give sorrow words," and, oh God, they do.

He was going out to be with the guys. I told him to take his jacket. Those were my last words to him.

My little 12-year-old daughter was stabbed to death in our back yard by my son's best friend. He had spent the night at our house and gone to church with us that very morning. Her little skiing outfit is still in the closet. I can't give it away.

When our child was killed, it took over a week to find her body. The D.A.'s office treated us like we were the criminals. Whenever we telephoned to find out what was happening, they brushed us off. They wouldn't tell us when the trial was happening. They wouldn't tell us anything.

Our daughter was killed by her ex-husband in our front yard with her children watching. *Bang! Bang! Bang!* He shot her, then himself right there on the front lawn . . .

Friends were supportive at first, at the time our son was killed, but now they avoid us. They don't know what to say, what to do. If you bring up your child's death, they change the subject. I keep getting the feeling that they think I should be able to put his death behind me by now and get on with my life. People have no idea what you go through when something like this happens to you.

My wife and I went to the sheriff's office to apply for victim compensation funds. A deputy rifled through a few drawers and said, "Don't know nothin' about these funds. Why don't ya'll write to Ann Landers? She helps people."

My husband and I are getting a separation. We just have different ways of dealing with our son's death. He wanted to get rid of all his clothes right away. I wanted to keep them. He said he had to move on in his life and I'm still grieving. "Until death do us part" has new meaning for me.

My daughter's killer can possibly get out on parole in another year. He's only served six years. I can't bear the thought that he would be out a free man and she is buried in the ground and dead forever. Six years is nothing. This isn't justice. My husband and I are planning to attend the parole hearing.

I lost my job. Just couldn't pull it together. I'd be staring out of the window and couldn't concentrate. They let me go last week.

Vernon starts to talk about Faith. His voice breaks and he can't speak. The room is silent.

Afterward, in the parking lot Elizabeth and Vernon walk with me over to my car. I thank them for inviting me to the meeting. They don't say much. They don't have to. *Late have I loved thee* — the words of St. Augustine in his *Confessions* well up within me. I put the key into the door of the car to unlock it and decide that, whatever it takes, I am going to help murder victims' families — as many as I can. I don't yet know how, but I'll find out.

The leader had said that the group was small tonight, just a dozen people. Thank God. So much tragedy seated around one table. But courage too, and, at times, ironic humor. People talked and cried and offered encouragement and validation: "No, you're not crazy. I've been through the mood swings you're talking about . . . Don't let that minister pressure you into forgiveness that you do not feel . . . You're not alone in feeling guilt. I felt a lot of guilt too, I still do sometimes, but I know better how to handle it . . ."

I am surprised that so many feel victimized by the criminal justice system. Insensitivity by the D.A.'s office and the police seems to be almost everyone's experience. I am also surprised by people's frequent experience of abandonment by relatives and friends. I notice that most victims mentioned tonight were killed by someone they knew. I am startled to find out that the divorce rate of couples who have lost a child is 70 percent. I see that some favor the death penalty and some do not. I find out that four to seven months after the murder is a critical time for survivors because by then the shock and numbness wear off and the loss and rage set in. I discover new meaning for the word "anniversary." I learn that survivors may recount over and over again the terrible details of the murder because they are trying to take it in, trying to overcome their own disbelief.

Mourning and weeping in this valley of tears . . . a snatch of words from a prayer comes to me as I drive home. I know that for the twelve or so grieving people who have found their way to this group tonight, there are thousands of others who are traumatized and alone. The valley of the victimized in this country is wide and deep and growing.[3] In such a sea of pain what can one person do?

Better, I decide, to try to help ten real hurting people – or nine, or one – than to be overwhelmed and withdraw and do nothing – or write an academic paper on The Problem of Evil.

At the next Pilgrimage board meeting I propose that we inaugurate an assistance program for murder victims' families in New Orleans. Everyone agrees. We decide to locate the program where the homicide rate is highest – in the inner city.

Mandated by the board to pursue funding and resources, I approach churches for start-up funds, Hope House for office space, and the Mennonites for a volunteer.[4] I discover that a victim assistance program such as ours – a nonprofit, community-based group – can get federal funds. In 1984 Congress passed the Victims of Crime Act, which set up the Crime Victims' Fund, and these funds are partially dedicated to community-based victim assistance programs such as ours.[5] State law-enforcement agencies administer these funds, and victim assistance groups must apply through state agencies for grants. Federal funds are not available to individuals, but state victim compensation funds are. In 1975 only ten states offered such help to victims. Now almost all of the states offer some form of compensation to victims of violent crime for expenses such as medical care, counseling, lost wages, and funeral expenses.

But, as Elizabeth and Vernon Harvey learned, often the local law-enforcement officials, entrusted with administering state funds and educating the public about them, put little energy or enthusiasm into the task. The sheriff's deputy who advised the victim's family to write to Ann Landers exemplifies the problem. Most sheriffs' departments direct their energies toward punishing offenders, not helping victims.[6]

Maybe one day we'll integrate some of the principles of civil law into criminal justice, as Howard Zehr advises in his book *Changing Lenses: A New Focus for Crime and Justice*. Zehr points out that civil law defines wrongs as injuries and focuses on settlement and restitution to the victims.[7] This is not to suggest that retribution or punishment of the offender does not have a place in the administration of justice, but the question for our future is whether retribution should be the *only* emphasis. According to the Amnesty International polls taken in four states* mentioned earlier, the American

---

*Georgia, New Mexico, New York, and Virginia. For New Mexico, the option offered was thirty years before the possibility of parole instead of twenty-five. See note 21 to chapter 5.

people seem to prefer a system of criminal justice which combines punishment for offenders with restitution for victims. These polls show that support for the death penalty as punishment for felony murder drops to about 50 percent when people are offered the alternative of mandatory twenty-five years' imprisonment without possibility of parole coupled with restitution to the victim's family from the labor of the offenders.

But given the present system, where prisoners in state institutions make only pennies for their labors, there is no practical way for offenders to make financial restitution to their victims.

Not yet. But that is not to say that a way cannot be found in the future. The truth is that we need to reform our system of criminal justice, and the first step toward that reform is the honest admission that the course we are now pursuing is counterproductive. Even though we execute criminals — at staggering costs — violent crime continues to rise. Between 1988 and 1992 murders nationwide increased 14 percent.[8] The death penalty, although it sounds tough on crime, is actually a diversion of resources away from crime-fighting programs that truly make our streets and neighborhoods safer. Texas, for example, has more than three hundred persons on death row and executes more of its citizens each year than any other state, yet its murder rate remains one of the highest in the country. The state spends approximately $2.3 million on each capital case, a grossly disproportionate outlay of resources which forces cut-backs in other crucial areas of crime control. It is estimated for example, that prisoners in Texas, because of economic cut-backs in the criminal justice system, serve only 20 percent of their sentence and rearrests are common.

In contrast, New York City, in a state with no death penalty, reduced its crime rate dramatically in the first four months of 1992 — murders declined by 11 percent — which many attribute to increased community policing. In 1990 the city had 750 foot officers on the streets. Today there are 3,000.[9]

Similarly, in New Orleans in 1992, the year ended with a 21 percent decrease in the murder rate, halting a three-year stretch of record-breaking murder rates, a decline which police readily attribute to two federal drug-fighting programs and beefed up police patrols in high-crime areas. Said police spokesperson, Sergeant Marlon Defillo: "We are taking more guns off the street before they can be used in more crimes."[10]

The question arises: how many laid off police officers is one execution worth?

As I go about setting up the victim assistance group in New Orleans, I know I have everything to learn. I send off for packets of information from victim assistance programs around the country[11] and telephone people who seem to have effective programs.

How do human beings who have been devastated by the murder of a loved one recover from such a loss and pick up their lives again? What helps? What hinders?

Janet Yassen, crisis services coordinator of the Victims of Violence Program in Cambridge, Massachusetts,[12] tells me that people who come seeking help most often need at least a year for the rage, grief, and loss to settle so that they can begin to integrate what happened to them. The feelings of rage never entirely go away, she says, but gradually, over time, the "volume" goes down, and victims can accept other emotions — appreciation of beauty, ambition, friendship, trust. She emphasizes how gradual the healing is and how the steps can't be short-circuited. Even after many years, she says, certain situations — the anniversary of the crime or reading about a similar event in the newspaper — can cause the rage and hurt to resurface.

In August 1988, we succeed in establishing the New Orleans victim assistance group. We've gotten start-up funds from a few church groups, a small office at Hope House, and the Mennonite Volunteers send Dianne Kidner to launch the organization. Four years earlier I had worked to set up legal assistance for death-row inmates. Now, at last, I have done something to help victims.

The first thing I do is take Dianne to visit the Harveys. She is eager to get their ideas about needs of victims and possible programs. When I call to arrange the visit, Elizabeth suggests a potluck meal, so I bring baked beans and Dianne brings a pie. Elizabeth has made potato salad, and Vernon barbecues hamburgers.

Outside by the barbecue pit Vernon and I sip bourbon highballs and he tells me about different jobs he's had in construction and how he almost died in World War II when his ship was torpedoed. He tells how he was fished out of the sea unconscious, presumed dead, and almost dumped into a body bag when someone happened to notice that he was alive.

This only emphasizes the randomness of Faith's death. I don't know what to say and we're both quiet for a while. The only sound comes from the hamburgers sizzling on the grill, and I remember what Robert had said about the electric chair: "I know it fries your ass."

During the meal, the talk mostly centers on Dianne's work with victims. Dianne says she hopes the program will empower people, so she's thinking of not using the word "victim" in the name of the program. She tries out the name "Survive."[13] The Harveys like it.

One day in July 1989, I get a telephone call from Elizabeth Harvey. She is worried about Vernon, who is recuperating from open-heart surgery. She says he's been talking about giving up. "That's just not Vern," she says, and she wonders if I can pay him a visit. "If anybody can get him fighting, you can," she says.

That very afternoon I go to visit him in New Orleans Veterans' Hospital. He and Elizabeth both looked washed out. Elizabeth has been driving back and forth across the Lake Pontchartrain Causeway to see him each day while working as a cashier in a department store.

"The damn doctors lied to me," Vernon says to me as soon as I walk in. "They didn't tell me I was going to hurt like this. If I had known, I would never have let them cut me," and he shows me the red gash down the middle of his chest. He's lying on a stretcher in the hall near his room waiting to go to X ray.

Elizabeth tells how she and Vern have recently spent three days in court with a murder victim's relatives from Ohio. "Their daughter was killed near the state park in Mandeville," Elizabeth says, "and here they come for the trial all alone, not knowing the court procedures or anything. Vern and I explained to them what was going to happen in court."

Vernon fidgets on the stretcher. "You wait forever in this damn place," he says.

"Know what they should've done with Willie?" he says. "They should've strapped him in that chair, counted to ten, then at the count of nine taken him out of the chair and let him sit in his cell for a day or two and then strapped him in the chair again. It was too easy for him. He went too quick."

He says he's been thinking of a much more effective way to prevent murders. "What we do is fry the bastards on prime-time TV, that's what we oughta do. Show them dying in the electric chair, say, at eight at night, and see if that doesn't give second thoughts to anybody thinking of murder."

I say that maybe what an execution does is show that the state can kill as well as anyone else, and that what people learn from such

an example is that when you have a really bad problem with someone, what you do is kill him.

Vernon says I have *got* to be kidding, and here we go again,
Vernon and I playing our familiar roles, jousting with each other
about the death penalty.

I tell him that the people doing the thinking and the people doing
the killing are not the same people.

"That's because we're not executing *enough* of 'em," Vernon
retorts. "We have to make executions more frequent and more
consistent. No exceptions."

"But money and race and politics and the discretion we leave to
D.A.'s is always going to keep it from being a uniform and fair
process," I say, "and even locale plays a part. Some states have the
death penalty and some don't."

Vernon is getting some color in his face.

Elizabeth looks relieved.

An attendant has now appeared to bring Vernon to X ray. "What
we really oughta do," he says as his stretcher begins to move away,
proving to me just how effective my arguments have been, "we
oughta do to them exactly what they did to their victim. Willie
should've been stabbed seventeen times, that's what we oughta do
to them."

I tell him to hang in there and I'll be coming back with an apple
pie.

One evening in January 1991, I'm facing another doorknob and
taking a deep breath before I turn it. Behind it are members of
Survive, the victim assistance group begun by Dianne Kidner and
now directed by Mary Riley, another Mennonite volunteer. During
the two years Dianne worked with victims she mostly helped individuals, but now Mary has moved the organization toward group
self-help and has begun weekly gatherings on Monday nights in one
of the conference rooms at the Loyola University law school. Under
Mary's direction, membership has been steadily growing and it now
numbers about forty people — mostly indigent black women trying
to cope with the death of sons, daughters, spouses, parents. Mostly
sons — almost all of them killed with guns. *Bang, bang, bang, bang,
bang, bang, bang.* If sounds of the killings could be accumulated and
played back, it would sound like a war — which, in fact, it is. The
Louisiana Weekly, a black-owned newspaper, ran a full page listing
the name and race of the 323 homicide victims in New Orleans in

1990 (284 were black) with the headline: "For the City of New Orleans, Saddam Hussein Was Not the Only Horror of the Year."[14]

And Dr. Frank Minyard, Orleans Parish coroner, in a recent newspaper interview said, "Between AIDS, drugs, murder, police, prisons . . . You talk about genocide: by the year 2000 we will have lost a whole generation. There will be no more black males between the ages of 30 and 40."[15]

I open the door.

I feel prepared for what I will hear tonight. "Braced," maybe, is a better word because almost every week at Hope House staff meetings I hear stories of shoot-outs and deaths in the St. Thomas Housing Development.

As the stories begin, I think of the plagues visited on Egypt recorded in the Book of Exodus. The last plague was the worst — the slaying of the firstborn sons of the Egyptians. The Israelites who had put lamb's blood over their doorposts were spared by the Avenging Angel. But no one here tonight seemed able to get the blood on the doorpost in time, and some have been visited by the Avenging Angel more than once.

> How do I introduce myself — as the mother of six or the mother of four? I guess I'll say six even though two of my sons were killed, both of them shot, five months apart. I've been angry at God and confused because I have really tried to do right, go to church every Sunday, and give a good home to my kids and I thought that would protect us.

> My son was abducted and shot twelve times. It was just a few days before he was to appear as a witness to a drug-related murder. He had seen two boys killing someone. We had gotten threats and I had called the D.A.'s office and asked for protection. I sent my other son to the country to stay with kinfolk. They was callin' and threatenin' him too.

> Well, they know me at City Hall, yes, they do, because I still get out there with my picket sign and I let them know I know my son was set up to be killed by the police. He had been dating a white girl, a policeman's daughter, and I'm gonna stand up to 'em 'til the day I die.

> My son was shot by his girlfriend. She just got a gun and shot him in the eye, his right eye, and I'm going to

have to quit my second job so I can pay more attention to my younger daughter. I'm so worried about that child.

I keep wanting to stay in bed and sleep and not get up. If I can just get through my boy's birthday, then Christmas . . . I've lost three children: the first was a crib death, my three-year-old died of hepatitis, and now my twenty-four-year-old son was shot to death.

I had to drop out of LPN [licensed practical nurse] school for the second time now. Got a bad case of nerves.

I keep waitin' for my boy to knock on the door. Seven times, that was his little knock and I'd say, "Who's there?" and he'd say, "Me, Baby," and the newspaper told it wrong. They talked about my boy's murder like it was just another drug-related murder. They don't know who shot my boy. The killer's still out there somewhere.

My eighty-three-year-old father was shot in cold blood. I think it was because he was speaking out about crime in the neighborhood.

My son was a crack cocaine addict. I called his parole officer and tried to get him to arrest him but the officer said my boy was hopeless, that it was no use. They found him shot.

I went to several stores where they sell guns — not to buy one exactly, I just asked about buying one. It was so easy. All I had to do was show a picture ID . . . All these young kids are totin' guns — handguns, sawed-off shotguns, .357 Magnums, Uzis. Even thirteen-year-olds have guns. They go in people's houses and steal them.

As each of the women speaks, a litany punctuates the testimonies — "Oh, Lord . . . Yes, Lord . . . Jesus . . . Say it . . . Amen . . . Jesus, help us . . . God makes a way out of no way" — and sometimes soft moans and tears and heads bent down and then raised up, and at times hands reaching to clasp another hand.

Some talk of considering suicide, of staying in bed and sleeping, of numbing the pain with alcohol or drugs. They talk of confusion and bewilderment. But mostly they talk about carrying on. The struggle for physical survival — meeting utility and rent payments, putting food on the table, taking sick children to Charity Hospital — helps keep them going. Except for the one woman who pickets in front of city hall, it seems to be a given, a fact of life, that no one expects anything from the criminal justice system.

A pattern emerges: of the forty or so members of Survive, only one hopes to see her child's murderer brought to trial. *Maybe*, another member cautions. She, too, had thought her child's killer would be brought to trial, only to be told that the charges had been dropped because of "insufficient evidence."

One case in forty of a perpetrator brought to trial is not a very good track record for a D.A.'s office. I soon discover that in the majority of these cases the perpetrator is still at large, or, if apprehended, kept in jail for a short while, then freed. A good number of Survive members have never been interviewed by investigating officials. Some have never seen a document of any kind — a medical or autopsy report or even a death certificate.

Granted, even the most fair-minded law enforcement officials face a substantial challenge in a city as crime-ridden as New Orleans. First there is the sheer volume of homicides, where in a single weekend there might be as many as four murders, especially in poor black neighborhoods, where most homicides take place.[16] The police are not legally required to investigate every reported crime.[17] Then there is the difficulty of getting witnesses to come forward. Blacks in low-income housing projects are reluctant witnesses because they both distrust the police and fear retaliation from drug dealers. Nor are police investigators eager to conduct investigations in violence-ridden neighborhoods.

In such circumstances "equal protection of the laws," a Fourteenth Amendment right, is indeed a challenge. Yet some tough cases show that where there is resolve, results can be expeditious.

A recent New Orleans case comes to mind of a judge's son who was murdered. The young man, who had been to a bar, was killed in the street near the bar in the early-morning hours. There were no witnesses to the crime, yet within four days of vigorous investigation two suspects were arrested, charged, and jailed. A high bond was set, and the suspects were kept in jail pending trial.[18]

In 1989, there were 249 homicides in New Orleans. Eighty-five percent of the victims were black. Sixteen offenders were convicted and jailed.[19]

My hunch is that the large number of "unsolved" murders of black victims is not unique to New Orleans, but I discover that the Bureau of Justice Statistics does not track the race of the victim in its records of "unsolved" murders.

The "Chattahoochee Report," whose findings were presented

to the House Judiciary Subcommittee on Civil and Constitutional Rights of the Georgia House of Representatives on July 9, 1991, revealed strong racial bias in the way some D.A.s prosecute murder cases. The study of murder cases in a six-county area in Georgia from 1973 to 1990 found that although blacks comprised 65 percent of murder victims and whites, 35 percent, the death penalty was sought in 85 percent of murder cases that involved white victims but only in 15 percent of those cases that involved black victims.[20]

The section of the "Chattahoochee Report" entitled "Victims' Families: A Contrast in Black and White" could have been transcribed from a Survive meeting. Numerous black families in Columbus County, where the death penalty has been vigorously sought, testified that despite the D.A.'s protestation that he always met with victims' families, he had not in fact ever visited them. In contrast, the study shows, when the victim was white, the D.A. was solicitous of the family's feelings, often paying them courtesy visits at their homes and then announcing at a press conference that he would seek the death penalty.

The report cites one such highly publicized case in Columbus in which the homicide victim was the daughter of a prominent white contractor: "D.A., William J. Smith, phoned to ask the contractor personally what punishment he wanted the D.A. to seek. When the contractor told him to go for the death penalty, Smith told him that was all he needed to hear. He secured a death sentence and was rewarded with a $5,000 contribution — his largest single contribution — to run for judge in the next election."[21]

In cases involving black victims, however, the report states, "not only did none of the murders of their relatives lead to a capital trial, but officials often treated them as criminals:

- Jimmy Christian was informed by the police in 1988 that his son had been murdered. That was the last he heard from any officials. He was never advised of any court proceedings. When an arrest was made, he heard about it on the street. He was not informed of the trial date or the charges.
- Johnny Johnson came home from church in 1984 to find the body of his wife, her throat cut. His one contact with officials occurred when he was briefly jailed on suspicion of her murder.
- Mildred Brewer witnessed the shooting of her daughter in 1979. Instead of being allowed to accompany her in the ambulance to the hospital, she was taken to police headquarters and ques-

tioned for three hours — during which her daughter died. When a suspect was arrested, tried and sentenced, Mrs. Brewer heard nothing from the D.A.[22]

And so it goes.

The Survive meeting ends, heads all bowed in prayer. Later, people cluster in small groups, chatting and sipping drinks that some of the women have provided. All the sorrow and loss is overwhelming, yet I don't feel devastated. There's something in the women themselves that strengthens me. I think of the rallying cry of black women of South Africa: "You have struck the women. You have struck the rock." Maybe it's because black people, especially black women, have suffered for such a long, long time. Seasoned sufferers, they have grace, tenacity, a great capacity to absorb pain and loss and yet endure. *God makes a way out of no way.* For these women this is no empty, pious sentiment. It is the air they breathe, the bread they eat, the path they walk.

A ripple of laughter bubbles up from one end of the room and I see Shirley Carr slip her arm comfortingly around another woman's shoulders. Shirley was the first to speak tonight, telling of her two sons killed five months apart. She's worked through the paralysis of her grief and is now able to accompany others through the phases and seasons of denial and guilt, rage and loss, withdrawal and despair. Mary sees that when her term of service is up, Shirley will likely take over directorship of the group. Development of self-help and local leadership is important in the Mennonite philosophy.

Mary Riley and I have become friends, and we look for ways to build bridges between our two organizations — Pilgrimage, our abolitionist group, and Survive. When people join Pilgrimage, besides inviting them to become pen pals to death-row inmates, we also encourage them to volunteer their services to Survive or to other victim assistance groups in their town or city.

Lloyd LeBlanc, the father of young, murdered David. With him, I end this narrative.

In the years immediately after Pat Sonnier's Pardon Board hearing, my encounters with Lloyd were friendly but tentative. We talked on the telephone, wrote notes. I paid a few visits. My first visits to his home in St. Martinville had been especially difficult for Eula, Lloyd's wife. The thought of someone coming into her house who had befriended her son's murderers was at first too much for her. When I would come, she would leave the house. It's better now.

One day two years ago in a telephone conversation, Lloyd said that he goes to pray every Friday from 4:00 to 5:00 A.M. in a small "perpetual adoration" chapel in St. Martinville, and I asked if I might join him. He said he would like that very much. I know I want to do this, even if it's four o'clock in the morning. Words of Rainer Maria Rilke come:

> Work of the eyes is done, now
> go and do heart-work.[23]

I drive into Baton Rouge the night before to shorten the distance of the drive, and Louie comes to sleep over at Mama's house so we can save time in the morning. Good brother that he is, he says I should not make the trip alone. We have figured that if we leave Baton Rouge at 2:45 we can reach St. Martinville by 4:00. Louie fills the thermos with coffee.

Riding in the dark across Acadian Louisiana reminds me of when I was eight years old and I would get up with Mama during Lent to go to early-morning Mass. I remember the still, cold air, the feeling of mystery that is always there in the dark when you are awake and the rest of the world is asleep.

In his note Lloyd has told me how he prays for "everyone, especially the poor and suffering." He prays for "the repose of the soul" of David and for his wife, Eula. He prays in thanksgiving for his daughter, Vickie, and her four healthy children. It is the grandchildren — little Ryan, Derek, Megan, and Jacob — who have brought Eula back to life — but it has taken a long, long time. For a year after David's murder, Lloyd had frequently taken her to visit David's grave. Unless he took her there, he once told me, "she couldn't carry on, she couldn't pick up the day, she couldn't live." For three years his wife had cried, and he said the house was like a tomb and he found himself working long hours out of the house "to keep my sanity."

Once, during one of my visits, he took me to his office — he is a construction worker — and showed me the grandfather clock he was making after his day's work was done. "It's good to keep busy," he says.

Lloyd LeBlanc prays for Loretta Bourque and her family. The Bourques had been more anxious than he to witness the execution of Patrick Sonnier. The day before the Pardon Board was to hear Pat's appeal, members of the Bourque family had visited Lloyd to urge him to attend the hearing and press for the death sentence. A few months earlier, trying to evade witnessing the execution, Lloyd had asked his brother to take his place, but the brother had a heart attack and couldn't.

There, at the Pardon Board hearing, Lloyd LeBlanc had done what was asked of him. Speaking for both families, he asked that the law of execution be carried out. But after the execution he was troubled and sought out his parish priest and went to confession.

Now, Lloyd LeBlanc prays for the Sonniers — for Pat and for Eddie and for Gladys, their mother. "What grief for this mother's heart," he once said to me in a letter. Yes, for the Sonniers, too, he prays. He knows I visit Eddie, and in his letters he sometimes includes a ten-dollar bill with the note: "For your prison ministry to God's children." And shortly before Gladys Sonnier's death in January 1991, Lloyd LeBlanc went to see her to comfort her.

Louie and I drive Interstate 10 West, then turn off at Breaux Bridge for the last twenty miles. We go through Parks, the last place David and Loretta were seen alive, and drive into the parking lot of the very old wooden church of St. Martin of Tours. Light shines in a steady slant from the tall stained-glass window of the chapel. Red, green, and yellow speckle the grass. All around is darkness. Nearby, large hundred-year-old oak trees spread their branches.

I tap the door of the chapel and a young woman with long dark hair lets us in with a quiet smile. She has a blanket around her. Her hour of vigil has been from three to four o'clock. We find out that she has eight children. Her husband preceded her in prayer earlier in the night. Louie and I are glad to get out of the cold. The fall weather is setting in.

Inside the chapel I see a sign hand-printed in black letters on white paper, a quotation from the Gospel of John: "Because you have seen me, you believe. Blessed are those who do not see and yet believe." The round wafer of bread consecrated at Mass is elevated in a gold vessel with clear glass at the center so the host can be seen. Gold rays, emanating outward, draw the eye to the center. Two pews along the back wall. Two kneelers, four red sanctuary candles on the floor. On the wall a crucifix and a picture of Mary, the mother of Jesus.

At five minutes to four Lloyd drives up. "You made it," he says, "I'm glad you're safe, you know those highways," and I introduce him to Louie. The chapel is warm and close and filled with silence and the smell of beeswax. Lloyd and I kneel on the prie-dieux. He takes his rosary out of his pocket. Louie, in the pew behind us, already has his rosary in his hands.

We "tell" the beads, as the old French people used to say. *One at a time — Hail Mary, Holy Mary, Hail Mary, the mysteries of Christ and our own, life and joy, suffering and death — we round the beads one by one, a circle and round we go, dying and behold we live, the soul stretched taut, the soul which says: No more, I can take no more. Hail Mary, Holy Mary, breathed in and breathed out, linking what eyes cannot see but what the heart knows and doubts and knows again.*

Holding a rosary is a physical, tangible act — you touch and hold the small, smooth beads awhile and then let go. "Do not cling to me," Jesus had said to Mary Magdalene. The great secret: *To hold on, let go. Nothing is solid. Everything moves. Except love — hold on to love. Do what love requires.*

We pray the sorrowful mysteries. Jesus agonizing before he is led to execution. Jesus afraid. Jesus sweating blood. Were there beads of sweat on David's brow when he realized the mortal danger? Was it when the kidnappers turned the car down a road that he knew ended in a cane field? Was it when he was told to lie face down on the ground? His mother had bought him a new blue velour shirt that he was wearing that night. Standing by the kitchen sink, he wrapped his arms around himself and patted the new shirt and said, "Mama, this is going to keep me warm at the game tonight."

And Loretta . . . her last evening of life at a football game . . . She had seen friends there, laughed and talked and cheered her team, safe in the globe of stadium light, unaware of the dark road soon to be hers.

Lloyd LeBlanc has told me that he would have been content with imprisonment for Patrick Sonnier. He went to the execution, he says, not for revenge, but hoping for an apology. Patrick Sonnier had not disappointed him. Before sitting in the electric chair he had said, "Mr. LeBlanc, I want to ask your forgiveness for what me and Eddie done," and Lloyd LeBlanc had nodded his head, signaling a forgiveness he had already given. He says that when he arrived with sheriff's deputies there in the cane field to identify his son, he had knelt by his boy — "laying down there with his two little eyes sticking out like bullets" — and prayed the Our Father. And when he came to the words: "Forgive us our trespasses as we forgive those who trespass against us," he had not halted or equivocated, and he said, "Whoever did this, I forgive them." But he acknowledges that it's

244

a struggle to overcome the feelings of bitterness and revenge that well up, especially as he remembers David's birthday year by year and loses him all over again: David at twenty, David at twenty-five, David getting married, David standing at the back door with his little ones clustered around his knees, grown-up David, a man like himself, whom he will never know. Forgiveness is never going to be easy. Each day it must be prayed for and struggled for and won.

NOTES

CHAPTER ONE

1. Dorothy Day established soup kitchens and shelters for the poor in New York City. With Peter Maurin she published a newspaper, *The Catholic Worker*, (Current address: 36 East First Street, New York, New York 10003). Her life story is told in *The Long Loneliness* (San Francisco: Harper and Row, 1952).
2. *Statistical Abstract of the U.S.*, 110th ed., Washington, D.C. 20402: U.S. Government Printing Office, 1988.
3. Donald L. Barlett and James B. Steele, *America: What Went Wrong?* (Kansas City: Andrews and McMeel, 1992), p. xiii.
4. *The Louisiana Weekly* (New Orleans), a black-owned newspaper, told of the U.S. Department of Justice survey in an article by Jeff White, "Black Leaders React to Police Brutality Survey," May 30, 1992.

   Also see Kevin Bell, "Black Males: Police Abuse Common," *Times-Picayune*, January 7, 1993, and the companion article in the same issue by Sheila Grissett and Scott Aiges: "Officers Defend Marsalis Arrest." Branford Marsalis, bandleader of *The Tonight Show*, was stopped for speeding by New Orleans police, frisked, handcuffed, and brought to jail, even though he says that he cooperated fully with police and signed the speeding ticket. Marsalis, speaking of the incident before a national audience on *The Tonight Show* (January 4, 1993), attributed his abusive handling by police to the fact that he is black.

Also see Art Harris, "New Orleans' Poor Blacks Fear Police Brutality," *Sunday Advocate*, Baton Rouge, June 14, 1981.

5. Langston Hughes, "Warning," *The Panther and the Lash: Poems of Our Times* (New York: Alfred A. Knopf, Inc., 1989).

6. Louisiana Department of Safety and Corrections, P.O. Box 94304, Capitol Station, Baton Rouge, Louisiana 70804; "Probation and Parole, 1990," Bureau of Justice Statistics of the U.S. Department of Justice, November, 1991, Washington, D.C.; Marc Mauer, "Americans Behind Bars: One Year Later," February 1992, The Sentencing Project, 918 F Street NW, Suite 501, Washington, D.C. 20004, (202) 628-0871; William J. Chambliss, "Trading Textbooks for Prison Cells," June 1991, National Center on Institutions and Alternatives, 635 Slaters Lane, Suite G-100, Alexandria, Virginia 22314.

7. Marc Mauer, "Young Black Men and the Criminal Justice System: A Growing National Problem" (the Sentencing Project, February 1990).

8. Jason DeParle, "A Matter of Life and Death," *Times-Picayune*, April 7, 1985, p. 14.

9. Section 1 of the Thirteenth Amendment (enacted December 18, 1865): "Neither slavery nor involuntary servitude, except as a punishment for crime whereof the party shall have been duly convicted, shall exist within the United States, or any place subject to their jurisdiction."

10. James S. Liebman, "More than 'Slightly Retro': The Rehnquist Court's Rout of Habeas Corpus Jurisdiction in *Teague v. Lane*," *New York University Review of Law and Social Change* 18: pp. 537–635, p. 541.

Hugo Adam Bedau notes that from 1967–1982 over 2,000 death sentences were vacated on constitutional grounds. See *The Death Penalty in America* (New York: Oxford University Press, 1982), p. 68.

11. "We never held that prisoners have a constitutional right to counsel when mounting collateral (federal or state post-conviction litigation) attacks to their convictions [and we] decline to so hold today": *Pennsylvania v. Finley*, 481 U.S. 551 (1987). This Supreme Court decision was reaffirmed in *Coleman v. Thompson*, 111 S. Ct. 2546 (1991).

12. After deliberating upon the sentence for Elmo Patrick Sonnier for some time, the jury requested information about Sonnier's eligibility for work release if he were given a life sentence. In fact, regulations of the Department of Corrections stipulated that inmates convicted of murder were ineligible for such programs, but the judge did not have a copy of the regulations, and from his instruction the jury ascertained that if they sentenced Sonnier to life imprisonment he might possibly qualify for work release. The Louisiana Supreme Court determined the judge's instruction "incomplete and misleading" and

remanded for resentencing January 28, 1980, *State v. Sonnier*, 379 So. 2d 1336 (La. 1980).

13. The time sequence of the Sonnier trials and retrials was as follows:

> *April, 1978* Elmo Patrick Sonnier tried, convicted, and sentenced to death.
> *September, 1978* Eddie Sonnier tried, convicted, and sentenced to death.
> *1979* Eddie Sonnier's death sentence overturned by the Louisiana Supreme Court.
> *January, 1980* Elmo Patrick Sonnier's death sentence overturned by the Louisiana Supreme Court and remanded for a new sentencing trial.
> *March, 1980* Elmo Patrick Sonnier resentenced to death.

14. Arthur S. Miller and Jeffrey H. Bowman, *Death by Installments: The Ordeal of Willie Francis* (Westport, Connecticut: Greenwood Press, Inc., 1988).

15. *Glass v. Louisiana*, 471 U.S. 1080 (1985), pp. 1086–1087.

16. Dr. Hillman's affidavit was presented as part of a defense brief in *Sawyer v. Whitley*, 772 F. Supp. 297 (U.S. District Court, E.D., Louisiana, 1991).

17. "Reflections on the Guillotine" in *Resistance, Rebellion, and Death*, by Albert Camus, trans. Justin O'Brien (New York: Vintage Books, 1974), pp. 225–226. All subsequent references to Camus' work are from this essay, in this translation, and are cited by page number in the text. Reprint of the 1961 edition published by Knopf, New York.

CHAPTER TWO

1. Two books published by The Center for Louisiana Studies (P.O. Box 40831, Lafayette, Louisiana 70504), give a graphic account of Angola's history. They are Anne Butler and C. Murray Henderson's *Angola — The Louisiana State Penitentiary: A Half Century of Rage and Reform* (1990) and *The Wall Is Strong: Corrections in Louisiana* Burk Foster, Wilbert Rideau, and Ron Wikberg, eds. (1991).

   Rideau, an Angola inmate, and Wikberg, recently released from prison, coauthored *Life Sentences: Rage and Survival Behind Bars* (New York: Times Books, 1992).

2. Ron Wikberg, "Death Watch: The Horror Show," *The Angolite* 15 no. 5, September/October, 1990): p. 36. (Louisiana State Penitentiary, Angola, Louisiana 70712.)

3. C. Murray Henderson, warden at Angola from 1968–1975, says, "Usu-

ally murder is committed in the heat of passion and discharges something in the psyche, with the result that the individual rarely repeats
the offense ... Surprisingly, murderers ... have the lowest rate of
recidivism of any group of offenders" (Butler and Henderson, *The
Wall Is Strong*, p. 51.)

The Federal Bureau of Investigation gives no estimate of murders
of "passion." The term is ambiguous and hard to measure. In its 1989
Uniform Crime Report the FBI estimated that 54 percent of murders
were between family or acquaintances, 13.1 percent between strangers,
and 33.1 percent unknown.

CHAPTER THREE

1. Source: The Loyola Death Penalty Resource Center, 210 Baronne
   St., Suite 608, New Orleans, Louisiana 70112, (504) 522-0578.
2. With permission from the mother of Robert Wayne Williams, photographs of his charred body were published by the prison magazine.
   Ron Wikberg, "Death Watch: The Horror Show," *The Angolite* 15 no.
   5, (September/October, 1990) (Louisiana State Penitentiary, Angola,
   Louisiana 70712).
3. Trial Transcript, *State of Louisiana v. Elmo Patrick Sonnier*, Supreme
   Court of the State of Louisiana, No. 63293, vol. 7, pp. 1205–1206.
4. Of the 3,829 executions under state authority in the United States
   from 1930 to 1980, 2,307 (60 percent) occurred in Southern states.
   See Hugo Adam Bedau, *The Death Penalty in America*, 3d ed. (New
   York: Oxford University Press, 1982) pp. 58–61.
5. Jill Smolowe, "Must This Man Die?" *Time*, May 18, 1992, pp. 40–44;
   Peter Applebome, "Execution Stirs Up Troubling Questions," *New
   York Times*, May 22, 1992.
6. *Keeney v. Tamayo-Reyes*, 112 S. Ct. 1715 (1992); see Peter Applebome,
   "Indigent Defendants, Overworked Lawyers," *New York Times*, May
   17, 1992.
7. Marcia Coyle, Fred Strasser, and Marianne Lavelle, "Fatal Defense:
   Trial and Error in the Nation's Death Belt," *The National Law Journal*
   12, no. 40 (June 11, 1990): pp. 30–44. To research this special report
   The National Law Journal conducted a six-month, six-state investigation of capital defense in the South, poring over 100 trial transcripts
   and interviewing 150 attorneys, judges, prosecutors, and experts in
   capital law. The following instances of ineffectiveness of counsel are
   among those documented in the report:

   - In a postconviction affidavit, the defense attorney's investigator
     said he witnessed his boss, Emmett Moran, shoot up with cocaine

during trial recesses and use speed, alcohol, Quaaludes, morphine and marijuana after court sessions. The trial judge found no "credible evidence" of intoxication and ruled that Mr. Moran was not ineffective. Five Florida Supreme Court justices upheld the conviction. Moran's client, Jerry White, is on death row.

- In October 1989, the Fifth U.S. Circuit Court of Appeals refused to call inadequate this twenty-nine-word defense by counsel Jon Wood at Jesus Romero's sentencing trial in San Antonio: "You are an extremely intelligent jury. You've got that man's life in your hands. You can take it or not. That's all I have to say." The court said: "Had the jury returned a life sentence the strategy might well have been seen as a brilliant move."

- In Lee County, Alabama, at 6:00 P.M., just after the jury in the capital murder trial of James Wyman Smith returned a guilty verdict, the judge asked if prosecution and defense were prepared to proceed with the penalty phase. The following exchange is recorded in the trial transcript:

Thomas E. Jones (Defense Counsel): No, sir, we are not.

Court: I hate to send the jury back to a motel another night. What do you lack being ready?

J. Michael Williams (Defense Counsel): Judge, I haven't even read the statute about it.

At 7:00 P.M. the judge then recessed the trial until 8:30 the next morning, at which time Mr. Smith was sentenced to death.

8. In February 1992, New Orleans public defender Rick Teissier, whose caseload tops 700 clients a year, filed a motion in state court arguing the state's public defender program was unconstitutional. See Keith Woods, "Impoverished System Poor Defense," *Times Picayune*, February 24, 1992; also Richard Lacayo, "You Don't Always Get Perry Mason," *Time*, June 1, 1992.

The American Bar Association's Criminal Justice Section's Project on Death Penalty Habeas Corpus found "the inadequacy and inadequate compensation of counsel at trial the principal failing" of the administration of capital punishment. See Ira P. Robbins, "Toward a More Just and Effective System of Review in State Death Penalty Cases," *American University Law Review* 40 (Fall, 1990): pp. 1–296.

9. The stringent standard for ineffective assistance of counsel was set in the 1984 ruling of the U.S. Supreme Court in *Strickland v. Washington* (466 U.S. 668).

"Effective Assistance: Just a Nominal Right?" Coyle, Strasser, and Lavelle, "Fatal Defense," p. 42.

10. Michael T. Kroll, "Louisiana Execution Moves State Back to the 19th Century," *Pacific News Service*, week of May 14–18, 1990.

NOTES

11. Racial discrimination in the application of the death penalty for rape is patently clear. Of the 455 persons executed for rape in the United States, 405 were black. The overwhelming majority of the executions — 443 — took place in the South. In *Coker v. Georgia*, 433 U.S. 992 (1977), the Supreme Court ruled the death penalty for rape unconstitutional. See Hugo Adam Bedau, *The Death Penalty in America*, 3d ed. (New York: Oxford University Press, 1982) pp. 58–61.

12. In *Batson v. Kentucky*, 476 U.S. 79 (1986) the U.S. Supreme Court ruled that "equal protection of the laws" of the Fourteenth Amendment prohibits the prosecutor from excusing potential jurors simply on the basis of race. But instances of black defendants facing an all-white or nearly all-white jury continue with some frequency. An example comes from the area surrounding Columbus, Georgia. The "Chattahoochee Report," an extensive study of the effects of race in death-penalty trials in the Chattahoochee Judicial District of Georgia, revealed that from 1976 to 1990, in eight of the ten cases where blacks were convicted in capital cases, the "impartial" jury they faced were all white or nearly all white (one black juror). See Fig. 6 of "Chattahoochee Judicial District: Buckle of the Death Belt," published in July 1991 by the Death Penalty Information Center, 1606 20th Street NW, Washington, D.C. 20009, (202) 347-2531. (This report is also cited in chapter 11.)

13. *State of Louisiana v. Gaskin*, 412 So. 2d 1007 (La. 1982).

14. David C. Baldus, George G. Woodworth, and Charles A. Pulaski, Jr., *Equal Justice and the Death Penalty: A Legal and Empirical Analysis* (Boston: Northeastern University Press, 1990).

15. *McCleskey v. Kemp*, 107 S. Ct. 1756 (1987). The U.S. Government's General Accounting Office (GAO) scrutinized over two dozen studies of racial bias in capital sentencing and found them to be "remarkably consistent" in their conclusion that killers of whites are more likely to receive the death penalty than killers of blacks. The GAO found the correlation of race present "at all stages of the criminal justice process," including the prosecutor's decision to charge a defendant with a capital offense or the decision to proceed to trial rather than plea-bargain. The research projects they reviewed took into account factors such as prior criminal records, heinousness of the crime, and the number of victims.

    See the GAO Report to Senate and House Committees in the Judiciary, "Death Penalty Sentencing: Research Indicates Pattern of Racial Inequalities," GAO/GGD 90-57, February 1990. Copies of the report may be obtained from the U.S. General Accounting Office, P.O. Box 6015, Gaithersburg, Maryland 20877, (202) 275-6241.

16. Coyle, Strasser, and Lavelle, "Fatal Defense," pp. 32, 38.

17. After the Supreme Court reinstated the death penalty in 1976, 42

executions took place by May 1985, and, of these, 36 (85 percent) occurred in Texas, Louisiana, Georgia, and Florida. Of the 179 executions taking place by June 30, 1992, 114 (63.7 percent) occurred in these four states. Source: *Death Row, USA*, June 1992, NAACP (National Association for the Advancement of Colored People) Legal Defense and Educational Fund, Suite 1600, 99 Hudson St., New York, NY 10013, (212) 219-1900.

18. In Louisiana and Mississippi, attorneys who represent indigent defendants in capital trials are given a maximum fee of $1,000 to investigate, prepare and try cases. In Georgia the fee is even less — $50 to $150 for counsel at trial (which is waivable) and no more than $500 for preparation and investigation for trial and appeal expenses. See Coyle, Strasser, and Lavelle, "Fatal Defense," pp. 32–33.

    According to Steve Bright, Alabama now pays defense counsel $20 per hour, up to a limit of $2,000 a case for out of court preparation. See Steve Bright, "In Defense of Life: Enforcing the Bill of Rights on Behalf of Poor, Minority, and Disadvantaged Persons Facing the Death Penalty," *Missouri Law Review* 57 (Summer, 1992): pp. 849–870, especially note 55, (1992).

19. Judge Lois Forer of the Court of Common Pleas in Philadelphia in her book, *Money and Justice* bluntly sums up the disparities in our court system toward rich and poor: " . . . the legal system is divided into two separate and unequal systems of justice: one for the rich, in which the courts take limitless time to examine, ponder, consider, and deliberate over hundreds of thousands of bits of evidence and days of testimony, and hear elaborate endless appeals and write countless learned opinions; the other for the poor, in which hasty guilty pleas and brief hearings are the rule and appeals are the exception." See *Money and Justice: Who Owns the Courts?* (New York: Norton, 1984), p. 9.

20. For the past three years, 1990–1992, the number of people sentenced to death has been 260 a year. (See Capital Punishment 1991, Bureau of Justice Statistics, October, 1992) In 1991 the number of murders was about 25,000. (See *Washington Post*, August 30, 1992, at A13) Thus, only about 1 percent of murderers get the death penalty. In 1992 there have been 29 executions. Assuming there will be 25,000 murders this year, that amounts to one execution for every 860 murders.

    In an article, "The Death Penalty and the Risk of Execution Today," Hugo Adam Bedau demonstrates why the risk of execution for murder in the United States is so low: police make arrests in about two out of three murders, and of those arrested, prosecutors are able to get a conviction in about two thirds of these cases; it is difficult for courts to get a conviction of an accused felon without a confession, which felons are reluctant to give without an inducement — namely, a plea bargain or reduced charges; capital trial juries tend to grant more life sentences than death sentences even in Southern states where the death penalty is most vigorously sought; and appellate courts, state and federal, nullify many death sentences because trial courts violate due process. See *Lifelines*, January–March 1991, p. 2, published by The National Coalition to Abolish the Death Penalty, 1325 G St. N.W., LL-B, Washington, D.C. 20005, (202) 347-2411.

21. *Penry v. Lynaugh* 109 S. Ct. 2934 (1989).

In Georgia, on June 24, 1986, Jerome Bowden, a thirty-three-year-old black man with an IQ of 65, was executed for the murder of Kathryn Stryker. The only incriminating evidence against Bowden was his "confession," which was typed by the police because Bowden could neither read nor write. In his last statement he thanked the prison for taking care of him. See "Jerome Bowden's 11th Hour" in Robert Perske's *Unequal Justice?* (Nashville: Abingdon Press, 1991).

See also John Blume and David Bruck, "Sentencing the Mentally Retarded to Death: An Eighth Amendment Analysis," *Arkansas Law Review* 41 (1988): pp. 725–764.

22. *Thompson v. Oklahoma*, 487 U.S. 815, 108 S. Ct. 2687 (1988). See Victor Streib, *Death Penalty for Juveniles* (Bloomington: Indiana University Press, 1987).

In its October 1992 report *United States of America: The Death Penalty and Juvenile Offenders*, Amnesty International described its findings in the cases of twenty-three juvenile offenders sentenced to death and suggested that safeguards in capital punishment law had not been met in many cases. The report noted that the majority of juvenile offenders on death row came from acutely deprived backgrounds and that many were of below-average intelligence, had been seriously abused as children, and suffered from mental illness or brain damage. AI called on the twenty-four states which permit the execution of 15- to 17-year-old offenders to bring their legislation into line with international standards which stipulate that no one may be executed for crimes committed below the age of eighteen. The report is available from Amnesty International Publications, 1 Easton Street, London WC1X 8DJ, United Kingdom; 322 Eighth Avenue, New York, New York 10001, (212) 807-8400.

23. *Ford v. Wainwright* (407 U.S. 399 (1986). See Kent S. Miller and Michael L. Radelet, *Executing the Mentally Ill: The Criminal Justice System and the Case of Alvin Ford* (Newbury Park, California: Sage Publications, 1993).

24. Stephen J. Adler, "The Cure That Kills." *American Lawyer*, September, 1986. See Michael L. Radelet and George W. Barnard, "Treating Those Found Incompetent for Execution: Ethical Chaos with Only

One Solution," *Bulletin of the American Academy of Psychiatry and the Law* 16 (1988): pp. 297–307.

25. The Louisiana Supreme Court ruled that Perry could *not* be forcibly medicated. "An incompetent prisoner cannot be forced to take drugs that might make him sane enough to be executed." *State v. Perry*, 608 So.2d 594 (La. 1992) No. 91-K P- 1324 (La., October 19, 1992).

    See G. Linn Evans, "*Perry v. Louisiana:* Can a State Treat an Incompetent Prisoner to Ready Him for Execution?" *Bulletin of the American Academy of Psychiatry and the Law* 19 (1991): pp. 249–270.

26. See Jason DeParle in, "A Matter of Life or Death," *Times Picayune*, April 7, 1985. This survey of 504 Louisiana murder cases eligible to receive the death penalty concluded that "race, locale, and luck" play a large role in determining which criminals are spared and which are condemned to die.

    See also M. Dwayne Smith, "Patterns of Discrimination in Assessments of the Death Penalty: An Assessment of Louisiana," *Journal of Criminal Justice* 15 (1987): pp. 279–286.

    See also Ronald J. Tabak, "The Death of Fairness: The Arbitrary and Capricious Imposition of the Death Penalty in the 1980's," *New York University Review of Law and Social Change* 14, no. 4 (1986): pp. 798–848.

27. Louisiana Revised Statutes 14:30(1).

28. Trial Transcripts, *State of Louisiana v. Elmo P. Sonnier*, pp. 1077–1078 and 1145–1147.

29. *Clark v. Louisiana State Penitentiary*, 694 F. 2d 159 (Fifth Circuit, 1982). Colin Clark, convicted of first-degree murder in East Baton Rouge Parish and sentenced to die in August 1979, received a new trial because the Fifth Circuit Court of Appeals ruled that the improper jury instruction violated his Fourteenth Amendment rights. The new trial won him a sentence of life imprisonment, which he is serving today in the Louisiana State Penitentiary.

30. One week before trial, Sonnier's defense attorney filed a flurry of pretrial motions. All were denied by the court, some because they were filed after March 6, the deadline for pretrial motions. Trial Transcripts, *Louisiana v. Elmo P. Sonnier*, pp. 36–94.

31. The U.S. Catholic Bishops first issued a statement opposing capital punishment in 1974, then in 1980 issued a more expanded and comprehensive statement, arguing, in part, the "discriminatory nature" of the death penalty in a society where "those condemned to die are nearly always poor and disproportionately black . . ." The bishops' "Statement on Capital Punishment" (1980) may be obtained from the U.S. Catholic Conference, 3211 Fourth St. NE, Washington, D.C. 20017, (202) 541-3000

32. Raul X. Rosales, S.J., "Jesuits Fight for Life," *The Maroon*, October 31,

NOTES

1986 (Loyola University, New Orleans, Louisiana 70118); "Connick Replies" (letter to editor), *The Maroon*, December 5, 1986.

33. Kevin Pedro Kelly, "Priests Take Both Sides in Death Penalty Debate," *The National Catholic Reporter*, July 3, 1981.

34. John Maginnis, *The Last Hayride* (Baton Rouge: Gris Gris Press, 1984), p. 207.

35. Toney Anaya, former governor of New Mexico, answering what he called "the moral dictates of conscience," commuted to life all death sentences before he left office. See Richard E. Meyer, "New Mexico Death Sentences Commuted," *The Los Angeles Times*, November 27, 1986.

Before leaving office, Governor Richard Celeste commuted the death sentences of eight prisoners in Ohio, including those of four women. He said that strong racial bias had put a disproportionate number of black people on Ohio's death row, and he was also concerned about mental illness and mental retardation among death-row inmates. However, the state appealed seven of these commutations after Celeste left office, so the fate of these prisoners is as yet unresolved. See "At End of Term, Ohio Governor Commutes Death Sentences of 8," *New York Times*, January 12, 1991.

CHAPTER FOUR

1. "During his life on earth, he offered up prayer and entreaty, aloud and in silent tears, to the one who had the power to save him out of death, and he submitted so humbly that his prayer was heard. Although he was Son, he learnt to obey through suffering . . ." Letter to the Hebrews 5:7, 8. All quotations from Scripture are from *The Jerusalem Bible* (Garden City, New York: Doubleday & Co., Inc., 1966). Subsequent citations are by book, chapter, and verse in the text.

CHAPTER FIVE

1. George Bernard Shaw, *Saint Joan* (New York: Penguin, 1966), pp. 153–154.

2. C. Paul Phelps died suddenly on March 9, 1993. He was sixty years old. After retirement from the Department of Corrections he ran (with considerable success) a private probation agency and works with first-time offenders to prevent their going to prison. Counseling, supervision, education, and job training were centerpieces of the program.

3. In December 1948, the United Nations General Assembly adopted

without dissent the Universal Declaration of Human Rights. Article 3 of the Universal Declaration states, "Everyone has the right to life." Article 5 states, "No one shall be subjected to torture or to cruel, inhuman, or degrading treatment or punishment." The United States signed the declaration but Congress did not ratify it. Copies of the U.N. Declaration of Human Rights are available from Amnesty International. (See note 22 of chapter 3 for address.)

4. For information about the victims' advocacy group contact the Office of Justice and Peace of the Catholic Diocese of Lafayette, 1408 Carmel Avenue, Lafayette, Louisiana 70802, (318) 261-5545.

5. In New York, over the period 1907–1963, there were on average two more homicides in the month following an execution. See William J. Bowers and Glenn L. Pierce, "Deterrence or Brutalization: What Is the Effect of Executions?" *Crime and Delinquency* 26 (1980): pp. 453–484.

Also see William C. Bailey, "Murder and Capital Punishment in the Nation's Capital," *Justice Quarterly* 1 (1984): pp. 211–233; and William J. Bowers, "The Effect of the Death Penalty Is Brutalization, not Deterrence," in Kenneth C. Haas and James A. Inciardi's *Challenging Capital Punishment: Legal and Social Science Approaches* (Newbury Park, California: Sage, 1988).

6. For a thorough treatment of the death penalty as deterrent, see Hugo Adam Bedau, *The Death Penalty in America*, 3d ed. (New York: Oxford University Press, 1982), pp. 93–185.

Also see Raymond Paternoster, *Capital Punishment in America* (Lexington, Massachusetts: Lexington Books, 1991), pp. 217–245; and Roger Hood's monograph published for the United Nations, *The Death Penalty: A Worldwide Perspective* (Oxford, England: Oxford University Press, 1989), pp. 117–148.

For an annotated bibliography on deterrence and other facets of the death penalty in the United States, see Michael L. Radelet and Margaret Vandiver's *Capital Punishment in America: An Annotated Bibliography* (New York: Garland Publishing, Inc., 1988).

7. See Amnesty International USA's, *When the State Kills . . . The Death Penalty: A Human Rights Issue* (1989), pp. 11, 12.

8. See Walt Philbin, "Major Crime Declines in New Orleans," *Times-Picayune*, November 7, 1987. But despite the general decline in crime, the murder rate in New Orleans increased 16.3 percent in the third quarter, the time period immediately after the spate of executions.

By contrast, during the same time period, death penalties handed down by Louisiana juries declined sharply. From 1982 to 1987 juries averaged ten death sentences a year, but in the two-and-a-half years following the rash of executions, juries handed down only two death sentences. See Jason DeParle, "Abstract Death Penalty Needs Real

Executions: Did a Spate of Executions Affect Juries?" *New York Times*, June 30, 1991.

9. The July 26, 1991, CNN/Gallup public opinion poll indicated that of the 76 percent who said they were in favor of the death penalty, 13 percent cited deterrence as a reason, 19 percent cited protection, and 50 percent, revenge. (News Information, Cable News Network, 2200 Fletcher Avenue, Fort Lee, New Jersey 07024.)

In contrast, an earlier 1977 Harris survey cited 59 percent of respondents saying they believed that "executing people who commit murder deters others from committing murder." This was only one year after the U.S. Supreme Court reinstated the death penalty in *Gregg*, and as yet only the execution of Gary Gilmore in Utah (January 17, 1977) had been carried out. However, by July 1991, when the CNN/Gallup Poll was taken, 150 criminals had been put to death with no detectable decrease in violent crimes occurring. See Louis Harris, *The Harris Survey* (New York: Chicago Tribune, New York. News Syndicate February 7, 1977).

10. Ted Gest and Jo Ann Tooley, "Data Base," *U.S. News and World Report*, May 6, 1991: "Public's view of the best way to reduce crime: more executions — 33%; more crime prevention measures — 65%."

11. Marcia Blum, a graduate of Northeastern University Law School, directed the Louisiana Capital Defense Project for the first year. From her efforts and those of Judith Menadue, who followed her, has arisen the Loyola Death Penalty Resource Center, 210 Baronne Street, Suite 608, New Orleans, Louisiana 70112, (504) 522-0578.

12. Amnesty reports that these ten countries, which each carried out over fifty executions between 1985 and mid-1988, account for 83 percent of all executions recorded. See Appendix 17, Table 1 of *When the State Kills* (p. 263). In the same source, Amnesty reports "as of August 1988, no fewer than 28 prisoners in 12 U.S. states were under sentence of death for crimes committed when they were below 18 years of age" (*When the State Kills*, p. 38).

13. See Appendix 15 of *When the State Kills*, for Amnesty's worldwide list of abolitionist and retentionist countries.

14. *When the State Kills*, p. 7.

15. *Furman v. Georgia*, 408 U.S. 238 (1972).

16. Currently 36 states authorize the death penalty for some types of murder: Alabama, Arizona, Arkansas, California, Colorado, Connecticut, Delaware, Florida, Georgia, Idaho, Illinois, Indiana, Kentucky, Louisiana, Maryland, Mississippi, Missouri, Montana, Nebraska, Nevada, New Hampshire, New Jersey, New Mexico, North Carolina, Ohio, Oklahoma, Oregon, Pennsylvania, South Carolina, South Dakota, Tennessee, Texas, Utah, Virginia, Washington, and Wyoming.

The death penalty is also authorized under the Federal Air Piracy

Act, 1974 (49 U.S.C. 1472–3) and under the Uniform Code of Military Justice (UCMJ), which lists a dozen crimes — felony murder, espionage, and desertion among them — as punishable by death when committed in time of war. In 1985 President Ronald Reagan signed into law an amendment to the UCMJ extending the death penalty for espionage by a member of the armed services during peacetime (10 U.S.C. 906 (a)). Federal law also authorizes the death penalty for murders committed in the course of major drug activities (21 U.S.C. 848 (e) and witness tampering where a death results (18 U.S.C. 1512).

17. *Gregg v. Georgia*, 428 U.S. 153 (1976).

18. Historically, a majority of U.S. citizens have consistently favored imposing the death penalty on murderers, at least as measured by responses to the question: "Do you favor or oppose the death penalty for murderers?" In 1936, 62 percent said they favored the death penalty; in 1953, 68 percent; in 1972, 53 percent; in 1977, 67 percent; in 1986, 70 percent; and in 1991, 76 percent. Only in 1966, when those favoring the death penalty registered at 42 percent, has public support been less than a majority.

See H. Erskine's survey of nationwide and statewide polls on the death penalty from 1936 to 1969: "The Polls: Capital Punishment," *Public Opinion Quarterly* 34 (1970): pp. 290–307; Hugo Bedau's "American Attitudes Toward the Death Penalty" in *The Death Penalty in America*, pp. 65–92; and Robert M. Bohm, "American Death Penalty Opinion, 1936–1986: A Critical Examination of the Gallup Polls," in Robert M. Bohm, ed., *The Death Penalty in America: Current Research* (Cincinnati: Anderson Publishing Co., 1991), pp. 113–145.

19. See the annual Uniform Crime Reports of the Federal Bureau of Investigation (U.S. Department of Justice, Washington, D.C. 20530).

20. Glenn L. Pierce and Michael L. Radelet, "The Role and Consequences of the Death Penalty in American Politics," *New York University Review of Law & Social Change* 18 (1990–1991): pp. 711–728, esp. p. 714.

21. See George Gallup, "The Death Penalty," Gallup Reports 244 and 245 (January/February, 1986), pp. 10–16.

A number of surveys of public opinion about capital punishment by Amnesty International have consistently found far less support for capital punishment when those interviewed were presented with specific alternatives to death, such as life without parole, and when the question about capital punishment was asked, not in the abstract: "Do you favor or oppose capital punishment for murderers?" but in the concrete: "Do you favor or oppose capital punishment for juveniles, the mentally retarded, those who have suffered child abuse," etc. Some Amnesty International polls are summarized in James Alan Fox, Michael L. Radelet, and Julie Bonsteel, "Death Penalty Opinion in

the Post-Furman Years," *New York University Review of Law and Social Change* 18 (1990–91): pp. 499–528, at p. 525.
22. Austin Sarat and Neil Vidmar, "Public Opinion, the Death Penalty, and the Eighth Amendment: Testing the Marshall Hypothesis" *Wisconsin Law Review* 1976 (1976): pp. 171–197.

   See also Robert M. Bohm, Louise J. Clark, and Adrian F. Aveni, "Knowledge and Death Penalty Opinion: A Test of the Marshall Hypothesis," *Journal of Research in Crime and Delinquency* 28 (1991): pp. 360–387.
23. With Bill Quigley and Barbara Major I helped to found Pilgrimage for Life (now named Louisiana Coalition to Abolish the Death Penalty). It is located at Hope House, 916 St. Andrew St., New Orleans, Louisiana 70130, (504) 522-5519.

CHAPTER SIX

1. For a probing exploration of the relationship between religion and the practice of retribution, see Susan Jacoby's *Wild Justice: The Evolution of Revenge* (New York: Harper and Row, 1983).
2. See Table 1 in Fox, Radelet, and Bonsteel's "Death Penalty Opinion in the Post-Furman Years." Over a fifteen-year period — from 1972 to 1988 — a composite 73.3 percent of Catholics and 71.4 percent of Protestants favored death for first-degree murderers while support in the overall population registered at 71.2 percent.
3. See *The Death Penalty: The Religious Community Calls for Abolition*, published by the National Coalition to Abolish the Death Penalty and the National Interreligious Task Force on Criminal Justice. Copies may be obtained from NCADP, 1325 G. Street NW (LL-B), Washington, D.C. 20005, (202) 347-2411.

   See also Philip English Mackey's work in which he illustrates that some of the most vocal defenders of the death penalty in America a century ago were Christian clergymen: "An All Star Debate on Capital Punishment, Boston, 1854," *Essex Institute Historical Collections* 110 (July, 1974): pp. 181–199.
4. In the 1980 "Statement on Capital Punishment," the U.S. Catholic Bishops state: "Allowing for the fact that Catholic teaching has accepted the principle that the state has the right to take the life of a person guilty of an extremely serious crime . . ."

   The state's right to execute criminals is a long-standing teaching in the Catholic Church. Augustine (354–430) argued that the wicked might be "coerced by the sword" in order to protect the innocent, and Thomas Aquinas (1225–1274) declared the killing of "evildoers" lawful when "directed to the welfare of the whole community."

NOTES

For a historical perspective on the Catholic Church's position supporting government's right to use force against its citizens, see chapter 5 of Elaine Pagels, *Adam, Eve, and the Serpent* (New York: Vintage Books, 1989), pp. 98–126.

5. These estimates, computed by Glenn L. Pierce and Michael L. Radelet, were based on an estimated population of 248,239,000 and utilized statistics from the U.S. Department of Justice, 1989 (supra note 4, at 48), and the U.S. Department of Commerce, Statistical Abstract of the United States, 1989, pp. 78, 84 (1990). See Glenn L. Pierce and Michael L. Radelet, "The Role and Consequences of the Death Penalty in American Politics," *New York University Review of Law and Social Change* 18, no. 3 (1990–1991): pp. 711–728, esp. p. 714.

6. Paul Slovic, Baruch Fischhoff & Sarah Lichtenstein, "Facts Versus Fears: Understanding Perceived Risk," in *Judgment Under Uncertainty: Heuristics and Biases* Daniel Kahneman, Paul Slovic, and Amos Tversky, eds., (1982), p. 467.

7. See Pierce and Radelet, "The Role and Consequences of the Death Penalty in American Politics," op. cit., p. 713.

8. David von Drehle, "The Death Penalty: A Failure of Execution," *Miami Herald*, July 10, 1988. See also Robert L. Spangenberg and Elizabeth R. Walsh, "Capital Punishment or Life Imprisonment? Some Cost Considerations," *Loyola of Los Angeles Law Review* 23 (1989): pp. 45–58; Margot Garey, "The Cost of Taking a Life: Dollars and Sense of the Death Penalty," *University of California-Davis Law Review* 18 (1985): pp. 1221–1273; and Massachusetts Bar Association, "The Dollar and Human Costs of the Death Penalty," in *A Special Issue on the Death Penalty*, April 1992.

9. Massachusetts Bar Association, "Costs of the Death Penalty."

Chapter Seven

1. Susan Jacoby, *Wild Justice: The Evolution of Revenge* (New York: Harper and Row, 1983), pp. 5, 10.

2. *Crime and Justice Facts*, Bureau of Justice Statistics, 1987.

In 1979 the Louisiana legislature repealed the ten years-six-months release procedure (La. R. S. 15:571.7), which had been operative since 1926, and mandated a life sentence "without benefit of probation, parole, or suspension of sentence" for a number of crimes: first-degree murder — when juries fail to vote unanimously for the death penalty (La. R.S.14:30); second-degree murder (La. R.S. 14:30.1); aggravated rape (La. R.S. 14:42); and aggravated kidnapping (R.S.14:44). In 1976 the legislature mandated that those convicted of possession of heroin with intent to distribute must serve a life sentence with no possibility of parole (R.S.40: 966). See Bryan Denson, "Punishment: Life Means Life in Louisiana," *Houston Post*, July 14, 1991.

3. Jacoby, *Wild Justice*, p. 289.

4. *Ibid.*, p. 11.

5. See Julian H. Wright, "Life-Without-Parole," *Vanderbilt Law Review* 43, pp. 530–568.

   According to research conducted by the National Coalition to Abolish the Death Penalty, as of August 1992, seventeen death-penalty states have "true" life-sentences-without-parole: Alabama, Arkansas, California, Connecticut, Delaware, Illinois, Louisiana, Maryland, Missouri, Montana, Nevada, New Hampshire, Oklahoma, Oregon, Pennsylvania, South Dakota, and Washington; and twelve death-penalty states have "life-without-parole" sentences where parole is possible after a minimum number (at least twenty) of years served: Arizona, Colorado, Florida, Kentucky, Indiana, Nebraska, New Jersey, North Carolina, Ohio, South Carolina, Tennessee, and Texas. Of non-death-penalty states eight have "true" life-sentences-without-parole: Hawaii, Iowa, Maine, Massachusetts, Michigan, Rhode Island, Vermont, and West Virginia; and three have minimum time served statutes: Alaska, Kansas, and North Dakota. Ten states have unspecified life sentences. Of these the death-penalty states are: Georgia, Idaho, Mississippi, New Mexico, Utah, Virginia, and Wyoming; and the non-death-penalty states are: Minnesota, New York, and Wisconsin.

   See the "Alternative Sentencing Summary" Nov. 1993, published by the National Coalition to Abolish the Death Penalty (see note 20, chapter 3).

6. *Ibid.*, pp. 542–543. Kentucky's Truth in Sentencing Act in 1986 (Ky. Rev. Stat. Ann. 439.3401(3) [Michie/Bobbs-Merrill Supp. 1988]) mandates that violent offenders serve at least 50 percent of the terms of years imposed against them before becoming eligible for parole.

7. See Elizabeth Leech, "Kansas Senate Votes Down Death Penalty," *Kansas City Times*, April 4, 1987.

8. K.S.A. 21–4622, effective July 1, 1990.

9. South Carolina Constitution, article IV:14.

10. Amnesty International polls conducted in six states consistently showed that citizens prefer life imprisonment to death when offered a choice between the two alternatives. Presented with the choice, support for the death penalty in Georgia (Dec., 1986) registered at 46 percent; in Kentucky (Dec., 1989), 36 percent; in Maryland (Nov., 1988), 45 percent; in Massachusetts (Sept., 1990), 44 percent; in New Mexico (Oct., 1990), 50 percent; in New York (March, 1991), 36 percent, and in Oklahoma (Dec., 1988), 48 percent. See note 21 in chapter 5.

11. The same Amnesty International polls show that when offered this

alternative, only 42 percent of the residents of Georgia still preferred the death penalty, 38 percent of the residents of New Mexico, 41 percent of New Yorkers, and 27 percent of Virginians.

12. This idea is also found in social science literature. See Gresham M. Sykes and David Matza, "Techniques of Neutralization: A Theory of Delinquency," *American Sociological Review* 22 (December 1957): pp. 664–670.

13. The juvenile records of Robert Lee Willie are held at the St. Tammany Parish Sheriff's Office, Covington, Louisiana.

14. *State v. Willie*, 410 So.2d 1019 (La. 1982).

15. Trial Transcripts, *State of Louisiana v. Robert Lee Willie*, Supreme Court of the State of Louisiana, No. 81-KA-0242: vol. 7, pp. 451–452.

16. *Robert Lee Willie v Ross Maggio, Jr.*, 737 F.2d 1372 (5th Cir., 1984).

17. See John Fahey, "Second Killer Gets Life in Faith Hathaway Case," *Times-Picayune*, October 25, 1980.

18. Robert Lee Willie: Legal Chronology

May 28, 1980: Murder of Faith Hathaway.

May 30, 1980: Kidnapping of Mark Brewster and his teenage girlfriend.

June 3, 1980: Arrest in Hope, Arkansas, on charges of kidnapping and rape (Brewster and girlfriend).

June 30–July 1, 1980: In federal court Willie and Vaccaro plead guilty to kidnapping (Brewster and girlfriend) and receive three 30-year sentences to be served in a federal penitentiary.

October 20–23, 1980: Willie goes to trial in state court, Washington Parish, for the murder of Faith Hathaway. The jury finds him guilty and sentences him to death. At the same time, in the same courthouse, Vaccaro's jury finds him guilty and sentences him to life imprisonment.

November 13, 1980: Willie and Vaccaro, on trial in state court in Baton Rouge, are each sentenced to four life sentences for aggravated rape, kidnapping, and attempted murder (Brewster and girlfriend).

January 25, 1982: The Louisiana Supreme Court overturns Willie's death sentence and orders a new sentencing trial.

June 28, 29, 1982: At a second sentencing trial the jury once again sentences Willie to death.

August, 1983: Willie is sentenced in a state district court to a life sentence for second-degree murder of Sheriff Deputy Wagner.

NOTES

November 7, 1983: Willie is released from federal prison and sent to death row at Angola.

CHAPTER EIGHT

1. In 1984 Louisiana Pardon Board members were paid $28,900 annually; the chairperson, $34,700. Source: Louisiana Department of Safety and Corrections Capital Station, P.O. Box 94304, Baton Rouge, Louisiana 70804, (504) 342-6740.
2. Jason DeParle, "A Matter of Life or Death," *Times-Picayune*, April 7, 1985, p. 6.
3. John Fahey, "Mother Is Sentenced to Jail for Aiding Wanted Son," *Times-Picayune*, February 13, 1981.
4. Liz Scott, "A Patron for the Condemned," *New Orleans Magazine*, April 1985, pp. 66–71.
5. Jonathan Eig, "Picking Up the Pieces," *The Angolite* 16, no.3 (May/June 1991): pp. 46–50. The article is a reprint of the article "A Tough Lesson" in the *Dallas Morning News*, March 25, 1991.

   The Baton Rouge *Morning Advocate* published numerous articles about the bribes-for-pardon scandal, from September 4, 1986, when Marsellus was indicted, until August 30, 1989, when he was paroled from the Federal Correctional Institute at Fort Worth, Texas.
6. Along with State Representative Joseph A. Delpit, Marsellus was indicted on state conspiracy, corrupt influencing, and public bribery charges. Marsellus settled the state charges in a plea agreement that called for his cooperation in the state's case against Delpit. He pleaded guilty to conspiracy to commit mail fraud, a federal offense, and served time in a federal, not a state penitentiary.
7. The date of Marilyn Hampton's release, June 9, 1986, is recorded at the Louisiana Department of Safety and Corrections, P.O. Box 94304, Capitol Station, Baton Rouge, Louisiana 70804-9304. Records in this office state that she was given a sentence of only twelve years for first-degree murder, but records of the Fourth Judicial Court of Louisiana in Ouachita Parish (Docket No. 38292) where Hampton was tried, convicted, and sentenced, give the original sentence as life imprisonment.
8. Joe Morris Doss, an Episcopal priest and attorney who helped represent Knighton during his appeals, has written a monograph about Earnest Knighton, Jr.'s case, *The Death Penalty — Law and Morality: A Case Study* (Cincinnati: Forward Movement Publications, 1988): 412 Sycamore Street, Cincinnati, Ohio 45202.

263

NOTES

CHAPTER NINE

1. The story is told in the Gospel of Matthew, chapter 2.
2. The account of Riley is told by San Quentin death-watch officer, Joseph Ferretti, who participated in 126 executions and kept a notebook of the first 117. See Michael A. Kroll, "The Fraternity of Death," at pp. 16–26 in Michael L. Radelet (ed.), *Facing the Death Penalty: Essays on a Cruel and Unusual Punishment* (Philadelphia: Temple University Press, 1989).
3. See Albert Nolan, O.P., *Jesus Before Christianity* (Maryknoll, New York: Orbis Books, 1976). This book, with its telling title, is the most compelling book about Jesus that I have ever read.
4. Elaine Pagels, *Adam, Eve, and the Serpent* (New York: Vintage Books, 1989), p. xxv.
5. Jacoby, *Wild Justice*, pp. 336–337.

   Among Catholics in the United States the Catholic Worker Movement, begun by Dorothy Day and Peter Maurin in the early part of this century, embraces nonviolence as a way of life as well as a tactic for social transformation (see note 1, chapter 1).

   The Aims and Means of the Catholic Worker Movement's charter states: " 'Blessed are the peacemakers, for they shall be called children of God.' (Matthew 5:9) Only through nonviolent action can a personalist revolution come about, one in which one evil will not be replaced simply by another. Thus, we oppose the deliberate taking of life for any reason, and see every oppression as blasphemy. Jesus taught us to take suffering upon ourselves rather than inflict it upon others, and He calls us to fight against violence with the spiritual weapons of prayer, fasting and non-cooperation with evil . . ."

   Also within the Catholic tradition, Pax Christi (Peace of Christ) seeks to implement nonviolence "in thought, word, and action." The international organization sponsors retreats and conferences and publishes numerous materials on nonviolence. (Pax Christi USA, 348 East Tenth Street, Erie, Pennsylvania 16503, (814) 453-4955.

CHAPTER TEN

1. Walter Berns, *For Capital Punishment: Crime and the Morality of the Death Penalty* (New York: Basic Books, 1979), pp. 269–270.
2. Quoted from Associated Press dispatches by Henry Schwarzschild, "Homicide by Injection," *New York Times*, December 23, 1982.
3. See John K. Wiley, Associated Press Writer, "Delaying Hanging Crueler Than Death, Lawyer Says," *Times-Picayune*, January 5, 1993.

4. John Laurence, *The History of Capital Punishment* (New York: Citadel Press, 1983).

5. John Pope, "Execution by Injection Tonight," *Times Picayune*, November 14, 1991.

6. Gallup found that six in ten of those who favor the death penalty agree that "the poor are more likely than those of average or above average income to receive the death penalty for the same crime." See "Death Penalty Support Remains Strong," *The Gallup Poll Monthly* no. 309 (June 1991).

   Also see Robert H. Thomas, and John D. Hutcheson, Jr., "Georgia Residents' Attitudes Toward the Death Penalty, the Disposition of Juvenile Offenders, and Related Issues" (City Center for Public and Urban Research, Georgia State University, University Plaza, Atlanta, Georgia 30303, December 1986).

7. When Californians who favored the death penalty were asked, "Suppose it were proved that a mistake had been made and an innocent person had been executed," 63 percent said they would still support the death penalty. See John Balzar, "75% Support Death Penalty in California," *Los Angeles Times*, August 19, 1985.

8. "Harper's Index," *Harper's*, July 1992. Source: Research USA (1992), 645 North Michigan Avenue, Suite 640, Chicago, Illinois 60611, (312) 337-1992.

9. ABC/Washington Post Poll, September 1989.

10. Michael L. Radelet, Hugo A. Bedau, Constance Putnam, *In Spite of Innocence: Erroneous Convictions in Capital Cases* (Boston: Northeastern University Press, 1992).

11. *Ibid.*, pp. 60–73.

12. *Ibid.*, pp. 276, 318.

13. *Ibid.*, pp. 197–213.

14. *Ibid.*, pp. 300–301.

15. *Ibid.*, p. 289.

16. Michael L. Radelet, "People Released from Death Row since 1970 with Evidence of Innocence," unpublished paper, University of Florida, department of sociology, Gainesville, Florida 32611, March, 1992.

17. Radelet, Bedau, Putnam, *In Spite of Innocence*, pp. 5–10.

18. David Margolick, "25 Wrongfully Executed in U.S., Study Finds," *New York Times*, November 14, 1985.

Chapter Eleven

1. Willie Lawrence Celestine, executed July 20, 1987. Willie was one of the two clients—Robert Willie, the other—whom Millard Farmer

asked me to befriend when he came to visit me in October, 1984 (see page 115 at the end of chapter 5).

2. Sterling Rault was executed on August 24, 1987. His was the 992nd confirmed legal execution in Louisiana since 1722. For documentation on legal executions in the United States, contact Watt Espy, Capital Punishment Research Project, Box 277, Headland, Alabama 36345, (205) 693-5225.

3. The U.S. Bureau of Justice Statistics records 23,438 homicides in 1990. For information on U.S. crime, contact Justice Statistics Clearinghouse, U.S. Department of Justice, Washington, D.C. 20531, (800) 732-3277.

4. The Mennonites promote programs of nonviolent social change. For information on Mennonite Volunteers, contact the Mennonite Central Committee, 21 South 12th Street, PO Box 500, Akron, Pennsylvania 17501-0500, (717) 859-1151.

5. The National Organization for Victim Assistance (NOVA) publishes a Directory of Victim Assistance Programs and Resources in states and municipalities across the United States. This broad-based organization publishes a newsletter, holds an annual national conference and conducts training for victims' advocates. Contact: 1757 Park Road N.W., Washington, D.C. 20010, (202) 232-6682.

6. There are exceptions. In New York state, The Genessee County Community Victim Assistance Program is a model example of collaboration between law enforcement officials and the community in attending to victims' needs. Contact: *Community Victim Assistance Program*, Genesee County Sheriff's Department, County Building No. 1, Batavia, New York, (716) 344-2550, ext. 226.

7. Howard Zehr, *Changing Lenses: A New Focus for Crime and Justice* (Scottdale, Pennsylvania: Herald Press, 1990), pp. 215–216.

8. Source: Uniform Crime Reports for the U.S., FBI, U.S. Department of Justice, Washington, D.C. 20535.

9. See "Millions Misspent: What Politicians Don't Say About the High Costs of the Death Penalty," a report by the Death Penalty Information Center, October 1992, pp. 3–9. Contact: 1606 20th St. NW, Washington, D.C. 20009 (202) 347-2531.

10. Walt Philbin, "N.O. Murders Down by 61," *Times-Picayune*, January 1, 1993.

11. The following are some national organizations and programs which offer victim assistance:

> *National Organization for Victim Assistance* (see note 5 above)
> *National Victims Resource Center* (P.O. Box 6000, Rock-

ville, Maryland 20850, (800) 627-6872. Publishes victim-related books and articles and maintains a legislation data base containing state crime victim compensation statutes.

National Victims Center. The organization has two main offices:

- Victim Services and Membership: 307 West 7th Street, Suite 001, Fort Worth, Texas 76102, (817) 877-3355.
- Programs, Public Policy, Training Programs, Media Office, and Library: 2111 Wilson Blvd, Suite 300, Arlington, Virginia 22201, (703) 276-2880.

Parents of Murdered Children and Other Survivors of Homicide Victims. The organization publishes a directory of POMC Chapters throughout the United States, a newsletter, and articles and pamphlets on victim-related topics. Headquarters: 100 East Eighth Street, B-41, Cincinnati, Ohio 45202, (513) 721-5683.

Victim Offender Reconciliation Program. Directed by the Office of Criminal Justice, Mennonite Central Committee (see note 4 above). Publishes articles and pamphlets on victim assistance and on the process of victim-offender reconciliation. The latter brings victim and offender into direct communication so that grievances of the victim can be expressed and remorse and reparation of the offender can be rendered — A fragile process and not always possible or successful, but sometimes producing amazing results.

A victim-offender reconciliation program was initiated by inmates at Sing-Sing Prison who wanted to express remorse for their crimes. (For information on meetings, which are held in Sing Sing Prison, contact Russ Immarigeon, 27 Phud Hill Road, Hillsdale, New York 12529.)

Murder Victims Families for Reconciliation. Provides information about the needs and concerns of victims' families who are opposed to the death penalty. Core members of the group have had a family member murdered, but membership in the group is open to anyone. Office: 2093 Willow Creek Road, Portage, Indiana 46368, (219) 763-2170.

12. Victims of Violence Program, Cambridge Hospital, 1493 Cambridge Street, Cambridge, Massachusetts 02139, (617) 498-1284.
13. Survive continues to provide assistance. Office: Children's Bureau of New Orleans, 921 Canal St., New Orleans, Louisiana 70112, (504) 525-2366.

NOTES

14. *Louisiana Weekly*, January 26, 1991.

15. Allen Johnson, Jr., "Dr. Minyard Sees 'Drug Holocaust' Among Blacks," *Louisiana Weekly*, December 9, 1990.

16. The question arises: why the propensity to violence in the black community? For a good start in answering that question, I recommend Charles E. Silberman's book, *Criminal Violence, Criminal Justice* (New York: Vintage Books, 1980). Silberman points out that, since the 1970s and into the present, blacks in the United States commit a disproportionate percentage of violent crimes, and then explores the question of whether the propensity to violence is part of the cultural baggage blacks carried with them from Africa or something blacks have learned through their experience in this country. Interestingly, he points out that the homicide rate in black Africa, whence blacks came, is the same as that of western Europe, significantly below the rate of either white or black America. He then explores historically the black experience of the "American dream," beginning with slavery, and when he's finished one wonders, as he does, why blacks in poor, inner-city communities are not more violent than they are.

17. "Almost without exception the courts have refused to interfere with this exercise of discretion [by police]. Courts have determined that citizens may not sue police to force them to make arrests." David Austern, *The Crime Victims Handbook* (New York: Viking Penguin, Inc., 1987), p. 7.

18. Walt Philbin, "Tulane Student Slain in Parking Lot near Oak Street Bar," *Times-Picayune*, October 27, 1990; Walt Philbin, "3 Booked in Rapes, Murder Uptown." *Times-Picayune*, October 30, 1990.

19. Michael Perlstein, "Most Killers Escape Prison Sentence, City Records," *Times-Picayune*, January 13, 1991.

20. "Chattahoochee Report," p. 3.

21. *Ibid.*, pp. 9, 10.

22. *Ibid.*, pp. 11, 12.

23. Rainer Maria Rilke, *The Selected Poetry of Rainer Maria Rilke*. (New York: Vintage, 1984).

INDEX

Index

ABC Evening News, 213–15
"abuse of the writ," 45
Adam, Eve, and the Serpent (Elaine Pagels), 195, 196
Adams, James, 220
Adams, Randall Dale, 219, 220
AFDC (Aid to Families with Dependent Children), 8
Alexander, Herbert R., 154
Alford, William, Jr., 161
    at Pardon Board hearing for Willie, 165–69
Alvord, Gary, 50
American Civil Liberties Union in Louisiana, 112
Amnesty International, 105, 232–33
    investigation into death penalty around the world, 113–14
Angola
    death house, 35, 36, 72–73
    first reforms at, 24–25
    guards at, 71
    history of, 24
    "Red Hat" disciplinary cell block, 25
    See also Death Row
Angolite, The, 169, 170

appeal (federal habeas) of the death penalty, 46
    Pat Sonnier, 45–54
        appeal to the governor, 53
            denied, 54
        federal habeas appeal weakened, 46
        final appeal turned down, 86
        review of trial, 47–48, 51–54
            ineffectiveness of counsel, 52–53
    Robert Lee Willie
        petition for relief in federal court, 154–55
            denied, 155–56
Aryan Brotherhood at Marion, 182, 188
Auburn Prison, New York, 18
Augustine, Saint, 196, 231

Baham, Michael, 44
Bahlinger, Sister Kathleen, 63, 66, 67
    makes funeral arrangements for Sonnier, 75, 97–98
Baldwin, Timothy, 158, 170–72
Barker, Dr. Ann, 77, 82–83, 96–97, 125
Bedau, Hugo A., 218–19, 220, 221
Berns, Walter, 215–16

INDEX

Bible, the
"proof texts" on the death penalty, 193–95
Blackburn, Frank C., 35, 104, 120, 176–77, 190, 191
at Willie's execution, 210
meets with Sister Helen, 121–25
position on spiritual advisors, 121
position on the death penalty, 122–23
black male homicide victims, 236–37
Blum, Marcia, 157, 163, 164
Bourque, Loretta, 4, 242, 244
newspaper descriptions of the crime, 15
Bourque family, 11, 12, 17
at execution of Sonnier, 93–94
Brennan, Justice William F., 19–20, 114
Brewer, Mildred, 240–41
Brewster, Mark, 146
Brown, Anthony Silah, 219
Brown-McGeehee Funeral Home, 213, 221
Bundy, Ted, 144
Bureau of Justice Statistics, 239
Burke, Dracos
at Pardon Board hearing for Sonnier, 63–66
speaks against bill to abolish death penalty, 113, 115
Bussie, Fran, 75

Camus, Albert ("Reflections on the Guillotine"), 21–22, 35, 74, 89, 123, 148, 216, 221
capital punishment. See death penalty
Carr, Shirley, 241
Catholic Church reform movement to practice social justice, 5
Changing Lenses: A New Focus for Crime and Justice (Howard Zehr), 232
"Chattahoochee Report," 239–40
Christian, Jimmy, 240
Christianity and the death penalty, 122–124 195–96
Clarion Herald, 110
Clark issue, 51, 52
Coleman, Roger Keith, 46
Colon, Chava, 14–15
asks Sister Helen to become pen pal to Sonnier, 3, 4
"Complaint for Declaratory and Injunctive Relief" filed by death-row inmates, 151

Confessions (St. Augustine), 231
Connick, Harry, Sr., 54
Coody, Maj. Kendall, 179–81
Craft, John
preparation for Willie's Pardon Board hearing, 157–59
presentation to the Pardon Board, 165
crime
"index crimes," relevance of death penalty to, 129
homicides in New Orleans, 239
public's view of, 129
racial bias in prosecution of murder cases, 240
reduction of, in New York City and New Orleans, 233
rise in homicide rate after executions, 110
rise in rate of violent crime, 233
risk of felon-type murders, 128–29

Dalton, Sam, 58
Daniels, Dr. Lionel, 66
Day, Dorothy
account of her time in jail, 34
on social justice, 5
"Death Belt," 49
juries imposing sentences in, 116
death house at Angola, 72–73
last hours of Sonnier, 84–88
last hours of Willie, 204–11
death penalty
abolition of, in England, 221
as applied in Southern states, 3
arguments against, 130
Augustine and, 196
as a deterrent to crime, 110
biblical texts on, 193–95
Christianity and, 122–24, 195–96
"coarsening" effect on society, 215–16, 218
discrimination in capital crimes sentencing, 48, 49
and the Eighth Amendment, 114–15
by electrocution, 18–20
euphemisms for, 216
execution of juveniles, insane, and mentally retarded, 50
by hanging, 18
"index crimes," relevance of death penalty to, 129

information campaign about, 128

for innocent people, 218–19

introduction of death by electrocution in the U.S., 1890, 18

investigation into, around the world, 113–14

by lethal injection, 216–18

moral complexity of, 102–3

moral contradiction in, 22

moral dilemma over, 21

opinion of U.S. citizens on, 116, 232–33

opposed, with no-parole sentences, 144

procedural requirements for federal appeals, 46

for rape declared unconstitutional, 48

reinstatement by the U.S. Supreme Court, 39

removal of constitutional protection against, 45–46

ruled "arbitrary and capricious," 46, 51

seminar on at Loyola University, 223–25

Supreme Court admits discrepancy that correlates with race, 49

in U.S., two-year study of, 218–19, 220, 221

U.S. Catholic Bishops' statement, 54, 124

death row, 11

Angola, description of, 27

cell in, 13

class-action suit by inmates, 151,

Sonnier moved to death house, 60 178, 179

Willie moved to death house, 183

DeGirolama, John, 158–59

DeParle, Jason, 198

Department of Corrections

changes on death row, 178, 179

Doss, Father Joseph, 109, 158

Drake, Henry, 219

dress code (wearing the habit) for nuns, 25–26

drugs

drug-fighting programs, 233

in St. Thomas housing project, 8

Dybdahl, Tom, 36, 44, 97, 111–12, 121

Edwards, Gov. Edwin, 53

rejects Sonnier's final clemency appeal, 87

meeting about Sonnier's appeal for clemency, 55–57

political implications of clemency, 61–62

Eighth Amendment, 46, 114–15

electrocution, 18–20

the apparatus, 104

introduced in U.S., 18

pain of, 20

See also death penalty; execution

Elizabeth (Willie's mother)

at funeral of son, 221–22

at Pardon Board hearing, 165

time in jail, 161–62

visits son for last time, 199–201

England, abolition of death penalty, 221

"equal protection of the law," 239

Evans, John Louis, 19

execution

cost of v. life imprisonment, 129–30

expenditures on capital cases, 233

of innocent people, 220–21

methods of, 217

preparation of the prisoner for, 207

process in Louisiana, 104–5

public, 218

Farmer, Marion, 158, 159, 160

at Pardon Board hearing Willie, 165–69

presentation, 167–68

Farmer, Millard, 42, 90–94, 219

agrees to help Sonnier, 43

convinces Sister Helen to be spiritual advisor to Robert Lee Willie, 117

meeting with governor about Sonnier's appeal for clemency, 55–57

appeal fails, 87

prepares for Pardon Board hearing, 58–62

at hearing, 63–66

prepares petitions for appeals, 44, 46–47

suggests legal office for death-row inmates, 112

federal appeal, 14

Fisher, Brad, 55, 55–57

at Pardon Board hearing for Sonnier, 63–66

meeting with governor about Sonnier's appeal for clemency, 55–57

Flavin, Sister Lilianne, 53, 107, 108

denied request to counsel death-row inmate, 120

given approval to serve as spiritual advisor, 125

For Capital Punishment: Crime and the Morality of the Death Penalty (Walter Berns), 215–16

Ford v. Wainwright, 50

INDEX

Forster, E. M., 120
Francis, Willie, 19
Frey, Bishop Gerald, 109
funeral arrangements
  for Sonnier, 66, 67, 97
  for Willie, 213, 221–22
Furman v. Georgia, 1972, 46, 51, 114, 115, 117

Gandhi, Mohandas, 196, 197
Gaskin case, 48
Gauthier, Elsie, 7
Gilmore, Gary, 144
Glass, Jimmy, 32
Glass v. Louisiana, 19
Goodwin, Nancy, 85, 109
Gregg v. Georgia, 1976, 45–46, 114–15
"Gruesome Gerty," 184
guards at Angola, 71

habeas corpus appeal, 14
Hampton, Marilyn, 170, 171, 172
Hand, Lawrence, 66
Hannan, Archbishop Philip, 54, 55
"Hard 40" statute, 143
Harvey, Elizabeth, 12, 133–40
  at abolition campaign, 226–27
  at Sterling execution, 227–28
  at Willie's execution, 210
  describes events leading up to crime, 133–35
  pain and grief, 144
  at seminar on death penalty at Loyola University, 223–24, 225
  speaks at Pardon Board hearing for Willie, 168
  talks about execution of Willie, 212
    to Peter Jennings, 214
Harvey, Lizabeth, 136, 212
  at Sterling execution, 227–28
Harvey, Vernon
  first meeting with Sister Helen, 131–40
  need for retribution, 137–40
  pain and grief, 144
  recounts scene and murder, 136–37
  at seminar on death penalty at Loyola University, 223–24, 225
  speaks at Pardon Board hearing for Willie, 168
  at Sterling execution, 227–28
  talks about execution of Willie, 212
    to Peter Jennings, 214

undergoes open-heart surgery, 235–36
  at Willie's execution, 210
Hathaway, Faith, 12, 128, 133–35, 159
"Heel-string Gang," 24
Hemby, Dennis Buford, 119
Hillman, Dr. Harold, 20
Hodge, James, 75
homicide victims
  of blacks, 239
  in New Orleans, 43
Hope House, 3
  begun in 1969, 8
  staff meeting, 117
Hughes, Langston, 9
Hugo, Victor, 221

"index crimes," 116, 129
innocent people
  execution of, 220–21
  sent to death row and later released, 219, 220
insane people, execution of, 50

Jacoby, Susan, 142–43, 196–97
Jennings, Peter
  interview about Willie's execution, 213–15
Jent, William, 219
Johnson, Johnny, 240
Jones, Willie Leroy, 124
juveniles, execution of, 50

Keeney v. Tamayo-Reyes, 1992, 46
Kegel, Martha, 112
Kemmler, William, 18
Kidner, Dianne, 234, 235, 236
King, Martin Luther, 196, 197
Knighton, Ernest, 115, 158, 174

Larose, Joseph, 110
LeBlanc, David, 4, 242, 245
  newspaper descriptions of his murder, 15
LeBlanc, Eula, 11, 12, 241–42
LeBlanc, Lloyd, 11, 12, 17
  at execution of Sonnier, 93–94
  at Pardon Board hearing for Sonnier, 64–65
  prayers of, 241–45
  what an apology means to the family, 42
legal office for death-row inmates, 112
legal system, 45
Lesurques, 221

lethal-injection form of the death penalty, 216–18
life imprisonment
  average time served, 142–43
  cost of v. execution, 129–30
  statute reformulated, 24
Livingston, Bob, 139
Louisiana Capital Defense Project, 157
Louisiana Coalition on Jails and Prisons. *See* Prison Coalition
Louisiana State Penitentiary at Angola. *See* Angola
Louisiana Weekly, 236
Loyola University
  seminar on the death penalty, 223–24, 225
Lundy, George, 54, 55

McClesky v. Kemp, 1987, 49
MacMurdo, Sister Alice, 26
Maggio, Warden Ross, 35, 77–78, 87, 216
  gives permission for Eddie and Pat to visit, 70–71
Maginnis, John, 57
Major, Barbara, 116
Marion federal penitentiary
  killings at, 189–90
  Willie's time at, 188–89
Marsellus, Howard, 61, 62
  conversation with Sister Helen, 169–74
  at Pardon Board hearing for Sonnier, 63–66
  at Pardon Board hearing for Willie, 167, 168
  sentenced for taking bribes, 158
Marshall, Justice Thurgood, 117
measured retribution, 143–44
Mennonite Volunteers, 234
mentally retarded, execution of, 50
Miller, Earnest Lee, 219
Minyard, Dr. Frank, 237
murder rate
  in states with the death penalty, 110
Murray, Julian, 115

Neal, Sister Marie Augusta, S.N.D.deN.
  on social justice, 5–6
  New Orleans Magazine, 111, 163
  Scott's interview with Harveys, 175
Nursey, Joe, 60, 85, 86, 95
  meets with Edwards about Sonnier's appeal for clemency, 55–57

October walk, 125, 128–31
Orleans Parish Jail, 26
Ott, Bishop Stanley, 53
  celebrates Sonnier's funeral Mass, 99, 107
  meeting with governor about Sonnier's appeal for clemency, 55–57
  speaks to abolish death penalty, 113, 115

Pagels, Elaine, 195, 196
Pardon Board, 44
  bribery of, 172–73
  hearing about Sonnier, 63–66
    clemency denied, 66
  influence of politics on, 158
  hearing about Willie
    preparation for, 157–63
    presentations, 163–69
    request denied, 168
Parents of Murdered Children, 228–31
Pellicci, Vincent, 158–59
Penry v. Lynaugh, 50
Penton, Chaplain, 89, 181–82, 208
Perry, Michael Owen, 50
Peters, Mary James, 170
Phelps, C. Paul, 78–79
  expedites deal for Marilyn Hampton, 171–72
  discusses death penalty with Sister Helen, 101–5
Pilgrimage for Life, 126, 198
  inaugurates assistance program for murder victims' families, 232
  members encouraged to join Survive, 240
  week-long abolition campaign, 226–27
police in New Orleans, complaints against, 9
polygraph test
  request for by Willie, 186–87, 190, 191
  results of, 202–3
postconviction relief, 14
"poverty law," 48
Prejean, Helen
  accusations against, 120, 121
  confronted by Lloyd LeBlanc, 64–65
  conversation with Howard Marsellus, 169–74
  conversation with Maj. Coody, 179–81
  enjoys friendship of black people for first time, 10
  fainting episode at prison, 79–80, 124–25
  family background and early life, 6–7
  first meeting with Vernon Harvey, 131–40

INDEX

Prejean, Helen (*cont.*)
  goes on retreat, 112–13
  her life in St. Thomas housing project, 4, 10
  interview at Angola, 23, 25
  interview with Liz Scott, 110–11
  at meeting of Parents of Murdered Children, 229–31
  meets with Warden Blackburn, 121–25
  moral conviction against the death penalty, 31, 123–24
  moral dilemma over death penalty, 21
  offering help to victims' families, 32
  prays with Lloyd LeBlanc, 242–45
  and Pat Sonnier
    becomes "spiritual adviser," 23, 26
    at the execution, 90–94
    first visit with, 26–31
    last visits in the death house, 71–77, 80–82, 84–88
    letters, 11–14
    meets with governor about clemency appeal, 55–57
    at Pardon Board hearing, 63–66
    reads files and transcripts, 14–17, 58–60
    requests to be at execution, 57
    visits his family, 106–7
  returns to St. Thomas housing project, 107–8
  and Robert Lee Willie
    becomes spiritual adviser, 117–19
  at funeral, 221–22
  letters to Willie, first, 120
  prepares for Pardon Board hearing, 160–63
  preparing him for execution, 199–209
  presentation to the Pardon Board, 166–67
  reads trial transcripts and newspaper clippings about trial, 151, 152–56
  visits, 145–51
    before execution, 176–80
    in death house, 184–90
  seminar on death penalty at Loyola University, 223–25
  talks to Peter Jennings about execution of Willie, 213–15
  talks to reporters about Willie, 213
  visits to Eddie Sonnier, 32–34, 69–70
Prejean, Louie, 82, 242–45
Prejean, Mary Ann, 82
Prison Coalition, 3
prison hospital, 79–80
prison confinement rate in the U.S., 9
"proof texts" from the Bible, 193–95

Quigley, Bill, 60, 95, 112, 120
  at the execution of Sonnier, 90–94
  class-action suit for death-row prisoners, 127–28
  files last petitions for Sonnier, 74, 76
  lawsuit to improve death-row conditions, 151
  presents Baldwin's case to Pardon Board, 170
  takes issue of death penalty to the people, 115–16
Quigley, Debbie, 60, 125

Rabelais, Capt. John, 76–77, 79–80, 89–91, 185, 189
Rabenhorst Funeral Home, 97, 98
racial discrimination
  in application of death penalty for rape, 251
  in capital crimes sentencing, 48, 49
  in prosecution of murder cases, 240
  system of, in Louisiana, 7
Radelet, Michael L., 218–19, 220, 221
Rault, Sister Ruth, D.C., 227
Rault, Sterling, 227–28
Reagan, President, 139, 140, 216
"Red Hat," 25
Rees, Rachelle, 159
"Reflections on the Guillotine" (Albert Camus), 21–22, 35, 74, 89, 123, 148, 216, 221
regulations for visitors, Louisiana Dept. of Corrections, 26
restitution by offenders, 144
Richardson, James, 219
Riley, Leandress, 190–91
Riley, Mary, 236, 241
Rilke, Rainer Maria, 242
Roberts, Bill, 171

St. Martinville, La., 4
St. Pierre, Sister Therese, 8
St. Thomas housing project
  dope buying and selling, 8
  Helen's apartment, 4–5
  relatives in prison, 9–10
  single mothers, 8
  stories of shoot-outs and deaths in, 237–38

treatment of residents by police, 9
violent crime rate in, 7
Sarat, Austin, 117
Scardina, Sister Leigh, 125
Schaff, Sister Lory, 8, 63, 66, 67, 75
Scott, Liz, 110, 163, 164
    interview with Harveys, 175
Sisters of St. Joseph of Medaille, 5
Smith, Virginia, 48
Smith, William J., 240
social justice as mandate of Catholic Church,
    5
social program funds slashed, 9
Sonnier, Eddie, 4, 126
    attends Pat Sonnier's funeral, 98–99
    confesses to the murders, 41–42
    disciplinary reports, 33
    first visit by Sister Helen, 33–34
    found guilty and death sentence over-
        turned, 16
    last visit with Sonnier, 70–71
    letter to Governor Edwards, 69, 71, 74–75
        appears in Times–Picayune, 83–84
Sonnier, Gladys, 68, 94, 106–7
Sonnier, Patrick
    account of trials, 16–17
    accuses Eddie of the murders, 16
    claims not to have committed the murders,
        39
    confesses to the murders, 16
    describes his remorse, 38–39
    early background as told to Sister Helen,
        28–31
    the execution, 91–94
    final appeal turned down, 86
    final meal, 86–87
    final words to Mr. LeBlanc, 93
    found guilty and sentenced to death, 16
    funeral, 97–100
        arrangements, 66, 67
    last effects sent to Sister Helen, 100
    last hours on day of execution, 84–88
    last letter to Eddie, 88–89
    last visits with Sister Helen in the death
        house, 71–74, 75–77, 80–82
    last visit with Eddie, 70–71
    letters to Sister Helen, 12–13, 18, 32
    letter to Governor Edwards, 73, 75
    life on death row, 13
    newspaper descriptions of the crime,
        15
    Pardon Board denies clemency, 66

    petition for appeal denied, third date of
        execution issued, 54
    petition for stay of execution filed, 36, 37,
        40
        denied, 42
    preparations for the electrocution, 89–91
    preparations for Pardon Board hearing,
        58–62
    "prison adjustment potential," 55
    receives execution date, 34
    resentenced to death at second sentencing
        trial, 17
    spiritual preparation for his death, 80–81
    suicide attempt, 39
    tells Sister Helen about the murders, 38
    terror of electrocution, 20
    trial
        autopsy report, 59
        jury selection, 45
Sonnier, Star, 99, 100
Spenkelink, John, 144
spiritual advisors to death-row inmates
    opposition to women as, 120–21
    training sessions for, 111–12
"Statement on Capital Punishment," 124
Stogumber, Chaplain, 100–101
Stoval, Rev. James, 53
"Strap-down Team," 180, 210
strip searches
    of inmates, 34
    of visitors to prisons, 26
Survive, 236, 239, 241

Tabak, Ronald J., 154, 155
Tafero, Jesse, 19
Taylor, Johnny, 56
Texas Court of Criminal Appeal, 219
Thin Blue Line, The, 219, 220
Thomas, Assoc. Warden Roger, 80
Thompson v. Oklahoma, 50
Times–Picayune
    article about Willie, 198
    letters to the editor about Sonnier's fu-
        neral, 108–9
tranquilizing medication, 34
Treen, David, 58
Tunkle, Kimellen, 44, 95
    meeting with governor about Sonnier's
        appeal for clemency, 55–57

Uniform Crime Reporting Program of the
    FBI, 116

INDEX

Universal Declaration of Human Rights, 103
U.S. Catholic Bishops' statement on capital punishment, 54, 124
U.S. Supreme Court
   admits discrepancy that correlates with race, 49
   death penalty not forbidden by Eighth Amendment, 46
   on death penalty by electrocution, 18, 19
   denies Sonnier's appeal and issues third date of execution, 54
   federal habeas appeal gutted, 46
   Ford v. Wainwright, 50
   Furman v. Georgia, 1972, 46, 51, 114, 115, 117
   Glass v. Louisiana, 19
   Gregg v. Georgia, 1976, 45–46, 114–15
   Keeney v. Tamayo-Reyes, 1992, 46
   McClesky v. Kemp, 1987, 49
   Penry v. Lynaugh, 50
   Thompson v. Oklahoma, 50
   refuses to hear Willie's case, 156
   reinstatement of the death penalty, 39

Vaccaro, Joseph
   admits shooting Brewster, 152
   sentenced to life in federal prison, 119
van den Haag, Ernest, 221
Vandiver, William, 19
victim advocacy in the Catholic community, 109
victim impact statement, 225
"Victims' Families: A Contrast in Black and White," 240
Victims of Violence Program, Cambridge, Mass., 234
victims of violent crime
   assistance programs for, 225
      compensation, 232
      cuts in, 226–27
      funds for, 232, 234
      in New Orleans, 234
      Survive, 236
   divorce rate of couples who have lost a child, 231
   Parents of Murdered Children, 228–31
   rights of, 224–25
   treatment of black victims, 240–41
Vidmar, Neil, 117
Vodicka, John, 3

Wagner, Louis, 119
"Warrant of Execution in Capital Case," 34
Watson, Willie, 54–55
Wild Justice: The Evolution of Revenge (Susan Jacoby), 142
Will, George, 215, 216
Williams, Robert Wayne, 43, 44, 55
Williams, Rose, 55–57
Willie, Robert Lee, 12, 117
   admiration for Hitler, 187–88, 191
   date of execution set, 176
   describes his part in crime, 145–47
   dies in electric chair, 211
   first visit with Sister Helen, 126–28
   funeral of, 221–22
   interviews with reporters, 182–83
   involvement with drugs, 205–6
   jobs he once held, 206–7
   last meal, 204–5
   last phone calls, 208, 209–10
   letters to Sister Helen, 120
   meets Vaccaro while in jail, 153
   moved to death house, 183
   Pardon Board
      denies request, 168
      presentation, 165–67
   past record, 119, 152–53
   racist feelings for blacks, 203–4
   requests polygraph test, 186–87, 190, 191
      results of, 202–3
   sentenced to life in federal prison, 119
   time in Marion, 188–89
   trial
      appeal petition denied, 154–55
      review of transcripts, 153–55
   Supreme Court refuses to hear case, 156
   visits with mother and family for last time, 199–201
   visits with Sister Helen, 145–51
      before his execution, 176–80
witnesses to crime, reluctant, 239
witnesses to executions, 105
working poor, incomes of, 8

Yassen, Janet, 234

Zehr, Howard, 232
Zulke, Don Alan, 190, 192, 202